Consuming Passions

Consuming Passions

JONATHON GREEN

Fawcett Columbine • New York

A Fawcett Columbine Book

Published by Ballantine Books

Copyright © 1985 by Jonathon Green

All rights reserved under International and Pan-American Copyright Conventions. Published in the United States by Ballantine Books, a division of Random House, Inc., New York, and simultaneously in Canada by Random House of Canada Limited, Toronto. Originally published in Great Britain in 1985 by Sphere Books Limited.

Library of Congress Catalog Card Number: 86-90875

ISBN: 0-449-90208-0

Cover design by James R. Harris

Cover paintings by Ken Showell

Manufactured in the United States of America

First American Edition: November 1986

10   9   8   7   6   5   4   3   2   1

For my mother

CONTENTS

Consuming Passions

CHAPTER ONE

THE PLEASURES OF THE TABLE

Even an old boot tastes good if it is cooked over charcoal.

Anonymous   *Italian proverb*

Spread the table and the quarrel will end.

Anonymous   *Hebrew Proverb*

THE TABLE at which the King sat was richly decorated and groaned beneath the good fare placed upon it; for there was brawn, roast beef, venison pasty, pheasants, swan, capons, lampreys, pyke in latimer sauce, custard, partridge, fruit, plovers and a huge plum pudding which required the efforts of two men to carry. Afterwards plays were performed and there was much music and dancing . . .

Anonymous
description of Henry VII's Christmas feasting at Greenwich palace 1486

Elizabeth Tudor her breakfast would make
On a pot of strong beer and a pound of beefsteak
Ere six in the morning was tolled by the chimes –
Oh, the days of Queen Bess, they were merry Old Times!

Anonymous   Ballad, q. in *Good Cheer* by Frederick W. Hackwood 1911

WHAT SHOULD WE BE without our meals? They come to us in our joys and sorrows and are the most blessed break that dullness can ever know.

Anonymous q. in *Wine and Food* 1946

BEGIN WITH a Vermouth Amato in lieu of a cocktail. For hors d'oeuvre have some small crabs mashed up with sauce tartare and a slice of two of prosciutto crudo cut as thin as cigarette paper. After this a steaming risotto with scampi . . . some cutlets done in the Bologna style, a thin slice of ham on top and hot parmesan and grated white truffles and fegato alla veneziana complete the repast except for a slice of strachino cheese. A bottle of Val Policella . . . and a glass of fine Champagne and of ruby-coloured Alkermes for the lady, if your wife accompanies you, make a good ending. The Maître d'Hôtel will be interested in you directly he finds that you know how a man should breakfast.

Lt-Col. Nathaniel Newnham-Davis & Algernon Bastard
A Gourmet's Guide to Europe 1903

After a perfect meal we are more susceptible to the ecstasy of love than at any other time.

Dr Hans Bazli

GOOD LIVING is at once the luxury which costs the least; and perhaps of all pleasures it is the most innocent . . . at a banquet Wisdom may renew its moral forces. The bonds of society become narrowed, and rivals or enemies are merged into friends or guests. Persons who are entire strangers to each other share in the intimacy of the family, differences in rank are wiped out, weakness is united to power, manners are polished, and the mind takes fresh flight.

A. Beauvilliers *L'Art du Cuisinier* 1814

PART OF THE Bill of Fare for a Picnic of 40 Persons: A joint of cold roast beef, a joint of cold boiled beef, 2 ribs of lamb, 2 shoulders of lamb, 4 roast fowls, 2 roast ducks, 1 ham, 1 tongue, 2 veal-and-ham pies, 2 pigeon pies, 6 medium-sized lobsters, 1 piece of collared calve's head, 18 lettuces, 6 baskets of salad, 6 cucumbers.
Beverages: 3 doz. quart bottles of ale; ginger-beer, soda water and lemonade, of each 2 doz. bottles; 6 bottles of sherry, 6 bottles of claret, champagne à discrétion, and any other light wine that may be preferred, and 2 bottles of brandy. Take three corkscrews.

Mrs Isabella Beeton *The Book of Household Management* 1861

A SHOOTING PARTY LUNCHEON: Filets de Soles à la mayonnaise, Mouse de Homard frappé, Boeuf braise à la gelée, Langue à l'écarlate, Filets de Caneton à la Lorraine, Cailles poéllees à la Parisienne, Faisan en Robe de Chambre, Salade à la Japonaise, Bordure de Riz aux Prunes, Gateaux à l'Africaine, Bâtons Gruyère, Fromage, Dessert. (Fillets of Sole in Mayonnaise, Iced Lobster Soufflé, Braised Beef with Savoury Jelly, Dressed Ox-Tongue, Fillets of Duckling with Goose Liver Farce, Braised Stuffed Quails, Roast Pheasant in Crust, Japanese Salad, Border of Rice with Stewed Prunes, African Cakes, Savoury Cheese Fingers, Cheese, Dessert.)

Mrs Isabella Beeton *The Book of Household Management* 1861

I HAVE ALWAYS THOUGHT that there is no more fruitful source of family discontent than badly cooked dinners and untidy ways. Men are now so well served out of doors at clubs, hotels and restaurants – that to compete with the attractions of these places, a mistress must be thoroughly acquainted with the theory and practice of cookery as well as all the other arts of making and keeping a comfortable home.

Mrs Isabella Beeton *The Book of Household Management* 1861

LUNCHEON . . . is a very necessary meal . . . as a healthy person, with good exercise, should have a fresh supply of food every four hours. It should be a light meal; but its solidity must, of course, be, in some degree, proportionate to the time it is intended to enable you to wait for your dinner, and the amount of exercise you take in the mean time.

Mrs Isabella Beeton *The Book of Household Management* 1861

D INING IS THE PRIVILEGE of civilisation. The rank which a people occupy in the grand scale may be measured by their way of taking their meals . . . The nation which knows how to dine has learnt the leading lesson of progress. It implies both the will and the skill to reduce to order, and surround with idealisms and graces, the more material conditions of human existence; and wherever that will and that skill exist, life cannot be wholly ignoble.

Mrs Isabella Beeton *The Book of Household Management* 1861

. . . lunch was just ending. The landlord . . . said that we were unfortunately too late for a proper lunch, but they would see what they could do for us. Here is what

3

they did for us: Soupe, Jambon du pays, Confit d'oie, Omelette nature, Civet de lièvre, Riz de veau blanquette, Perdreau rôti, Fromage Roquefort, Fromage Cantal, Confiture de cerise, Poires, Figues. We ate everything; every dish was really distinguished . . . In addition there were three wines . . . The total bill, for two persons, was seven francs.

Arnold Bennett *Things that Have Interested Me*

Dine, v: to eat a good dinner in good company, and eat it slow. In dining, as distinguished from mere feeding, the palate and stomach never ask the hand, 'What are you giving us?'

Ambrose Bierce *The Devil's Dictionary* 1911

IT WAS A DINNER Nesset loved. First came Norfolk dumplings, light as puff-balls, made with real brewer's yeast, floating in rich brown hare gravy. Then jugged hare with red-currant jelly, roast potatoes, turnip-top salad, mashed swede, turnips and leeks, hot apple-pie and thick yellow cream. After that came home-baked bread and russet apples.

Mathena Blomefield *The Bulleymuung Pit* 1946

WHAT A BREAKFAST! Pot of hare: ditto of trout; pot of prepared shrimps: tin of sardines; beautiful beefsteak; eggs, mutton, large loaf and butter, not forgetting capital tea. There's a breakfast for you!

George Borrow *Wild Wales* 1862

SEATING THEMSELVES on the green sward, they eat while the corks fly and there is talk, laughter and merriment, and perfect freedom, for the universe is their drawing room and the sun their lamp. Besides, they have appetite, Nature's special gift, which lends to such a meal a vivacity unknown indoors, however beautiful the surroundings.

Jean-Anthelme Brillat-Savarin *La Physiologie du goût* 1825

The table is the only place where the first hour is not dull.

Jean-Anthelme Brillat-Savarin *La Physiologie du goût* 1825

A SHADY SPOT takes his fancy; soft grass welcomes him, and the murmur of the nearby spring invites him to deposit in its cool waters the flask of wine destined to refresh him. Then, with calm contentment, he takes out of his knapsack the cold chicken and golden-crusted rolls packed for him by loving hands, and places them beside the wedge of Gruyère or Roquefort which is to serve as his dessert . . .

Jean-Anthelme Brillat-Savarin *La Physiologie du goût* 1825

That all-softening overpowering knell
The tocsin of the soul – the dinner bell.

George Gordon, Lord Byron *Don Juan* 1821

All human history attests
That happiness for man – the hungry sinner! –
Since Eve ate apples, much depends on dinner.

George Gordon, Lord Byron *Don Juan* 1821

But man is a carnivorous production
And must have meals – at least once a day;
He cannot live, like woodcocks, upon suction,
But, like the shark and tiger, must have prey.

George Gordon, Lord Byron *Don Juan* 1819

But hark! a sound is stealing on my ear –
A soft and silvery sound – I know it well.
Its tinkling tells me that a time is near
Precious to me – it is the Dinner Bell.
O blessed Bell! Thou bringest beef and beer,
Thou bringest more good things than tongue can tell:
Seared is, of course, my heart – but unsubdued
Is, and shall be, my appetite for food . . .

C. S. Calverley *Beer*

THERE WAS A TABLE set out under a tree in front of the house, and the March Hare and the Hatter were having tea at it: a Dormouse was sitting between them, fast asleep, and the other two were using it as a cushion, resting their elbows on it and talking over its head. 'Very uncomfortable for the

Dormouse,' thought Alice; 'only, as it's asleep, I suppose it doesn't mind.' The table was a large one, but the three were all crowded together at one corner of it. 'No room! No room!' they cried out when they saw Alice coming. 'There's plenty of room!' said Alice indignantly, and she sat down in a large armchair at one end of the table.

Lewis Carroll (Charles Lutwidge Dodgson)
Alice's Adventures in Wonderland 1865

All people are made alike
They are made of bones, flesh and dinners.
Only the dinners are different.

Gertrude Louise Cheney *People* 1927

THE CAPTAIN GLANCED at the listing of food . . . Otardi, working as Beethoven, had written a score for the great artists beyond that glass wall to bring to vibrant harmonies: Beluga caviar . . . Dieppe turbot in golden mustard sauce! A saddle of veal with a daring onion sauce . . . there would be Basque rice and a courgettes au gratin . . . After that came a sorbet Dom Perignon to clear the mouth for some quail in aspic then 'les fromages somptueux' followed by small cakes, glazed fruit, petits fours.

Richard Condon *Arigato* 1972

The Sportsman's breakfast: first, a large bowl of salmon soaked in vinegar – a very common dish this . . . and a bottle of Port wine.

A Cosmopolite *A Sportsman in Ireland* 1897

I DON'T KNOW what you would call a regular life, but I mean by it a life in which one habitually breakfasts at eight.

Bishop Creighton q. in *Geoffrey Madan's Notebooks* 1981

I SHALL NOT QUICKLY FORGET my first dinner at Gaertner's. An onion tart, flat as a plate but still somehow oozing with cream, preceded a subtly flavoured sausage served hot with a mild and creamy horseradish sauce . . . followed by haricots verts fairly saturated in butter; we were then beguiled into eating a sweet called a vacherin glacé . . . an awe-inspiring confection of ice-cream, glacé fruits, frozen whipped cream and meringue, which left me temporarily speechless. But coffee and a glass of very good Kirsch soon put matters right.

Elizabeth David *French Provincial Cooking* 1960

THE CHARACTERISTICS OF DINNER: 1. That dinner is that meal, no matter when taken, which is the principal meal, i.e. the meal on which the day's support is thrown. 2. That it is therefore the meal of hospitality. 3. That it is the meal (with reference to both 1. and 2.) in which animal food predominates. 4. That it is the meal which, upon a necessity arising for the abolition of all but one, would naturally offer itself as the one.

Thomas De Quincey *The Casuistry of Roman Meals* 1839

HARVEY PROBABLY KNEW HOW to carve a goose, but it was his co-ordination that proved such a handicap. We all got large pieces of hot, crisp, juicy, oily goose and we had a large plate of those bread-rolls that come with great chunks of sea-salt and poppy seeds baked to the top of them. There was slivovice which Harvey liked and tiny pots of Turkish coffee of which he wasn't so fond. We ate in greedy silence.

Len Deighton *Funeral in Berlin* 1964

HEAPED UP ON THE FLOOR were turkeys, geese, game, poultry, brawn, great joints of meat, sucking pigs, long wreaths of sausages, mince-pies, plum-puddings, bartrels of oysters, red-hot chestnuts, cherry-cheeked apples, juicy oranges, luscious pears, immense twelfth-cakes, and seething bowls of punch that made the chamber dim with their delicious steam.

Charles Dickens *A Christmas Carol* 1843

A good soup, a small turbot, a neck of venison, ducklings with green peas, or chicken with asparagus, and an apricot tart, is a dinner for an emperor.

Earl of Dudley q. in Abraham Hayward *The Art of Dining* 1852

For my part, now, I consider supper as a turnpike through which one must pass, in order to get to bed.

Oliver Edwards q. in *The Life of Samuel Johnson* by James Boswell 1791

AN HONEST laborious countryman, with good bread, salt and a little parsley, will make a contented meal with a roasted onion.

John Evelyn

7

F is for Family . . . and the depths and heights of gastronomical enjoyment to be found at the family board. It is possible, indeed almost too easy, to be eloquently sentimental about large groups of assorted relatives who gather for Christmas, Thanksgiving or some such festival, and eat and drink and gossip and laugh together . . . The cold truth is that family dinners are more often than not an ordeal of nervous indigestion, preceded by hidden resentment and ennui and accompanied by psychosomatic jitters. The best way to guarantee smooth sailing at one of them is to assemble the relatives only when a will must be read.

M. F. K. Fisher *An Alphabet for Gourmets* 1949

THE TABLE HAD BEEN LAID under the wagon shed. It was laden with four sirloins, six fricassees of chicken, veal in the casserole, three legs of mutton, and, as a centre piece, a handsome roast suckling pig flanked with meat balls cooked in sorrel. Decanters of brandy stood at each corner, and bottles of sweet cider were frothing round their corks. The glasses had all been filled to the brim with wine in advance. Great dishes of yellow cream, which quivered whenever the table was shaken, bore on their smooth surfaces the initials of the newly-married couple picked out in hundreds and thousands.

Gustave Flaubert *Madame Bovary* 1856

Breakfast is a notoriously difficult meal to serve with a flourish.

Clement Freud *Freud on Food* 1978

To barbecue is a way of life rather than a desirable method of cooking.

Clement Freud *Freud on Food* 1978

On china blue my lobster red
Precedes my cutlet brown,
With which my salad green is sped
By yellow Chablis down.
Lord, if good living be no sin,
But innocent delight,
O polarize these hues within
To one eupeptic white.

Sir Stephen Gaselee *On China Blue* 1938

NOW TO THE BANQUET we press; Now for the eggs and the ham! Now for the mustard and cress! Now for the strawberry jam! Now for the tea of our host! Now for the rollicking bun! Now for the muffin and toast! Now for the gay Sally Lunn!

W. S. Gilbert *The Sorcerer* 1877

BY FIVE OR SIX HE WAS up having his 'morning' – a glass of ale or brandy, over which he reverently said a grace, which was brief when he was alone, longer when he was in company, before he visited his 'policy' and stables and fields. When breakfast was served at eight o'clock he was ready for the substantial fare of skink (a stew) or water gruel, supplemented by callops or mutton aided with ale. The bread consisted of oatmeal cakes or barley bannocks.

Henry Gray Graham *The Social Life of the Scotland in the 18th century* 1899

. . . AFTER A SHORT INTERVAL (Rat) reappeared, staggering under a fat, wicker luncheon-basket . . . 'What's inside it?' asked the Mole, wriggling with curiosity. 'There's cold chicken inside it', replied the Rat briefly, 'coldtonguecoldhamcoldbeefpickledgherkinssalad-freshrollscress-sandwichespottedmeatgingerbeerlemonadesodawater –' 'Oh stop, stop,' cried the Mole in ecstasies: 'This is too much!' 'Do you really think so?' enquired the Rat seriously. 'It's only what I always take on these little excursions; and the other animals are always telling me that I'm a mean beast and cut it very fine.'

Kenneth Grahame *The Wind in the Willows* 1908

EPILOGUE: But when all's said and written, there is nothing better than field mushrooms that you have gathered yourself, on toast, for breakfast.

Jane Grigson *The Mushroom Feast* 1975

All happiness depends on a leisurely breakfast.

John Gunther q. in *Newsweek* magazine 1970

A GOOD MEAL SOOTHES the soul as it regenerates the body. From the abundance of it flows a benign benevolence. A good and copious dinner begets a mellowing influence; it permeates the bosom with a bland philanthropy of sentiment, embracive of all classes, sects and races of man.

Frederick W. Hackwood *Good Cheer* 1911

Give me a little ham and egg
And let me be alone I beg
Give me my tea, hot, sweet and weak,
Bring me 'The Times' and do not speak.

A. P. Herbert   *A Book of Ballads*

Bring porridge, bring sausage, bring fish for a start,
Bring kidneys and mushrooms and partridge's legs.
But let the foundation be bacon and eggs.

A. P. Herbert   *A Book of Ballads*

A man may be a pessimistic determinist before lunch and an optimistic believer in the will's freedom after it.

Aldous Huxley   *Do What You Will* 1929

IT IS A GOOD RULE NEVER to start an argument just before breakfast or to enter into a quarrel just before supper. A quarrel that is unavoidable then is likely to be less bitter if the battlers hold off long enough to take a bite of food.

Arthur T. Jersild   q. in *Educational Psychology* ed. Charles Skinner

A man seldom thinks with more earnestness of anything than he does of his dinner.

Dr Samuel Johnson
Attributed in *Anecdotes of the late Dr Johnson* by Hester Lynch Thrale 1786

BEFORE DINNER men meet with great equality of understanding; and those who are conscious of their inferiority, have the modesty not to talk. When they have drunk wine, every man feels himself happy, and loses that modesty, and grows impudent and vociferous: but he is not improved; he is only not sensible of his defects . . . Wine makes a man more pleased with himself. I do not say that it makes him more pleasing to others.

Dr Samuel Johnson
q. in *The Life of Samuel Johnson* by James Boswell in 1791

Luncheon: as much food as one's hand can hold.

Dr Samuel Johnson   *Dictionary* 1755

. . . IN PARADISE . . . he will be waited on by 300 attendants while he eats, and shall be served in dishes of gold, whereof 300 shall be set before him at once, containing each a different kind of food, the last morsel of which shall be as grateful as the first, and will also be supplied with many sorts of liquors in vessels of the same metal; and to complete the entertainment, there will be no want of wine, which, though forbidden in this life, will yet be freely allowed in the next without danger, since the wine of Paradise will never inebriate though you drink it for ever.

The Koran, c. 650

BENEATH THE CANDELABRA, beneath the five tiers bearing towards the distant ceiling pyramids of home-made cakes that were never touched, spread the monotonous opulence of buffets at big balls: coraline lobsters boiled alive, waxy chaud-froids of veal, steely-tinted fish immersed in sauce, turkeys gilded by the oven's heat, rosy foie-gras under gelatine armour, boned woodcocks reclining on amber toast decorated with their own chopped guts, and a dozen other, cruel, coloured delights. At the end of the table two monumental silver tureens held limpid soup, the colour of burnt amber. Huge blond babas, Mont Blancs snowy with whipped cream, cakes speckled with white almonds, and green pistachio nuts, hillocks of chocolate covered pastry, brown and rich . . . pink ices, champagne ices, coffee ices, all parfaits and falling apart with a squelch at a knife cleft, a melody in major of crystallized cherries, acid notes of yellow pineapple, and those cakes called 'Triumphs of Gluttony', filled with green pistachio paste, and shameless 'Virgin' cakes, shaped like breasts.

Giuseppe de Lampedusa *The Leopard* 1960

IF FOOD did not exist it would be well-nigh impossible to get certain types off the phone, as one would be unable to say 'Look, I've got to run but let's have dinner sometime soon.'

Fran Lebowitz *Metropolitan Life* 1978

All's well that ends with a good meal.

Arnold Lobel *Fables* 1980

He may live without books – what is knowledge but grieving?
He may live without hope – what is hope but deceiving?
He may live without love – what is passion but pining?
But where is the man who can live without dining?

Edward Bulwer-Lytton, first Earl of Lÿtton *Lucile* 1860

PETER (THE GREAT) and his party sat down thirteen for supper and consumed five ribs of beef weighing three stone, a sheep, three-quarters of a lamb, a shoulder and a loin of veal, eight pullets and eight rabbits, and drank two and a half dozen bottles of sack, a dozen bottles of burgundy and unlimited beer and had six quarts of mulled sack before going to bed . . . they breakfasted on three quarts of brandy, half a sheep, nineteen pounds of lamb, seven dozen eggs, ten pullets and a dozen chickens.

Christopher Marsden *Palmyra of the North*

Men may talk of country Christmases and court gluttony,
Their thirty pound buttered eggs, their pies of carps' tongues,
Their pheasants drenched with ambergris, the carcases
Of three fat wethers bruised for gravy to
Make sauce for a single peacock: – yet their feasts
Were fasts compared with the City's
Three sucking pigs, served up in a dish,
Took from the sow as soon as she had farrowed,
A fortnight fed with dates and muskadine
That stood my master in twenty marks a piece;
Besides the puddings in their bellies, made
Of I know not what.

Philip Massinger *The City Madam* 1632

THE EXCELLENT LUNCH that the illustrious Crispi used to serve at Delmonico's at five o'clock in the afternoon . . . The incomparable orange blossom cocktails at Sherry's and the plates of salted nuts . . . The tavern cocktails at the Beaux Arts, each with its dash of absinthe . . . The Franziskaner Mai-bock at Luchow's . . . Dear old Sieg's noble Rhine wines at the Kaiserhof . . . the long-tailed clams and Spring onions at Rogers', with Pilsner to wash them down . . . The amazingly good American quasi-Pilsner, made by Herr Abner, on the Raleigh roof in Washington . . . The old-time Florestan cocktails – 50% London gin, 25% French vermouth and 25% Martini Rossi with a dash of Angostura bitters – drink half, then drink a glass of beer, then drink the other half . . . A Pilsner luncheon at the old Grand-Union, from one to six . . . A stray bottle of perfect sauterne, found in Rahway, New Jersey . . . a wild night spent drinking Swedish punch and hot water . . . Two or three hot Scotch nights . . . twenty or thirty Bass ale nights . . . five or six hundred Pilsner nights.

H. L. Mencken *'Bilder aus Schoner Zeit' in Prejudices, 4th series* 1924

The art of dining well is no slight art, the pleasure not a slight pleasure.

Michel de Montaigne *Essays* 1580 – 1588

Then, Dick, what a breakfast! oh, not like your ghost
Of a breakfast in England, your curs'd tea and toast;
But a sideboard, you dog, where one's eye roves about,
Like a Turk's in the harem, and thence singles out
One's paté of larks, just to tune up the throat;
One's small limbs of chicken, done en papillote
One's erudite cutlets, dress'd all ways but plain –
Or one's kidneys – imagine, Dick – done with champagne.
Then some glasses of Beaune, to dilute – or mayhap
Chambertin, which you know's the pet tipple of Nap.
Your coffee comes next, by prescription; and then, Dick's
The coffee ne'er failing, and – glorious appendix –
A neat glass of parfait-amour, which one sips . . .

Thomas Moore *The Fudge Family in Paris* 1818

Monday last was brought from Howick to Berwick, to be shipp'd to London . . . a pie, the contents whereof are as follows: 2 bushels of flour, 20 lb butter, 4 geese, 2 turkeys, 2 rabbits, 4 wild ducks, 2 woodcocks, 6 snipes, 4 partridges, 2 neat's tongues, 2 curlew, 7 blackbirds and 6 pigeons . . . It was near nine feet in circumference, weighs about twelve stones, will take two men to present it at table; it is neatly fitted with a case, a four small wheels to facilitate its use to every guest that inclines to partake of its contents at table.

Newcastle Chronicle
reporting the contents of a pie cooked for Sir Henry Grey, January 6, 1770

D INNERTIME IS THE most wonderful period of the day and perhaps its goal – the blossoming of the day. Breakfast is the bud. The dinner itself is, like life, a curve: it starts off with the lightest courses, then rises to the heavier, and concludes with light courses again.

Novalis (Friedrich von Hardenberg)

(THE GROWTH OF) LUNCHEON . . . marked the entry of a change in habits that cannot be called less than tremendous . . . men of business and affairs came to realise that their wives, fortified by lunch, could wait for dinner and that they themselves, if they ate a larger breakfast, could spend eight or nine consecutive hours in the office, interrupted only by the time given to a Maid of Honour and a glass of port. Similarly their wives were free of them for eight or nine hours at a stretch . . . they had the house to themselves, they had a meal to themselves, they had, like an exciting fresh toy, the afternoon . . . the figures for divorce rose steeply.

Arnold Palmer *Moveable Feasts* 1952

AMONG THE INNUMERABLE domestic casualties of recent years an unnoticed stillness in the air, a modest gap in the hall, commemorate negatively the once vibrant gong. It used to summon us to meals, mysterious affairs prepared out of sight by unseen hands and popping up deliciously, in a setting of snow and silver, every four hours. It even bade us, in the more splendid mansions and hotels, prepare ourselves for the supreme evening rite . . . It was the Victorians' monitory aperitif, the Edwardian version of the cocktail – and how, at its accents, those gastric juices flowed! Now that meals, like women, have lost their mystery, it is superfluous, it has gone.

Arnold Palmer *Moveable Feasts* 1952

AFTER THE . . . breakfast had been laid out but before it could be consumed, the entire family and staff spent ten minutes in the incense of its dishes, either looking at it and guessing the secrets of its hisses, pops and crackles, or kneeling to inhale the furniture polish and inspect, through open fingers, the carpet's design in crimson and blue. The prayers, like the meal that followed them (kedgeree, sausages, cold pheasant and the rest), laid a firm foundation for the Victorian day . . .

Arnold Palmer *Moveable Feasts* 1952

THE DEMAND (for a good breakfast) was significant, marking yet one more new world, the growth of a commercial age, the first cold-shouldering of leisure, the stigmatizing of contented acceptance of inherited means and status, a lengthening of the day, a competitive acceleration . . . It is possible to see in the British breakfast a link between the decay of taste which everywhere, but especially in England, accompanied the progress of the century and the quadrupling, in the years dividing Waterloo and Sedan, of our national income.

Arnold Palmer *Moveable Feasts* 1952

I CAN REMEMBER muffins always being served – well buttered, in a hot dish – at breakfast in an old-fashioned club in 1913 or 1914. Beside them a pot of blackcurrant jam would be posted; the mixture was delicious. Muffins for breakfast must . . . have been a casualty of the earlier war then impending. Muffins for any meal seem to be an unrecorded casualty of the last war. Of the famous brotherhood the crumpet, sometimes stony, sometimes rubbery, alone survives.

Arnold Palmer *Moveable Feasts* 1952

THE GROWTH OF business and businesslike habits, steadily justifying the ladies and pressing the dinner hour farther round the clock, was not well received by the stomach. English internal engines, designed for refuelling every four and a half hours, begin to labour when asked to run for six hours at a stretch. Once again wives and mothers took the situation in hand and found the remedy. They invented Afternoon Tea.

Arnold Palmer *Moveable Feasts* 1952

A MAN OF TASTE is seen at once in the array of his breakfast table . . . Chocolate, coffee, tea, cream, eggs, ham, tongue, cold fowl, all these are good, and bespeak good knowledge in him who sets them forth: but the touchstone is fish; anchovy is the first step, prawns and shrimps the second; and I laud him who reaches even to these; potted char and lampreys are the third, and a fine stretch of progression; but lobster is, indeed, matter for a May morning, and demands a rare combination of knowledge and virtue in him who sets it forth.

Thomas Love Peacock *Crotchet Castle* 1831

Above all (at dinner) drink very little. For a gourmet wine is not a drink but a condiment, provided that your host has chosen it correctly.

Edouard de Pomiane *Cooking with Pomiane* 1962

. . . THEY MADE READY supper, of extraordinary, besides his daily fare, were roasted sixteen oxen, three heifers, two-and-thirty calves, three-score-and-three fat kids, four-score-and-fifteen wethers, three hundred barrow pigs souses in sweet white wine, eleven-score partridges, seven hundred snipes and woodcocks, four hundred London Cornwall capons, six thousand pullets and as many pigeons, six hundred crammed hens, fourteen hundred leverets, three hundred and three buzzards, and one thousand and seven hundred cockerels . . . eleven wild boars . . . eighteen fallow deer . . . seven score pheasants, and some dozens of quests, cushats, ring-doves and wood-culvers; river-fowl, teals and auteals, bitterns, courtes, plovers, francolins, briganders, tyrasons, young lapwings, tame ducks, shovelers, woodlanders, herons, moorhens, criels, storks, comepetiers, oranges, flamans which are phoenicopters, terrigoles, turkies, arbens, coots, solingeese, curlews, termagants and water-wagtails, with a great deal of cream, curds and fresh cheese and store of soup, pottage and brewis, with variety. 'Without doubt, this was meat enough,' reflectively adds the historian Alcofribas.

François Rabelais *Gargantua* 1534

Here's a good dinner towards, thought I, when straight
Up comes a piece of beef, full horseman's weight,
Hard as the arse of Moseley, under which
The coachman sweats as ridden by a witch;
A dish of carrots, each of them as long
As tool to that fair countess did belong
Which her small pillow could not so well hide
But visitors his flaming head espied.
Pig, goose and capon followed in the read,
With all that country bumpkins call good cheer.

John Wilmot, 2nd Earl of Rochester
q. in *Consuming Passions* by Philippa Pullar 1970

Everything tastes better outdoors.

Claudia Roden *Picnic* 1981

THE SMELL of roasting meat together with that of burning fruit wood and dried herbs, as voluptuous as incense in a church, is enough to turn anyone into a budding gastronome.

Claudia Roden *Picnic* 1981

There is a vast difference between the savage and the civilised man, but it is never apparent to their wives until after breakfast.

Helen Rowland *A Guide to Men*

JOEL DUFFLE . . . chooses, as the first course, two quarts of ripe olives, twelve bunches of celery, and four pounds of shelled nuts, all this to be split fifty-fifty between them. Miss Violette Shumberger names twelve dozen cherry-stone clams as the second course, and Joel Duffle says two gallons of Philadelphia pepper-pot soup as the third . . . Violette puts in two five-pound striped bass, the heads and tails not to count in the eating, and Joel Duffle names a twenty-two pound roast turkey. Each vegetable is rated as one course, and Miss Violette Schumberger asks for twelve pounds of mashed potatoes with brown gravy. Joel Duffle says two dozen ears of corn on the cob, and Violette replies with two quarts of lima beans. Joel Duffle calls for twelve bunches of asparagus cooked in butter, and Violette mentions ten pounds of stewed new peas. This gets them down to the salad, and it is Joel Duffle's play, so he says six pounds of mixed green salad with vinegar and oil dressing, and now Miss Violette Shumberger has the final selection, which is dessert. She says it is a pumpkin pie, two feet across, and not less than three inches deep.

Damon Runyon *A Piece of Pie* 1950

WAVERLEY FOUND MISS BRADWARDINE presiding over the tea and coffee, the table loaded with warm bread, both of flour, oatmeal and barley meal, in the shape of loaves, cakes, biscuits and other varieties, together with eggs, reindeer ham, mutton and beef ditto, smoked salmon, marmalade and all the other delicacies which induced even Johnson himself to extol the luxury of a Scottish breakfast above that of all other countries. A mess of oatmeal porridge, flanked by a silver jug, which held an equal mixture of cream and buttermilk, was placed for the Baron's share of this repast.

Sir Walter Scott *Waverley* 1814

I think breakfast so pleasant because no-one is conceited before one o'clock.

Sydney Smith q. in *The Smith of Smiths* by Hesketh Pearson 1934

LIKE THE PLATONIC LOVER, a Platonic and imperishable vision – the ideal Picnic, the Picnic as it might be – the wonderful windless weather, the Watteauish landscape, where a group of mortals talk and feast as they talked and feasted in the Golden Age.

Logan Pearsall Smith q. in *Writers' Favourite Recipes* ed. G. Vincent 1978

A HIGHLAND BREAKFAST: One kit of boiled eggs: a second, full of butter; a third, full of cream; an entire cheese made of goat's milk; a large earthen pot, full of honey; the best part of a ham; a cold venison pastry; a bushel of oatmeal, made into thin cakes and bannocks, with a small wheaten loaf in the middle, for the strangers; a stone bottle full of whiskey, another of brandy, and a kilderkin of ale . . . Great justice was done to the collation by the guests.

Tobias Smollett *Humphrey Clinker* 1771

WITHOUT THE assistance of eating and drinking the most sparkling wit would be as heavy as a bad soufflé, and the brightest talent as dull as a looking-glass on a foggy day.

Alexis Soyer *The Modern Housewife* 1851

IT IS QUITE CERTAIN that too much attention cannot be given to the proper execution of, and in the intelligence displayed in, the order of a dinner. The dinner – being of each day, each season, each century – is not only an hereditary fashion, but also the soul of sociability . . . in all times, amongst all people, the good which has been done – and sometimes the evil – was always preceded or followed by a banquet.

Alexis Soyer *The Gastronomic Regulator* 1846

There on a slope of orchard, Francis laid
A damask napkin wrought with horse and hound,
brought out a dusky loaf that smelt of home,
And, half cut down, a pasty costly made,
Where quail and pigeon, lark and leveret, lay
Like fossils of the rock, with golden yolks
Imbedded and in jellied.

Alfred, Lord Tennyson

Next to eating good dinners, a healthy man with a benevolent turn of mind, must like, I think, to read about them.

William Thackeray

DINNER was made for eatin' not for talkin'.

William Thackeray *Fashnable Fax and Polite Annygoats*

SIR, Respect Your Dinner: idolize it, enjoy it properly. You will be many hours in the week, many weeks in the year, and many years in your life happier if you do.

William Thackeray q. in *Pleasures of the Table* by G. Ellwanger 1903

UNTIL THE 19th century, no one ever thought of eating eggs and bacon for breakfast, and now we know that a large breakfast for an average man is a crime against his own body. Let us resist the blandishments of bacon, the charms (now noticeably faded) of the sausage. Devilled grouse wantonly superimposed on kedgeree, kidneys and bacon following the porridge in its facile descent, fish-cakes the size of billiard balls, above all the two or three slices of ham which so often, so dreadfully often, rounded off the criminal proceedings.

The Times Leader on breakfast c. 1950

AND NOW LET us observe the well-furnished breakfast parlour at Plumstead Episcopi . . . The tea consumed was the very best, the coffee the very blackest, the cream the very thickest; there was dry toast and buttered toast, muffins and crumpets; hot bread and cold bread, white bread and brown bread, home-made bread and baker's bread, wheaten bread and oaten bread; and if there be other breads than these, they were there; there were eggs in napkins, and crispy bits of bacon under silver covers; and there were little fishes in a little box, and devilled kidneys . . . Over and above this, on a snow-white napkin . . . was a huge ham and a huge sirloin . . . Such was the ordinary fare at Plumstead Episcopi.

Anthony Trollope *The Warden* 1855

I ADVERTISE all such as have plethorick and full bodies, especially living at rest, and which are of a phlegmatick temperament, that they not only eschew the use of breakfasts, but also oftentimes content themselves with one meal in a day.

Tobias Venner *Via recta ad Vitam Longam* 1620

THE LEGITIMATE objects of dinner are to refresh the body, to please the palate, and to raise the social humour to the highest point; but these objects, so far from being studied, in general are not even thought of, and display and an adherence to fashion are their meagre substitutes.

Thomas Walker *The Original* 1835

SOLITARY DINNERS, I think, ought to be avoided as much as possible, because solitude tends to produce thought, and ihought tends to the suspension of the digestive powers.

Thomas Walker *The Original* 1835

A chief maxim in dining with comfort is to have what you want when you want it.

Thomas Walker *The Original* 1835

Only dull people are brilliant at breakfast.

Oscar Wilde *An Ideal Husband* 1895

AFTER a good dinner, one can forgive anybody, even one's own relatives.

Oscar Wilde *A Woman of No Importance* 1894

I hadn't the heart to touch my breakfast. I told Jeeves to drink it himself.

P. G. Wodehouse *My Man Jeeves* 1919

I don't know if you have ever noticed it, Jeeves, but a good, spirited kipper first thing in the morning seems to put heart into you.' 'Very true, sir, though I myself am more partial to a slice of ham.' For some moments we discussed the relative merits of ham and kippers as buckers-up of the morale, there being much, of course, to be said on both sides . . .

P. G. Wodehouse *The Mating Season* 1949

THERE IS NO spectacle on earth more appealing than that of a beautiful woman in the act of cooking dinner for someone she loves.

Thomas Wolfe *The Web and the Rock*

WE HAD FOR DINNER a Calf's Head, boiled Fowl and tongue, a Saddle of Mutton roasted on the Side Table, and a fine Swan roasted with Currant Jelly Sauce for the first Course. The second Course a couple of Wild Fowl called Dun Fowls, Larks, Blancmange, Tarts etc. etc. and a good Dessert of Fruit after amongst which was a Damson Cheese. I never eat a bit of Swan before, and I think it good eating with sweet sauce. The Swan was killed three weeks before it was eat and yet not the least bad taste in it.

James Woodforde *Diary of a Country Parson* January 28th, 1780

DINNER BOILED Tench, Peas Soup, a Couple of boiled Chicken and Pigs Face, hashed Calfs Head, Beans and roasted Rump of Beef with New Potatoes etc. Second Course roasted Duck and green Peas, a very fine Leveret roasted, Strawberry Cream, Jelly, Puddings &c. Dessert – Strawberries, Cherries and last Year's nonpareils . . . Coffee and Tea.

James Woodforde *Diary of a Country Parson* June 26th, 1792

AN EXQUISITE scent of olives and oil and juice rose from the great brown dish as Marthe, with a little flourish, took the cover off. The cook had spent three days over that dish. And she must take great care, Mrs. Ramsay thought, diving into the soft mass, to choose a specially tender piece for William Bankes. And she peered into the dish, with its shiny walls and its confusion of savoury brown and yellow meats, and its bay leaves, and its wine, and thought: This will celebrate the occasion . . .

Virginia Woolf *To the Lighthouse* 1927

THE LUNCH ON this occasion had begun with soles, sunk in a deep dish, over which the college cook had spread a counterpane of the whitest cream, save that it was branded here and there with brown spots like the spots on the flanks of a doe. After that came the partridges . . . many and various . . . with all their retinue of sauces and salads, the sharp and the sweet, each in its order; their potatoes, thin as coins but not so hard; their sprouts, foliated as rose-buds but more succulent. And no sooner had the roast and its retinue been done with than the silent serving man . . . set before us, wreathed in napkins, a confection which rose all sugar from the waves.

Virginia Woolf *A Room of One's Own* 1929

TO CALL IT A pudding and so relate it to rice and tapioca would be an insult. Meanwhile the wine glasses had flushed yellow and flushed crimson; had been emptied; had been filled. And thus by degrees was lit halfway down the spine, which is the seat of the soul, not that hard little electric light which we call brilliance, as it pops in and out upon our lips, but the more profound, subtle and subterranean glow which is the rich yellow flame of rational intercourse. No need to hurry. No need to sparkle. No need to be anybody but oneself. We are all going to heaven and Vandyck is of the company . . .

Virginia Woolf *A Room of One's Own* 1929

CHAPTER TWO

NOW TO THE BANQUET WE PRESS

I beg you come tonight and dine
A welcome waits you and sound wine
The Roederer chilly to a charm
As Juno's breasts the claret warm
The sherry of an ancient brand
No Persian pomp, you understand.
A soup, a fish, two meats and then
A salad fit for aldermen . . .
A dish of grapes whose clusters won
Their bronze in Carolinian sun.
Next cheese, for you the Neufchatel,
A bit of Cheshire like me well,
Cafe-au-lait or coffee black
With Kirsch or Kummel or Cognac.

J. B. Aldrich q. in *Wine and Food* 1947

I eat my peas with honey
I've done it all my life
It makes the peas taste funny
But it keeps them on the knife.

Anonymous *Manners*

Give the guest food to eat even though you yourself are starving.

Anonymous *Arab saying*

Seven make a banquet, nine make a noise.

Anonymous *Latin proverb 25*

THE COCKTAIL PARTY has the form of friendship without the warmth and devotion. It is a device either for getting rid of social obligations hurriedly en masse, or for making overtures towards more serious relationships, as in the etiquette of whoring.

Brooks Atkinson *Once Around the Sun* 1951

When asked out to dine by a P   on of Quality,
Mind and observe the most strict punctuality!
For should you come late, and make dinner wait,
And the victuals get cold, you'll incur, sure as fate,
The Master's displeasure, the Mistress's hate.
And though both may, perhaps, be too well-bred to swear,
They'll heartily wish you – I need not say where.

Richard Harris Barham *The Ingoldsby Legends* 1840

THE HALF-HOUR before dinner has always been considered as the great ordeal through which the mistress, in giving a dinner-party, will either pass with flying colours, or lose many of her laurels.

Mrs Isabella Beeton *The Book of Household Management* 1861

Etiquette, n: a code of social rites, ceremonies and observances, constituting a vulgarian's claim to toleration. The fool's credentials.

Ambrose Bierce *The Devil's Dictionary* 1911

I HAVE ALWAYS BEEN punctual at the hour of dinner, for I know that all those whom I kept waiting at that provoking interval would employ those unpleasant moments to sum up my faults.

Nicolas Boileau

Nothing is more pleasant than to receive your friends at your table; nothing more perfect if the food is good; but nothing more painful for them if it is bad. How pathetic that they should at the same time long to see you and dread your cooking. Think too, of their remarks afterwards, if they are only acquaintances.

X. Marcel Boulestin *Simple French Cooking for English Homes* 1923

LET THE NUMBER of guests not exceed twelve . . . so chosen that their occupations are varied, their tastes similar . . . the dining room brilliantly lighted, the cloth white, the temperature between 60° and 68°; the men witty and not pedantic, the women amiable and not too coquettish; the dishes exquisite but few, the wines vintage . . . the eating unhurried, the dinner being the final business of the day . . . the coffee hot . . . the tea not too strong, the toast artistically buttered . . . the signal to leave not before eleven and everyone in bed at midnight.

Jean-Anthelme Brillat-Savarin *La Physiologie du goût* 1825

THE HOST whose guest has been obliged to ask him for anything is a dishonoured man.

Baron Brisse *La Petite Cuisine* 1870

Swill champagne but sip claret.

Winston Churchill q. in *Way of Life* by John Boyd Carpenter 1982

I write these precepts for immortal Greece,
that round a table delicately spread,
Three, or four may sit in choice repast
or five at most. Who otherwise shall dine
Are like a troop marauding for their prey.

Dionysius of Halicarnassus *Thesmophorus* 50 BC

Food Throwers: Begun usually by estranged couples, once this victual flinging starts, everyone will do it . . . Should your dinner party have become an out of control concussion match with opponents catapulting croutons and petits pois across the mahogany, don't fight it, go with it. And when you have the desire to quell the uprising approach the original perpetrator from behind. There, slowly crown her with the contents of the fresh fruit salad bowl. But be warned. Although this immobilizes and rivets everyone's attention it also gives them new ideas.

J. P. Donleavy *The Unexpurgated Code* 1975

T O BE miserly towards your friends is not pretty. To be miserly towards yourself is contemptible.

Norman Douglas *Venus in the Kitchen* 1952

We should look for someone to eat and drink with before looking for something to eat and drink, for dining alone is leading the life of a lion or wolf.

Epicurus *Aphorisms – 300*

Since hunger is the most primitive and permanent of human wants, men always want to eat, but since their wish not to be a mere animal is also profound, they have always attended with special care to the manners which conceal the fact that at the table we are animals feeding.

John Erskine *The Complete Life*

When I demanded of my friend what viands he preferred,
He quoth: 'A large cold bottle and a small hot bird.'

Eugene Field *The Bottle and the Bird* 1889

G ASTRONOMICAL PERFECTION can be reached in these combinations: one person dining alone, usually upon a couch or a hillside; two persons, no matter of what sex or age, dining in a good restaurant; six people, of no matter what sex or age, dining in a good home. The six should be capable of decent social behaviour: that is, no two of them should be so much in love as to bore the others, nor, at the opposite extreme, should they be carrying on any sexual or professional feud which could put poison in the plates all must eat from.

M. F. K. Fisher *The Art of Eating* 1963

I prefer not to have among my guests two people or more, of any sex, who are in the first wild tremors of love. It is better to invite them after their new passion has settled, has solidified into a quieter reciprocity of emotions. (It is also a waste of good food, to serve it to new lovers.)

M. F. K. Fisher *Serve It Forth* 1937

D INING PARTNERS . . . should be chosen for their ability to eat – and drink – with the right mixture of abandon and restraint. They should enjoy food, and look upon its preparation and degustation as one of the human arts . . . Above all, friends should possess the rare gift of sitting. They should be able, no eager, to sit for hours – three, four, six – over a meal of soup and wine and cheese, as well as one of twenty fabulous courses.

M. F. K. Fisher *Serve It Forth* 1937

Congealed fat is pretty much the same, irrespective of the delicacy around which it is concealed.

Clement Freud *Freud on Food* 1978

It isn't so much what's on the table that matters, as what's on the chairs.

W. S. Gilbert q. in *Gilbert and Sullivan* by Hesketh Pearson 1935

T HE BEST NUMBER for a dinner-party is two: myself and a damn good head waiter.

Nubar Gulbenkian q. in *Observer* 1965

T HE INVETERATE DINER-OUT who is 'worth his salt' is always an acquisition to the company – a bright, chirrupy creature who is never at a loss when the conversation flags, who is ready with some anecdote, reminiscence or suggestive remark, which fans it immediately into flame again.

Frederick W. Hackwood *Good Cheer* 1911

The first four are necessary, namely: to know that God is the Provider; to be satisfied with what he has provided; to say 'In the name of God!' when beginning to eat and to say 'To God be thanks!' when you finish. The next four are customary, and it is well to observe them, though they are not required: to wash the hands before eating; to sit at the left of the table; to eat with three fingers; and to lick the fingers after eating. The last four are rules of particular politeness: to eat out of the dish that is immediately in front of you and out of your own side of the dish; to take small pieces; to chew the food well; and not to gaze at the others at the table with you.

Imam Hassan
Twelve Rules of Etiquette q. in *A Book of Middle Eastern Food* 1968

BEING SET AT THE TABLE, scratch not thyself, and take thou heed as much as thou canst not to spit, cough and blow at thy nose; but if it be needful, do it dexterously, without much noise, turning thy face sidelong.

Francis Hawkins *Youth's Behaviour* 1663

On the part of the guests . . . punctuality should be regarded as imperative; and the habitual want of it may be commonly set down to affectation or long-indulged selfishness. Rather than place the slightest restraint on himself the transgressor makes a whole party uncomfortable. It is no answer to say that they can sit down without him, for a well-selected company may be spoilt by a gap; and a late arrival causes discomfort and confusion in exact proportion to the care that has been in the preparatory arrangements.

Abraham Hayward *The Art of Dining* 1852

Nobody can write the life of a man, but those who have eat and drunk and lived in social intercourse with him.

Dr Samuel Johnson in *The Life of Samuel Johnson* by James Boswell 1791

DO YOU KNOW how helpless you feel if you have a full cup of coffee in your hand and you start to sneeze?

Jean Kerr *Mary, Mary*

Summer has an unfortunate effect on hostesses who have been unduly influenced by the photography of Irving Penn and take the season as a cue to serve dinners of astoundingly meagre proportions. These they call light, a quality which, while most assuredly welcome in comedies, cotton shirts and hearts, is not an appropriate touch at dinner.

Fran Lebowitz *Metropolitan Life* 1978

Civilised adults do not take apple juice with dinner.

Fran Lebowitz *Metropolitan Life* 1978

The rapturous, wild and ineffable pleasure
Of drinking at somebody else's expense.

Harry Leigh *Carols of Cockayne* 1869

When you ask one friend to dine,
Give him your best wine!
When you ask two,
The second best will do!

Henry Wadsworth Longfellow
q. in *Recreations of an Anthologist* by B. Matthews

It's all right, Arthur: the white wine came up with the fish.
Herman Mankiewicz
after vomiting across the dinner-table of a gourmet host . . . 1935

AT A DINNER-PARTY one should eat wisely but not too well, and talk well
but not too wisely.

W. Somerset Maugham *A Writer's Notebook* 1949

If the soup had been as warm as the claret . . .
If the claret had been as old as the chicken . . .
If the chicken had been as fat as our host . . .
It would have been a splendid meal.

Donald McCullough
After Dinner Grace 1960

A MAN SHOULD not so much respect what he eats, as with whom he eats.

Michel de Montaigne *Essays* 1588

Many social visits you think paid to yourself are paid to your bottles.

Austin O'Malley

Dining out is a vice, a dissipation of spirit punished by remorse. We eat, drink, and
talk a little too much, abuse all our friends, belch out our literary preferences and
are egged on by accomplices in the audience to acts of mental exhibitionism. Such

evenings cannot fail to diminish those who take part in them. They end on
Monkey Hill.

Palinurus (Cyril Connolly) *The Unquiet Grave* 1945

Society: A perfect dinner party for sixteen. Each person is as carefully chosen as
an instrument in an orchestra – yet how many of the guests would rather be
engaged that evening in a tête-à-tête? Or glad to leave early for a brothel?

Palinurus (Cyril Connolly) *The Unquiet Grave* 1945

IT IS MUCH EASIER to accept an invitation to dinner than to receive guests at
your own table . . . to invite relations, friends or business contacts to a meal is
a most complicated business . . . the guest's happiness is a matter of infinite
complexity. It depends on the host himself, on his humour, his health, his
business interests, his pastimes, the character of his wife, his education, his
appetite, his attitude towards his neighbour at table, his artistic sense, his
inclination to mischief, his good nature, and so on and so forth. So it is really not
worth worrying too much, or the problem of inviting guests to dinner would
become insoluble.

Edouard de Pomiane (Edouard Pozerski) *Cooking with Pomiane* 1962

For the dinner to be really good the host must feel a glow of inward joy during the
whole of the week which precedes it. He must await with impatience the day of
the party. He must ask himself every day what he can do to improve it . . .
Whatever such a host offers to his guests, I am sure that it will be good, because
he will have enjoyed the anticipation of it for a week beforehand and he will feel the
same joy for a week afterwards in his pleasure at having charmed his guests.

Edouard de Pomiane *Cooking with Pomiane* 1962

ONE SHOULD NEVER refuse an invitation to lunch or dinner, for one never
knows what one may have to eat the next day.

Edouard de Pomiane *Cooking with Pomiane* 1962

'Madam, I beg you not to trouble yourself with a bag; I will provide oats. But
before you commence your tedious sitting, I intend to give you a treat. Let us
have a dinner-party all to ourselves! May I ask you to bring up some herbs from

the farm-garden to make a savoury omelette? Sage and thyme, mint and two onions, and some parsley. I will provide lard for the stuff- lard for the omelette,' said the hospitable gentleman with sandy whiskers.

Beatrix Potter *The Tale of Jemima Puddleduck* 1908

Properly considered, the quality of the dinner is twice blest; it blesses him that gives and him that takes; a dinner with friendliness is the best of all satisfactory meetings – a pompous entertainment, where no love is, is the least satisfactory.

Punch July 1849

T HE ULTIMATE AIM of civility and good manners is to please: to please one's guest or to please one's host. To this end one uses the rules laid down by tradition: of welcome, generosity, affability, cheerfulness and consideration for others. People entertain warmly and joyously. To persuade a friend to stay for lunch is a triumph and a precious honour. To entertain many together is to honour them all mutually. It is equally an honour to be a guest.

Claudia Roden *A Book of Middle Eastern Food* 1968

I T IS IMPOLITE to hold the fork, the knife, or the spoon raised in the hand, to make motions with any of these things, to carry a piece of bread to the mouth with the knife, to make use at the same time of the spoon and fork, to wipe them with the tongue, or to thrust them into the mouth. Nothing is more impolite than to lick the fingers.

St John Baptist de la Salle
The Rules of Christian Manners and Civility 1695

When faced with a friteful piece of meat which even the skool dog would refuse do not screw up the face in any circs and sa coo ur gosh ghastly. This calls atention to oneself and makes it more difficult to pinch a beter piece from the next boy. Rice PUDINGS and jely in the pokcet are not a good micture with the fluff and ushual nauseating contents. Sometimes you can chiz a bit of pink mange into hankchief but it is apt to be a bit hard to manage when bloing the nose.

Geoffrey Willans and Ronald Searle *The Compleet Molesworth* 1958

T HE BEST HOST is not he who spends most money to entertain his guests, but he who takes the most intelligent interest in their welfare and makes sure that they will have a good time, something good to drink, something that is both good and new, if possible.

André Simon *The Concise Encyclopedia of Gastronomy* 1952

T HE COCKTAIL PARTY – a device for paying off obligations to people you don't want to invite for dinner.

Charles Merrill Smith *Instant Status* 1972

An excellent and well-arranged dinner is a most pleasing occurrence, and a great triumph of civilised life. It is not only the descending morsel, and the enveloping sauce – but the rank, wealth, wit and beauty which surround the meats – the learned management of light and heat – the smiling and sedulous host, proferring gusts and relishes – the exotic bottles – the embossed plate – the pleasant remarks – the handsome dresses – the cunning artifices in fruit and farina! The hour of dinner, in short, includes every thing of sensual and intellectual gratification which a great nation glories in producing.

Sydney Smith q. in *The Smith of Smiths* by Hesketh Pearson 1934

W E VENERATE THE CLERGY, honour the magistracy, look with deference to the nobility, and with regard to our equals, but far above all do we esteem those truly respectable persons who give dinners.

Lancelot Sturgeon *Essays on Good Living*

Some people are alarmed if the company are thirteen in number. The number is only to be dreaded when the dinner is provided but for twelve.

Lancelot Sturgeon *Essays on Good Living*

Two things are essential in life: to give good dinners and to make friends of women.

Prince de Talleyrand
q. in *'Pleasures of the Table'* by G. Ellwanger 1903

Eating should be done in silence, lest the windpipe open before the gullet, and life be in danger.

The Talmud 200 BC

Dinners are given mostly in the middle classes by way of revenge.

William Thackeray *The Book of Snobs* 1847

I T IS A VERY POOR consolation to be told that the man who has given one a bad dinner, or poor wine, is irreproachable in private life. Even the cardinal virtues cannot atone for half-cold entrées.

Oscar Wilde *The Picture of Dorian Gray* 1891

THERE WERE 20 of us at that Table and a very elegant Dinner the Bishop gave us. We had two courses of 20 Dishes each Course, and a Dessert after of 20 Dishes. Madeira, red and white Wines. The first Course amongst many other things were 2 Dishes of prodigious fine stewed Carp and Tench, and a fine Haunch of Venison. Amongst the second Course a fine Turkey Poult, Partridges, Pidgeons and Sweetmeats. Dessert . . . Mulberries, Melon, Currants, Peaches, Nectarines and Grapes. A most beautiful Artificial Garden in the Center of the Table . . . in the middle of which was a high round Temple supported on Pillars . . . wreathed round with artificial Flowers – on one side was a Shepherdess on the other a Shepherd . . .

James Woodforde *Diary of a Country Parson* September 4th, 1783

CHAPTER THREE

FLASH IN THE PAN

Too many cooks spoil the broth.

Anonymous *English proverb*

Always have a Chinese cook and never go into the kitchen!

Anonymous q. in *The Art of Eating* by M. F. K. Fisher 1963

T HE COOK . . . should be a judge of the season of every dish, as well as know perfectly the state of every article he undertakes to prepare. He must also be a judge of every article he buys; for no skill, however great it may be, will enable him to make good that which is really bad.

Mrs Isabella Beeton *The Book of Household Management* 1861

A GOOD COOK is . . . an artist whom one may bless after having eaten the courses he has served, an officer who will make one's table the envy of all who have shared its good cheer, a seneschal of grave mien and imposing presence, conscientious in his work, prolific in resources, proud of his art, who gives dignity to his labours.

M. Berchoux *Gastronomie*

A good cook is not necessarily a good woman with an even temper. Some allowance should be made for artistic temperament.

X. Marcel Boulestin *Simple French Cooking for English Homes* 1923

We may live without poetry, music and art;
We may live without conscience, and live without heart;
We may live without friends; we may live without books;
But civilised man cannot live without cooks.

Edward Bulwer-Lytton *Lucile* 1860

They had a cook with them who stood alone
For boiling chicken with a marrow-bone,
Sharp flavouring powder and a spice for savour.
He could distinguish London ale by flavour,
And he could roast and boil and seethe and fry,
Make good thick soup and bake a tasty pie . . .
As for blancmange, he made it with the best.

Geoffrey Chaucer *The Canterbury Tales* c. 1387

MOST OF THE WORLD'S great dishes were created by people who could not read and write.

Rupert Croft-Cooke *English Cooking* 1960

IT IS ODD how all men develop the notion, as they grow older, that their mothers were wonderful cooks. I have yet to meet a man who will admit that his mother was a kitchen assassin and nearly poisoned him.

Robertson Davies *The Table-Talk of Samuel Marchbanks* 1949

God sends meat, but the Devil sends cooks.

Thomas Deloney

To roast some beef, to carve a joint with neatness,
To boil up sauces and to blow the fire,
Is anybody's task; he who does this
Is but a seasoner and a brother-maker.
A cook is quite another thing. His mind
Must comprehend all facts and circumstances;
Where is the place and what the time of supper;
Who are the guests and who the entertainer;
What fish he ought to buy and where to buy it.

Dionysius of Halicarnassus *Thesmophorus* 50 BC

The true cook is the perfect blend, the only perfect blend, of artist and philosopher. He knows his worth: he holds in his palm the happiness of mankind, the welfare of generations yet unborn.

Norman Douglas *An Almanac*

ALL CULINARY TASKS should be performed with reverential love, don't you think so? To say that a cook must possess the requisite outfit of culinary skill – that is hardly more than saying that a soldier must appear in uniform. You can have a bad soldier in uniform. The true cook must have not only those externals, but a large dose of worldly experience. He is the perfect blend, the only perfect blend, of artist and philosopher. He knows his worth: he holds in his palm the happiness of mankind, the welfare of generations yet unborn . . .

Norman Douglas *South Wind* 1917

THERE IS NO HOPE for a cook who will not learn his own as well as other gourmets' limitations, and a man who has made one good Béchamel by rote . . . and then goes on to make impossible ones because of his lack of balance, perspective and plain common sense and modesty, is, to be blunt again, past recall.

M. F. K. Fisher *An Alphabet for Gourmets* 1949

WHAT UNSELFISH PEOPLE cooks are . . . Few people know better than they how important an element in fine eating is the furniture of the dining-room, the profound depths of the mahogany table-top, the glitter of crystal, the serene smoothness of silver, the Cuyp over the mantelpiece. What is their share? The kitchen sink, the loaded draining-board, the cat-like spit of the frying-pan, the soggy mess in the cullender.

Louis Golding *Wine and Food* 1943

The greatest animal in creation: the animal who cooks.

Douglas Jerrold

A master cook! Why, he is the man of men,
For a professor; he designs, he draws,
He paints, he carves, he builds, he fortifies,
Makes citadels of curious fowl and fish.
Some he dry-ditches, some moats around with broths,
Mounts marrow-bones, cuts fifty-angled custards,
Rears bulwark pies; and for his outer works,
He raiseth ramparts of immortal crust,
And teaches all the tactics at one dinner –
What ranks, what files to put his dishes in,
The whole art military! . . .
He is an architect, an engineer,
A soldier, a physician, a philosopher,
A general mathematician.

Ben Jonson

A GOOD COOK is the peculiar gift of the gods. He must be a perfect creature from the brain to the palate, from the palate to the finger's end.

Walter Savage Landor *Imaginary Conversations* 1824-1853

Cruelty, violence, and barbarism were the characteristics of the men who fed upon the tough fibres of half-dressed oxen; humanity, knowledge and refinement belong to the living generation, whose tastes and temperance are regulated by the science of such philosophers as Carème and such Amphitryons as his employers.

Lady Morgan *France in 1829-30*

B AD COOKS – and the utter lack of reason in the kitchen – have delayed human development longest and impaired it most.

Friedrich Nietzsche *Beyond Good and Evil* 1886

M. Bourgignon, our 'chef saucier' told me that by the time a chef is forty he is either dead or crazy.

David Ogilvy *Confessions of an Advertising Man* 1964

We'll dine and drink, and say if we think
That any thing can better be,
And when we have dined, wish all mankind
May dine as well as we . . .

Thomas Love Peacock *Crotchet Castle* 1831

I CONSIDER THE DISCOVERY of a dish which sustains our appetite and prolongs our pleasures as a far more interesting event than the discovery of a star, for we have always stars enough; and I shall not regard the sciences as sufficiently honoured or adequately represented amongst us until I see a cook in the first class of the Institute.

Henrion de Pensey
q. in *Pleasures of the Table* by G. Ellwanger 1903

. . . a priest, succinct in amice white
Attends; all flesh is nothing in his sight!
Beeves, at his touch, at once to jelly turn,
And the huge boar is shrunk into an urn:
The board with specious miracles he loads,
Turning hares to larks, and pigeons into toads.
Another (for in all what one can shine)
Explains the seve and verdeur of the vine.
What cannot copious sacrifice atone?
Thy truffles, Perigord! thy hams, Bayonne!

Alexander Pope *The Dunciad* 1728

IT WAS MY MOTHER who could accomplish anything, who herself had to admit that it might even be that she was actually too good . . . She could make jello, for instance, with sliced peaches hanging in it, peaches just suspended there, in defiance of the law of gravity. She could bake a cake that tasted like a banana. Weeping, suffering, she grated her own horseradish, rather than buy the pishachs they sold in a bottle at the delicatessen. She watched the butcher, as she put it, 'like a hawk', to be certain that he did not forget to put her chopped meat through the kosher grinder.

Philip Roth *Portnoy's Complaint* 1969

AMONG THE FAITHFUL, in the great kitchens of the world, Escoffier is to Carême what the New Testament is to the Old.

André Simon *The Concise Encyclopedia of Gastronomy* 1952

Cooks are in some ways very much like actors; they must be fit and strong, since acting and cooking are two of the most exacting professions. They must be blessed – or cursed, whichever way you care to look at it – with what is called the artistic temperament, which means that if they are to act or cook at all well, it cannot be for duds or dummies.

André Simon q. in *A Wine and Food Bedside Book* ed. C. Morny 1972

WHAT IS ASKED OF THE COOK? And what can be asked: To understand exactly the properties of everything he employs, to perfect, and correct, if necessary, the savours on which he operates; to judge with a true taste, to degustate with a delicate palate, to join the skilful address of the hand, and the prompt and comprehensive glance, to the bold but profound conceptions of the brain; and above all – it cannot be too often repeated – to identify himself so well with the habits, the wants, even the caprices and gastronomic eccentricities, of those whose existence he embellishes, that he may be able, not to obey them, but to guess them and even have a presentiment of them.

Alexis Soyer *The Pantropheon* 1853

A good cook is as useful as a good tutor.

Alexis Soyer *The Gastronomic Regulator* 1846

CHAPTER FOUR

THE JOY OF COOKING

COOKERY, or the art of preparing good and wholesome food, and of preserving all sorts of alimentary substances in a state fit for human sustenance, of rendering that agreeable to the taste which is essential to the support of life, and of pleasing the palate without injury to the system, is, strictly speaking, a branch of chemistry; but, important as it is both to our enjoyments and our health, it is also one of the latest cultivated branches of that science.

Frederick Accum *Cookbook* 1821

IT MAY BE SAFELY averred that good cookery is the best and truest economy, turning to full account every wholesome article of food, and converting into palatable meals what the ignorant either render uneatable or throw away in disdain.

Eliza Acton *Modern Cookery for Private Families* 1855

Cookery is the soul of every pleasure, at all times and to all ages. How many marriages have been the consequence of a meeting at dinner; how much good fortune has been the result of a good supper, at what moment of our existence are we happier than at table? There hatred and animosity are lulled to sleep, and pleasure alone reigns.

Anonymous q. in *F. Accum Cookbook* 1821

Point des Légumes, point de Cuisinière. (No vegetables, no cook.)
Anonymous *French saying*

AS IN THE FINE ARTS, the progress of mankind from barbarism to civilisation is marked by a gradual succession of triumphs over the rude materialities of nature, so in the art of cookery is the progress gradual from the earliest and simplest modes, to those of the most complicated and refined.

Mrs Isabella Beeton *The Book of Household Management* 1861

THE KITCHEN is the great laboratory of the household, and the much of the 'weal and woe' as far as regards bodily health, depends on the nature of the preparations concocted within its walls.

Mrs Isabella Beeton *The Book of Household Management* 1861

Cookery, n: a household art and practice of making unpalatable that which was already indigestible.

Ambrose Bierce *The Devil's Dictionary* 1911

FOR ART, there is no future, it's the living moment and then it's dead. That's wonderful. Cuisine is like a fireworks display, nothing remains. It is "une fête", rapid, ephemeral.

Paul Bocuse q. in *The Listener* 1976

THE SO-CALLED nouvelle cuisine usually means not enough on your plate and too much on your bill.

Paul Bocuse q. in *The Standard* 1985

Do not be afraid of simplicity. If you have a cold chicken for supper, why cover it with a tasteless white sauce which makes it look like a pretentious dish on the buffet table at some fancy dress ball?

X. Marcel Boulestin *Simple French Cooking for English Homes* 1923

The dangerous person in the kitchen is the one who goes rigidly by weights, measurements, thermometers and scales. I would say once more that all these scientific implements are not of much use, the only exception being for making pastry and jams, where exact weights are important.

X. Marcel Boulestin *What Shall We Have Today* 1931

Early produce is never as good as produce in season, and the pleasure of eating something because it is expensive has absolutely nothing to do with the taste of good cuisine.

X. Marcel Boulestin *Petits et grands plats* 1928

COOKERY IS NOT CHEMISTRY. It is an art. It requires instinct and taste rather than exact measurements.

X. Marcel Boulestin *Petits et grands plats* 1928

Cooking is a way of giving and making yourself desirable.

Michel Bourdin q. in *Time* magazine 1978

The discovery of a new dish does more for human happiness than the discovery of a new star.

Jean-Anthelme Brillat-Savarin *La Physiologie du goût* 1825

FRYING GIVES COOKS numerous ways of concealing what appeared the day before and in a pinch facilitates sudden demands, for it takes little more time to fry a four-pound carp than to boil an egg.

Jean-Anthelme Brillat-Savarin *La Physiologie du goût* 1825

Cooking is the oldest of the arts; for Adam was born fasting, and the new-born child has scarcely made its entry into this world before it utters cries which can only be quieted at its mother's breast. It is also of all arts the one which has done the most to advance the cause of civilisation; it was the need to cook which taught man to use fire; and it was by using that fire than man conquered Nature.

Jean-Anthelme Brillat-Savarin *La Physiologie du goût* 1825

WITH STUPIDITY and sound Digestion man may front much. But what, in these dull, unimaginative days, are the terrors of the conscience to the diseases of the liver? Not on Morality, but on Cookery, let us build our stronghold. There brandishing our frying-pan, as censer, let us offer sweet incense to the Devil, and live at ease on the fat things he has provided for his elect.

Thomas Carlyle *Sartor Resartus* 1838

SOME SENSIBLE PERSON once remarked that you spend the whole of your life either in your bed or in your shoes. Having done the best you can by shoes and bed, devote all the time and resources at your disposal to the building up of a fine kitchen. It will be, as it should be, the most comforting and comfortable room in the house.

Elizabeth David *French Country Cooking* 1951

One of the fallacies about the passing of judgement on cookery books is the application to the recipes of what is believed to be the acid test implied in the question do they work? . . . What one requires to know about recipes is not so much do they work as what do they produce if they do work?

Elizabeth David *Spices, Salt & Aromatics in the English Kitchen* 1970

How much cheese is a handful? How much more or less is a cupful? What is the capacity of a glass, a tumbler, or a soup ladle? What is the difference between a suspicion and a pinch? How much more is a good pinch? How much wine is a little, how many olives a few? When a book says a tin of chopped almonds or pomegranate juice what are you supposed to understand by that?

Elizabeth David *Spices, Salt & Aromatics in the English Kitchen* 1970

OBSERVING the frenzied shopping and cooking which goes on at Christmas-time one cannot help wondering if these prodigious efforts could not be spread out a little over the rest of the year. I do not mean, heaven forbid, that we should be forever cooking mammoth roasts, gigantic sirloins, whole sides of lamb and turkeys immense and bulging like captive balloons. It is not groaning boards we need so much as an orderly method of producing good quality everyday food without too much fuss or expense.

Elizabeth David *Spices, Salt & Aromatics in the English Kitchen* 1970

'Know your limitations' is a copybook maxim which could be applied more often when planning a meal; many a reputation for skillful entertaining has been founded on the ability to cook one dish to perfection . . .

Elizabeth David *French Country Cooking* 1951

. . . those . . . happy-go-lucky cooks who tell you, not without pride, 'of course I never follow a recipe, I just improvise as I go along. A little bit of this, a spoonful of that . . . it's much more fun really.' Well, it may be more fun for the cook, but it is seldom so diverting for the people who have to eat his products, because people who have a sure enough touch to invent successfully in the kitchen without years of experience behind them are very rare indeed. The fortunate ones gifted with that touch are those who will also have the restraint to leave well alone when they have hit on something good.

Elizabeth David *French Provincial Cooking* 1960

The ideal cuisine should display an individual character; it should offer a menu judiciously chosen from the kitchen-workshops of the most diverse lands and peoples – a menu reflecting the master's alert and fastidious taste . . .

Norman Douglas *South Wind* 1917

THE AMBITION of every good cook must be to make something very good with the fewest possible ingredients.

Urbain Dubois q. in *Esquire* June 1975

An unwatched pot boils immediately.

H. F. Ellis *Punch*

COOKERY IS NATURALLY the most ancient of the arts, as of all arts it is the most important.

George Ellwanger *Pleasures of the Table* 1903

A combination of the qualities of the scholar, the master cook, the painter, the gastronomer, the sportsman and the pantologist, assisted by the skill of the bookmaker and etcher, will be required to compose the cookbook par excellence.

George Ellwanger *Pleasures of the Table* 1903

All cooking is a matter of time. In general, the more time the better.

John Erskine *The Complete Life*

W HERE ROASTING is concerned, experience is the surest guide, as theory however precise, cannot replace the eye and the sureness which is the result of practice – one becomes a good roaster with a good deal of attention and observation and a little vocation.

Auguste Escoffier

The culinary art depends on the psychological state of society . . . wherever life is easy and comfortable, where the future is assured, it always experiences a considerable development. On the contrary, wherever life and its cares preoccupy the mind of man he cannot give to good cheer more than a limited place. Oftener than not, the necessity of nourishing themselves appears to persons swept up in the hurly-burly of business not as a pleasure but as a chore. They consider lost the time spent at table and demand only one thing: to be served quickly.

Auguste Escoffier q. in *'Food'* by Waverley Root 1980

C OOKERY IS THE ART of preparing food for the nourishment of the body. Progress in civilization has been accompanied by progress in cookery. (cf: Mary Lincoln: All civilised nations cook their food, to improve its taste and digestibility. The degree of civilisation is often measured by the cuisine.)

Fannie Farmer *The Boston Cooking School Cookbook* 1896

Any sensible person early in life learns how to prepare a number of appetising dishes and cooks them so often that he can produce them almost automatically.

J. G. Farrell q. in *'Writers' Favourite Recipes'* ed. G. Vincent 1978

C OOKERY . . . the art that contains everything that is elegant and courteous, and without which all the other arts are useless; that perfect, hospitable art which uses with equal success all the most excellent products of the air, the waters and the earth.

M. Fayot q. in *'Pleasures of the Table'* by George Ellwanger 1903

A RECIPE IS SUPPOSED to be a formula, a means prescribed for producing a desired result, whether that be an atomic weapon, a well-trained Pekingese, or an omelet. There can be no frills about it, no ambiguities . . . and above all no 'little secrets'. A cook who indulges in such covert and destructive vanity . . . is not honest, and therefore is not a good cook. He is betraying his profession and his art.

M. F. K. Fisher *With Bold Knife and Fork* 1968

A good recipe, for modern convenience, should consist of three parts: name, ingredients, method. The first will perforce give some sort of description . . . The ingredients should be listed in one column or two, rather than in a running sentence . . . The method should in most cases tell the temperature of the oven first, if one is needed, and in a real kitchen guide should indicate in the simplest possible prose what equipment will be used . . .

M. F. K. Fisher *With Bold Knife and Fork* 1968

CENTRAL HEATING, French rubber goods and cookbooks are three amazing proofs of man's ingenuity in transforming necessity into art, and, of these, cookbooks are perhaps most lastingly delightful.

M. F. K. Fisher *Serve It Forth* 1937

Don't be too daring in the kitchen. For example, don't suddenly get involved with shallots. Later, when you are no longer a Lonely Guy, you can do shallots. Not now. If you know coriander, stay with coriander and don't fool around. Even with coriander you're on thin ice, but at least you've got a shot, because it's familiar. Stay with safe things, like pepper.

Bruce Jay Friedman *The Lonely Guy Cookbook* 1976

COOKERY IS AS OLD as the world, but it must also remain, always, as modern as fashion.

Phileas Gilbert *La Cuisine de Tous les Mois* c. 1895

The economy of the kitchen is only a counterpart, in its simplicity or complication, its rudeness or luxury, of the economy of the State. The perfectibility of cookery indicates the perfectibility of society. The progress of cookery is the progress of civilisation.

Frederick W. Hackwood *Good Cheer* 1911

'Better first in a village than second in Rome' is a maxim peculiarly applicable to cookery.

Abraham Hayward *The Art of Dining* 1852

To cookery we owe well-ordered States
Assembling man in dear society
. . . The art of cookery drew us gently forth
From that ferocious life when, void of faith,
The Anthropophagian ate his brother.

Hesiod c. 750 BC

Cooking is like love – it should be entered into with abandon, or not at all.

Harriet van Horne *Vogue magazine* 1956

Women can spin very well, but they cannot write a good book of cookery.

Dr Samuel Johnson q. in *'The Life of Samuel Johnson'* by James Boswell 1791

THE ART OF USING up left-overs is not to be considered as the summit of culinary achievement.

Larousse gastronomique

MEN DO NOT HAVE to cook their food; they do so for symbolic reasons to show they are men and not beasts.

Edmund Leach *New York Review of Books* October 12th, 1967

People have been cooking and eating for thousands of years, so if you are the very first to have thought of adding fresh lime juice to scalloped potatoes try to understand that there must be a reason for this.

Fran Lebowitz *Metropolitan Life* 1978

Some people's food always tastes better than others, even if they are cooking the same dish at the same dinner. Now I will tell you why – because one person has much more life in them – more fire, more vitality, more guts – than others. A person without these things can never make food taste right, no matter what materials you give them, it is no use. Turn in the whole cow full of cream instead of milk, and all the fresh butter and ingredients in the world, and still that cooking will taste dull and flabby – just because they have nothing in themselves to give. You have got to throw feeling into your cooking.

Rosa Lewis
q. in *The Queen of Cooks – and some Kings* by Mary Lawton 1925

WHAT IS LITERATURE compared with cooking? The one is shadow, the other is substance.

E. V. Lucas *365 Days and One More*

Once learnt, this business of cooking was to prove an ever growing burden. It scarcely bears thinking about, the time and labour that man and womankind has devoted to the preparation of dishes that are to melt and vanish in a moment like smoke or a dream, like a shadow, and as a post that hastes by, and the air closes behind them, afterwards no sign where they went is to be found.

Rose Macaulay *Personal Pleasures*

If Medicine be ranked among those Arts which dignify their Professors . . . Cookery may lay claim to an equal, if not a superior distinction; to prevent disease, is surely a more advantageous Art to Mankind, than to cure them.

George Meredith
The Art & Science of Cookery unpublished manuscript c. 1850

Kissing don't last, cookery do.

George Meredith
q. in *Violets & Vinegar* by J. Cooper & T. Hartman 1980

Plain cooking cannot be entrusted to plain cooks.

Countess Morphy
q. in *The Art of Eating* by M. F. K. Fisher 1963

ALL THE BEST COOKING is simple. There is really nothing new in it. I have four thousand cookbooks dating back to 1503 and everything that is in 'nouvelle cuisine' was there two hundred years ago.

Anton Mosimann in *Now!* magazine 1981

The alimentary prospect now, as in all ages, closely resembles the political, and in an unending meal of food from tins transferred to cellophane wrappings and eaten at no set times we should not be far from mob rule. It is useless to repine. Indeed, the arts of cooking and eating, of selecting bottles and guests, may prove a trifling price for the blessing of living in the twentieth century. One can never be sure of the future. Therein lies the attraction of the past.

Arnold Palmer *Moveable Feasts* 1952

Which is the best cookery book? The one you like best, and which gives you that confidence that cannot be called forth to order, but which is instinctively felt. For myself I like those books which are not too complicated and which suggest ideas rather than being minutely detailed handbooks – I also like the kind of cookery book which evokes the good meals of the old inns of the past, for reconstitution of the past is a delicate pleasure . . . I do not by any means dislike the cookery book imbued with a certain fantasy, with initiative and daring ideas; but this characteristic must not be exaggerated. Mere freakishness is no passport to glory. It is not even to be recommended.

Pierre de Pressac *Considérations sur la cuisine* 1931

The kitchen is a country in which there are always discoveries to be made.

Grimod de la Reynière
Almanach des Gourmands 1804

D ISHES CARRY the triumphs and glories, the defeats, the loves and sorrows of the past.

Claudia Roden *A Book of Middle Eastern Food* 1968

Cookery means the knowledge of all herbs and fruits and balms and spices, and all that is healing and sweet in the fields and groves, and savoury in meats. It means carefulness and inventiveness, and willingness, and readiness of appliances. It means the economy of your grandmothers and the science of the modern chemist; it means much tasting and no wasting; it means English thoroughness and French art and Arabian hospitality; and in fine it means that you are to be perfectly and always ladies – loaf givers.

John Ruskin

ALTHOUGH IT ONLY takes four or five hours, unlike the year or so it takes to write a novel, cooking a curry is rather like cooking a book. There must be time for the actual work, and time for the contemplation. You must know the rules and the end to which the means are directed, but there has to be joy and experiment as well as knowledge: a sense, say, of characters (or ingredients) developing – and this is what takes the time . . . When you've finished it, curry is like a book . . . You can't eat much of it yourself, but get pleasure from the expressions of delight on the faces of the people you cook it for.

Paul Scott q. in *Writers' Favourite Recipes* ed. G. Vincent 1978

When men reach their sixties and retire they go right to pieces. Women just go right on cooking.

Gail Sheehy

The joy and thrill which great cooking . . . gives us cannot be repaid in the coin of the realm: they are gifts from the chef . . . and the debt which we owe (him) personally can only be discharged by applause or a kindly word of thanks. It costs so little and it is so right.

André Simon q. in *A Wine and Food Bedside Book* ed. C. Morny 1972

COOKERY IS A WHOLLY unselfish art: as 'art for art's sake' it is unthinkable. A man may sing in his bath every morning without the least encouragement, but no cook can cook just for his or her own sake in a like manner. All good cooks, like all great artists, must have an audience worth cooking for.

André Simon q. in *A Wine and Food Bedside Book* ed. C. Morny 1972

No science . . . is as complicated as the science of cookery, in pursuit of which every nation and clime differ in their mode, in order to produce the same results with nearly the same materials, no matter how these results may differ; yet there is no other plan than the following for them to adopt – they are, Roasting, Baking, Boiling, Stewing, Braising, Frying, Sautéing, Broiling . . .

Alexis Soyer *The Modern Housewife* 1951

No patent stove, no patent oven or apparatus of any kind are required. All that is necessary is an oven, a grid, and the paper bag . . . When in the homes of modest resource the contents of the paper bag that has passed through the culinary process are placed on the table, and the savoury smell has been succeeded by the delicious flavour, husband and children will join in the cry of homage to the new method of the ménagère, and exclaim 'Oh, mother, now we know what cooking is!'

Nicholas Soyer *Soyer's Paper-Bag Cookery* 1911

When we first began reading Dashiell Hammett, Gertrude Stein remarked that it was his modern note to have disposed of his victims before the story commenced. Goodness knows how many were required to follow as a result of the first crime. And so it is in the kitchen. Murder and sudden death seem as unnatural there as they should be anywhere else . . . Food is far too pleasant to combine with horror. All the same, facts, even distasteful facts, must be accepted, and we shall see how, before any story of cooking begins, crime is inevitable.

Alice B. Toklas *The Alice B. Toklas Cookbook* 1954

WHEN TREASURES are recipes they are less clearly, less distinctly, remembered than when they are tangible objects. They evoke, however, quite as vivid a feeling – that is, to some of us who, considering cooking as an art, feel that a way of cooking can produce something that approaches an aesthetic emotion. What more can one say? If one had the choice of again hearing Pachmann play the two Chopin sonatas or dining once more at the Café Anglais, which would one choose?

Alice B. Toklas *The Alice B. Toklas Cookbook* 1954

As if a cookbook had anything to do with writing.

Alice B. Toklas *The Alice B. Toklas Cookbook* 1954

What science demands more study? Every man is not born with the qualifications necessary to constitute a good cook. Music, dancing, fencing, painting and mechanics in general possess professors under twenty years of age, whereas in the first line of cooking pre-eminence never occurs under thirty. We see daily at concerts and academies young men and women who display the greatest abilities, but in our line nothing but the most consummate experience can elevate a man to the rank of chief professor. Cookery is an art appreciated only by a few individuals, and which requires . . . the most diligent and studious application. There are cooks and cooks – the difficulty lies in finding the perfect one.

Louis Eustache Ude *The French Cook* 1822

GOOD COOKING does not depend on whether the dish is large or small, expensive or economical. If one has the art, then a piece of celery or salted cabbage can be made into a marvellous delicacy; whereas if one has not the art, not all the greatest delicacies and rarities of land, sea or sky are of any avail.

Yuan Mei *Poems* trans. Arthur Waley 1956

COOKERY IS LIKE MATRIMONY – two things served together should match. Clear should go with clear, hard with hard, soft with soft . . . Into no department of life should indifference be allowed to creep – into none less than into the domain of cookery.

Yuan Mei q. in *Pleasures of the Table* by G. Ellwanger 1903

In no department of life, in no place, should indifference be allowed to creep; into none less than the domain of cookery.

Yuan Mei q. in *Food* by Waverley Root 1980

CHAPTER FIVE

THE MORE THE MERRIER

PLUS JE BOIS MIEUX JE CHANTE

The advantage of champagne consists not only in the exhilarating sparkle and play of its mantling life, where the beads that airily rise ever in pursuit of those that have merrily passed; but in the magnetism it possesses above all other wines – of tempting the fair sex to drink an extra glass.

St Ange

> Here's to champagne, the drink divine
> That makes us forget out troubles;
> It's made of a dollar's worth of wine
> And three dollar's worth of bubbles.

Anonymous

OYSTERS . . . are ungodly because they are eaten without grace; uncharitable, because they leave naught but shells; and unprofitable, because they must swim in wine.

Anonymous *Tarlton's Jests* 1611

There was a young gourmet of Crediton
Who took pâté de foie gras and spread it on
A chocolate biscuit
He murmured 'I'll risk it.'
His tomb bears the date that he said it on.

Anonymous q. in *The Chocolate Book* by Helge Rubinstein, 1981

Asparagus is a delicate fruite, and wholesome for everiebodie, and especially when it is thicke, tender and sweete, and no very much boiled, it giveth good stomach unto the sicke . . . it maketh a good colour in the face.

Anonymous *Maison Rustique* 1600

The way I gained my title's
By a hobby which I've got
of never letting others pay
However long the shot;
Whoever drinks at my expense
Are treated all the same,
From Dukes and Lords to cabmen down,
I make them drink Champagne.

Anonymous *Music hall song* 1895

An oyster, that marvel of delicacy, that concentration of sapid excellence, that mouthful before all other mouthfuls, who first had faith to believe it, and courage to execute? The exterior is not persuasive.

Henry Ward Beecher *Eyes and Ears*

Oysters are very unsatisfactory food for labouring men, but will do for the sedentary, and for a supper to sleep on.

A. J. Bellows *The Philosophy of Eating* 1970

Y OU FIRST PARENTS of the human race . . . who ruined yourself for an apple, what might you not have done for a truffled turkey?

Jean-Anthelme Brillat-Savarin *La Physiologie du goût* 1825

Some (foods) should be eaten before fully ripe, such as capers, asparagus, sucking pigs and pigeons . . . others, at the moment of perfection, such as melons, most fruit, mutton and beef . . . others, when they start to decompose, such as medlars, woodcocks, and especially pheasants; others, finally, after the methods of art have removed their deleterious qualities, such as the potato and the cassava root.

Jean-Anthelme Brillat-Savarin *La Physiologie du goût* 1825

I ONCE ATTENDED a dinner of gourmands . . . Following an admirable first course, there appeared, among other dishes, a huge Barbezieux cockerel, truffled fit to burst, and a Gibraltar-rock of Strasbourg foie-gras. This sight produced a marked, but almost indescribable effect on the company . . . Sure enough, all conversation ceased, for hearts were full to overflowing, the skilful movements of the carvers held every eye; and when the loaded plates had been handed round, I saw successively imprinted on every face the glow of desire, the ecstasy of enjoyment and the perfect calm of utter bliss.

Jean-Anthelme Brillat-Savarin *La Physiologie du goût* 1825

Whoever says 'truffles' utters a great word which arouses erotic and gastronomic memories among the skirted sex and memories gastronomic and erotic among the bearded sex.

Jean-Anthelme Brillat-Savarin *La Physiologie du goût* 1825

Champagne is exciting in its first effects and stupefying in its later ones, in other words it acts exactly like the carbonic acid gas it contains.

Jean-Anthelme Brillat-Savarin *La Physiologie du goût* 1825

THE OYSTER is unseasonable and unwholesome in all months that have not the letter R in their name.

Richard Buttes *Diet's Dry Dinner* 1599

Even for those who dislike Champagne . . . there are two Champagnes one can't refuse: Dom Perignon and the even superior Cristal, which is bottled in a natural-coloured glass that displays its pale blaze, a chilled fire of such prickly dryness that, swallowed, seems not to have been swallowed at all, but instead to have been turned to vapours on the tongue, and burned there to one sweet ash.

Truman Capote *Answered Prayers* 1975

CHAMPAGNE does have one regular drawback: swilled as a regular thing a certain sourness settles in the tummy, and the result is permanent bad breath. Really incurable.

Truman Capote *Answered Prayers* 1975

Give me Champagne and fill it to the brim,
I'll toast in bumpers ev'ry lovely limb;
I'll challenge all the heroes of the skies
To show a goddess with a Craven's eyes.
Why then averse to love? Ah, leave disdain,
Discard thy fickle undeserving swain,
and pledge thy lover in the brisk Champaign.

Lord Chesterfield *Witticisms* 1773

There is more simplicity in the man who eats caviar on impulse than in the man who eats grapenuts on principle.

G. K. Chesterton

A single glass of champagne imparts a feeling of exhilaration. The nerves are braced, the imagination is agreeably stirred; the wits become more nimble. A bottle produces the contrary effect. Excess causes a comatose insensibility. So it is with war: and the quality of both is best discovered by sipping.

Winston Churchill
q. in *The Wit of Sir Winston* 1965

GENTLEMEN, in the little moment that remains to us between the crisis and the catastrophe, we may as well drink a glass of champagne.

Paul Claudel *speech 1931*

Away with all this slicing, this dicing, this grating, this peeling of truffles! Can they not love it for itself? If you do love it, then pay its ransom royally – or keep away from it altogether. But once having bought it, eat it on its own, scented and grainy-skinned, eat it like the vegetable it is, hot and served in munificent quantities.

Colette (Sidonie-Gabrielle Colette) *Prisons et Paradis*

Spoil the child,
Spare the rod,
Open up the caviare
And say Thank God.

Noel Coward q. in *The Cynic's Lexicon* by Jonathon Green 1984

N O GOVERNMENT could survive without champagne. Champagne in the throats of our diplomatic people is like oil in the wheels of an engine.

Joseph Dargent quoted 1955

Champagne . . . takes its fitting rank and position (at a ball) amongst feathers, gauzes, lace, embroidery, ribbons, white satin shoes, and eau-de-Cologne, for champagne is simply one of the elegant extras of life.

Charles Dickens q. in *Wine and Food* 1937

The truffle is not an outright aphrodisiac, but it may in certain circumstances make women more affectionate and men more amiable.

Alexandre Dumas (père) *Grand dictionnaire de cuisine* 1873

For the true gourmand there are no blue eyes, white teeth or rosy lips that can take the place of a black truffle.

Fulbert Dumonteil q. in *Pleasures of the Table* by G. Ellwanger, 1903

A N OYSTER LIVES a dreadful but exciting life. Indeed, his chance to live at all is slim, and if he should survive the arrows of his own outrageous fortune and in the two weeks of his youth find a clean smooth place to fix on, the years afterwards are full of stress, passion and danger.

M. F. K. Fisher *Consider the Oyster* 1941

. . . the man who first put truffles into his paste of fat goose livers and spice and brandy . . . who first consummated this celestial wedding of high flavour should be rendered some special gastronomical salute . . . just as should the brave soul who first ate a tomato, and the equally hardy one who first evolved a Camembert cheese from a fermenting pudding of old cream. There is nothing much better in the Western world than a fine, unctuous, truffled pâté.

M. F. K. Fisher *An Alphabet for Gourmets* 1949

'I'd like to start with caviar and then have a plain grilled "rognon de veau" with "pommes soufflés". And then I'd like to have "fraises des bois" with a lot of cream. Is it very shameless to be so certain and so expensive?' She smiled at him enquiringly. 'It's a virtue, and anyway it's only a good plain wholesome meal.' . . . 'I myself will accompany Mademoiselle with the caviar, but then I would like a very small "tournedos", underdone, with "sauce Bearnaise" and a "coeur d'artichaut". While Mademoiselle is enjoying the strawberries, I will have half an avocado pear with a little French dressing. Do you approve?' The maître d'hôtel bowed.

Ian Fleming *Casino Royale* 1953

He was a very valiant man who first adventured on eating of oysters.

Thomas Fuller DD *The Worthies of England* 1662

The man sure had a palate covered o'er
With brass or steel, that on the rocky shore
First broke the oozy oyster's pearly coat,
And risked the living morsel down his throat.

John Gay *Trivia* 1716

TRUFFLES . . . anyone who does not declare himself ready to leave Paradise or Hell for such a treat is not worthy to be born again.

Maurice Goudeket *Close to Colette*

Give me champagne
I won't complain
If that's the best you can do.
But if you've got class
Fill my glass
With Oklahoma homebrew.

Tom T. Hall c. 1972

THE CALENDAR YEAR opens, gastronomically speaking, in a piano mood, and sweeps in a gradual crescendo through the magnificent promise of Spring to the fortissimo of early Summer, and so through the quiet rallentando of the game Autumn (a sudden sforzando for September oysters), when many fine flavours linger on our palate, to the almost solemn andante sostenuto of Christmastide, and those winter days when eating is not only a pleasure, but a necessary exercise.

Ambrose Heath *Good Food* 1932

And ah! oysters are here again. I see a vision of ecstatic epicures astride at oyster-bars with the glistening bivalves poised at expectant lips. Nothing but a hiatus, thus . . . expressive of indescribable delight, can give them adequate welcome. Let us give praise in a silence of gustatory anticipation!

Ambrose Heath *Good Food* 1932

Champagne has the taste of an apple peeled with a steel knife.

Aldous Huxley *Time Must Have a Stop* 1944

FIVE MUFFINS are enough for any man at any one meal, and the breast and wing of a chicken should suffice without attacking the fibrous legs. Very different, however, is the case of 'pâté de foies gras' sandwiches, oysters, and meringues. I cannot eat too many of these. I make it, therefore, my rule to consume very limited quantities of plain food in order to leave as much room as possible for delicacies.

E. V. Knox *Gorgeous Times*

THREE LACKEYS IN GREEN, gold and powder entered, each holding a great silver dish containing a towering macaroni pie . . . Good manners apart, though, the aspect of those monumental dishes of macaroni was worthy of the quivers of admiration they evoked. The burnished gold of the crusts, the fragrance of sugar and cinnamon they exuded, were but preludes to the delights released from the interior when the knife broke the crust; first came a smoke laden with aromas, then chicken livers, hard-boiled eggs, sliced ham, chicken with truffles in masses of piping hot, glistening macaroni, to which the meat juice gave an exquisite hue of suede.

Giuseppe de Lampedusa *The Leopard* 1960

For Champagne Charlie is my name
Champagne Charlie is my name,
Good for any game at night, my boys,
Good for any game at night, my boys,
Who'll come and join me in a spree?

George Leybourne *Champagne Charlie*

If you're given champagne at lunch, there's a catch somewhere.

Lord Lyons q. in *Geoffrey Madan's Notebooks* 1981

T HOU MOST BEAUTIFUL OF ALL, thou evening star of entremets – thou that delightest in truffles, and gloriest in a dark cloud of sauces – exquisite foie gras! – Have I forgotten thee? Do I not, on the contrary, see thee, smell thee, taste thee, and almost die with rapture of thy possession? What though the goose of which thou art a part, has, indeed, been roasted alive by a slow fire, in order to increase thy divine proportions – yet has not our almanack truly declared that the goose rejoiced amid all her tortures . . . because of the glory that awaited her? Did she not, in prophetic vision, behold her enlarged and ennobled foie dilate into pâtés and steam into sautés – the companion of truffles – the glory of dishes – the delight – the treasure – the transport of gourmands. O, exalted among birds – the apotheosised goose, did not thy heart exult even when thy liver parched and swelled within thee, from that most agonising death; and didst thou not, like the Indians at the stake, triumph in the very torments which alone could render thee illustrious?

Edward Bulwer-Lytton, first Baron Lytton *Pelham* 1828

At the end of a sentence I call for tea
At the end of a paragraph, bread and b.
At the end of a page chip potatoes and hake
At the end of a chapter fillet steak
But ah! when I finish the ultimate line
When I've brought to fulfillment the grand design
When I look at the thing and it's mine, all mine
Then it's Oysters, my love, with Cold White Wine!

Jan Morris q. in *Writers' Favourite Recipes* ed. G. Vincent, 1978

Champagne and orange juice is a great drink. The orange improves the champagne. The champagne definitely improves the orange.

Philip, Duke of Edinburgh
q. in *The Book of Royal Quotes* by Noel St. George 1981

THE AUTHOR . . . has always regarded the pleasures of good cheer as the first of the mind and the senses . . . is there a woman, however beautiful, who is worth those admirable red partridges of Languedoc . . . these pâtés de foie of geese and ducks which will forever celebrate the cities of Toulouse, Auch and Strassbourg; these stuffed tongues of Troyes; these sausages of Arles . . . Can one compare a pretty, simpering face with these splendid sheep of the Ardennes . . . whose flesh fairly melts in one's mouth? What comparison can be made between a piquante face and these pullets of Bresse? Who would oppose to these delights the caprices of a woman, her poutings, her vagaries, her refusals and even her favours?

Grimod de la Reynière *My Abnegation* 1797

The truffle . . . a delicious and luxurious piece of Dainty.

Sir Tancred Robinson 1693

The rather thick slices (of boiled beef), their velvet quality guessed at by every lip, rested languidly upon a pillow made of a wide slice of sausage, coarsely chopped, in which the finest veal escorted pork, chopped herbs, thyme, chervil. This delicate triumph of pork-butchery was itself supported by ample cuts from the breast and wing fillets of farm chickens, boiled in their own juice with a shin of veal, rubbed with mint and wild thyme. And to prop up this triple and magnificent accumulation, behind the white flesh of the fowls, (fed exclusively upon bread and milk), was the stout, robust support of a generous layer of fresh goose liver simply cooked in Chambertin.

Marcel Rouff *The Passionate Epicure*

'The bigger the better' is, though a common, not a universal rule; it does not, for instance, apply to fish, nor to mutton . . . But it generally applies to receptacles of wine, and to those of champagne very specially.

George Saintsbury *Notes on a Cellar-book* 1920

THERE'S NOTHING in Christianity or Buddhism that quite matches the sympathetic unselfishness of an oyster.

Saki (H. H. Munro)

A white coat worn over a violet waistcoat.
Duck eggs.
Shaved ice mixed with liana syrup and put in a new silver bowl.
A rosary of rock crystal.
Snow on wistaria or plum blossoms.
A pretty child eating strawberries.

Sei Shonagon *Elegant Things*

WHOLE TRUFFLES cooked in Champagne, or in any other way, are sheer extravagance. The only place of truffles in gastronomy is as a flavouring agent, and first of all in Foie Gras. This solid goose fat is improved beyond recognition when its complete lack of appeal to the olfactory senses is made good by the presence of some fresh truffles.

André Simon *The Concise Encyclopedia of Gastronomy* 1952

The Native (oyster) . . . should always be eaten uncooked and unspoilt by its beard being removed or palate-paralysing vinegars and sauces added to it. A squeeze of lemon is said to be permissable, but it is the thin end of the wedge of heresy.

André Simon *A Concise Encyclopedia of Gastronomy* 1952

His idea of heaven is eating pâté de fois gras to the sound of trumpets.

Sydney Smith q. in *The Smith of Smiths by Hesketh Pearson* 1934

'There must be two to eat a truffled turkey' says the gourmand . . . 'I and the turkey.'

Alexis Soyer *The Pantropheon* 1853

THE TRUFFLE! Beloved treasure that the earth conceals within her bosom – as she does the precious metals, which seems to have yielded grudgingly to the patient researches of the gastronomist.

Alexis Soyer *The Pantropheon* 1853

To open champagne at breakfast is premature, like uncovering the font at a wedding.

Pierce Synnott
q. in *A Wine and Food Bedside Book* ed. C. Morny 1972

Haschich Fudge (which anyone could whip up on a rainy day): this is the food of Paradise – of Baudelaire's Artificial Paradises: it might prove an entertaining refreshment for a Ladies' Bridge Club or a chapter meeting of the DAR. In Morocco it is thought to be food for warding off the common cold in damp winter weather and is, indeed, more effective if taken with large quantities of hot mint tea. Euphoria and brilliant storms of laughter; ecstatic reveries and extensions of one's personality on several simultaneous planes are to be complacently expected.

Alice B. Toklas *The Alice B. Toklas Cookbook* 1954

L AMENT THE MODERN AGE as we will. Declare with justice that we can no longer build or paint; that we have made all but the most remote corners of our countryside uninhabitable and destroyed the charms of travel. But in one thing we have it better than our great-great-grandfathers – the copious bounty of the harvest on those chilly battlefields of Champagne and of the invention and the industry in the dank chalk caves where miles of bottles lie maturing for our delight.

Evelyn Waugh *Vogue* 1965

Algernon: Why is it that at a bachelor's establishment the servants invariably drink the champagne? I ask merely for information. Lane: I attribute it to the superior quality of the wine, sir. I have often observed that in married households the champagne is rarely of a first-rate brand.

Oscar Wilde *The Importance of Being Earnest* 1895

CHAPTER SIX

THIS DRINK DIVINE

The cocktail is a pleasant drink;
It's mild and harmless – I don't think.
When you've had one, you call for two,
And then you don't care what you do.

George Ade *The Sultan of Sulu* 1902

GIVE A YOUNG MAN a twenty-mile tramp and a few pints of good beer, and he has nothing to envy for sheer animal content in the connoisseur's intellectual ecstasies over a great wine.

H. Warner Allen *Through the Wine Glass* 1954

Without a liqueur and a coffee the best of meals ends as tamely as a pretty mermaid.

H. Warner Allen *Through the Wine-Glass* 1954

Nor frost, nor snow, nor wind I trow,
Can hurt me if it would,
I am so wrapped within and lapped
With jolly good ale and old.

Anonymous *A Song of Ale* c. 1500

Bread is the staff of life, but beer is life itself.

Anonymous *English proverb*

Cider smiles in your face, and then cuts your throat.

Anonymous *English proverb*

There was a young lady of Kent
Who said that she knew what it meant
When men asked her to dine,
Gave her cocktails and wine,
She knew what it meant – but she went!

Anonymous in *The Limerick Book* ed. Langford Reed

Beer is all froth and bubble,
Whiskey will make you moan,
Plonk is another name for trouble,
But metho is out on its own.

Anonymous Aborigine q. in *Quadrant* magazine 1958

He that buys land buys many stones;
He that buys flesh buys many bones;
He that buys eggs buys many shells;
But he that buys good ale buys nothing else.

Anonymous *English proverb* c. 1450

Punch cures the Gout, the Cholic and the Phthisic,
And is to all men the very best Physic.

Anonymous c. 1750

THERE ARE TWO THINGS that a Highlander likes naked – and one of them
is malt whisky.

Anonymous *Scottish proverb*

Of all things thirst I count the worst,
And always stand in fear;
So when I goes out, I carries about
A little pint bottle of beer:
For I likes a little good beer:
So when I goes out I carries about
A little pint bottle of beer;
For I likes a little good beer.

Anonymous *I Likes a Drop of Good Beer*

The great utility of rum has given it the medical name of an antifogmatic. The quantity taken every morning is in exact proportion to the thickness of the fog.

Anonymous q. in *Massachussetts Spy* 1789

Phairson had a son
Who married Noah's daughter,
And nearly spoiled the flood
By drinking up ta water,
Which he quold haf done –
I, at least, pelieve it –
Had its mixture peen
Only half Glenlivet!

William Aytoun *The Massacre of Macpherson* 1845

They sell good beer at Haslemere
And under Guildford Hill.
At Little Cowfold as I've been told
A beggar may drink his fill:
There is a good brew in Amberley too
And by the bridge also;
But the swipes they take in at the Washington Inn
Is the very best beer I know.

Hilaire Belloc *West Sussex Drinking Song* 1908

Let's get out of these wet clothes and into a dry martini.

Robert Benchley q. in *George S. Kaufman* by Howard Teichmann 1972

BRANDY, n: a cordial composed of one part thunder-and-lightning, one part remorse, two parts bloody murder, one part death-hell-and-the-grave, two parts clarified Satan and four parts holy Moses!

Ambrose Bierce *The Devil's Dictionary* 1911

Quaff, v: emptying the 'sparkling wine' down your throat. When it's only whiskey, it's called swallowing.

Ambrose Bierce *The Devil's Dictionary* 1911

WHAT HARM in drinking can there be,
Since life and punch so well agree?

Thomas Blacklock *Epigram on Punch*

Ale . . . is much used in England to the detriment of many Englishmen; especially it killeth them which be troubled with the colic, and the stone, and the strangulion; for the drink is a cold drink; yet it doth make a man fat, and doth inflate the belly.

Andrew Boorde *The Breviarie of Health* 1598

Beer that is not drunk has missed its vocation.

Meyer Breslau *speech 1880*

AT FIRST they drink only a small glass of brandy in the morning, and that amount satisfies them for several years; then they double the dose . . . they drink a small glass in the morning and another at noon. They continue at that rate for two or three years; then they take to drinking regularly three times a day . . . Soon they are drinking at all hours and will have nothing but brandy flavoured with infusion of cloves; once that stage is reached it is certain that they have six months to live at the outside; they dry up, fever takes hold of them, they go into the hospital, and they are never seen again.

Jean-Anthelme Brillat-Savarin *La Physiologie du gout* 1825

To provoke, or sustain, a reverie in a bar, you have to drink English gin, especially in the form of the dry martini . . . Connoisseurs who like their martinis very dry suggest simply allowing a ray of sunlight to shine through a bottle of Noilly Prat before it hits the gin. At a certain period in America it was said that the making of a dry martini should resemble the Immaculate Conception, for, as Saint Thomas Aquinas once noted, the generative power of the Holy Ghost pierced the Virgin's hymen 'like a ray of sunlight through a window – leaving it unbroken.'

Luis Buñuel *My Last Breath* 1983

Freedom and Whisky gang thegither!

Robert Burns *The Author's Earnest Cry and Prayer*

There nought, no doubt, so much the spirit calms
As rum and true religion; thus it was,
Some plunder'd, some drank spirits, some sung psalms.

George Gordon, Lord Byron *Don Juan* 1819

Oh Beer! Oh Hodgson, Guinness, Allsopp, Bass!
Names that should be on every infant's tongue!
Shall days and months and years and centuries pass,
And still your merits be unrecked, unsung?
Oh! I have gazed into my foaming glass,
And wished that lyre could yet again be strung
Which once rang prophet-like through Greece and taught her
Misguided sons that the best drink was water . . .

C. S. Calverley *Beer*

FOR THE POOR, beer is a necessity, as tobacco is very nearly a necessity; it is only for people sufficiently rich and fashionable to be faddists that either is really a luxury.

G. K. Chesterton *All I Survey*

Most people hate the taste of beer – to begin with. It is, however, a prejudice that many have been able to overcome.

Winston Churchill q. in *The Wit of Sir Winston* 1965

A cocktail is to glass of wine as rape is to love.

Paul Claudel

On corn liquor: It smells like gangrene starting in a mildewed silo, it tastes like the wrath to come, and when you absorb a deep swig of it you have all the sensations of having swallowed a lighted kerosene lamp.

Irvin S. Cobb to the US Distillers' Code Authority

Lo! the poor toper whose untutor'd sense,
Sees bliss in ale, and can with wine dispense;
Whose head proud fancy never taught to steer,
Beyond the muddy ecstasies of beer.

George Crabbe *Inebriety* 1820

You can no more keep a martini in the refrigerator than you can keep a kiss there. The proper union of gin and vermouth . . . is one of the happiest marriages on earth and one of the shortest lived.

Bernard De Voto *The Hour* 1951

COGNAC . . . a sense of amusement, charm, excitement, all combined into the purest of pleasure.

Roy Andries de Groot *Esquire* April 1975

Sherry gives rise to no thoughts.

R. Druitt q. in *Geoffrey Madan's Notebooks* 1981

Ladies and gentlemen, I give you a toast; it is: Absinthe makes the tart grow fonder.

Hugh Drummond (cf: Mizner)
q. in Seymour Hicks *The Vintage Years* 1943

God made yeast as well as dough, and loves fermentation just as dearly as he loves vegetation.

Ralph Waldo Emerson *Essays* second series 1844

I HAVE FED purely upon ale; I have eat my ale, drank my ale, and I always sleep upon ale.

George Farquhar *The Beaux Stratagem* 1707

THERE'S NO SUCH THING as bad whiskey. Some whiskeys just happen to be better than others. But a man shouldn't fool with booze until he's fifty, and then he's a damn fool if he doesn't.

William Faulkner

There is nothing so deceitful as the spirits given us by wine. If you must drink, let us have a bowl of punch – a liquor I rather prefer, as it is nowhere spoken against in Scripture, and as it is more wholesome for the gravel, a distemper with which I am grievously afflicted.

Henry Fielding *Jonathan Wild the Great* 1743

A martini – shaken, not stirred.

Ian Fleming *Goldfinger* 1959

He who drinks small beer and goes to bed sober,
Falls as the leaves do fall, and dies in rank October;
But he who drinks strong beer and goes to bed mellow,
Lives as he ought to live, and dies an honest fellow.

John Fletcher q. in *The Penny Universities* by Aytoun Ellis 1956

See how it sparkles in the cup;
Oh how shall I regale!
Can any taste this drink divine,
And then compare rum, brandy, wine,
Or aught with happy Ale.

John Gay *A Ballad on Ale*

Three bottles of Champagne, two of Madeira, one of Hock, one of Curaçao, one quart of Brandy, one pint of Rum and two bottles of seltzer-water, flavoured with four pounds of bloom raisins, Seville oranges, lemons, white sugar-candy, and diluted with iced green tea instead of water.

George IV recipe for *Regent's Punch*

Whisky comes from the Gaelic "uisge-beatha" meaning "water of life". In the curious mind this will at once rouse wonder, perhaps even a contemplative effort to surprise the ancestral thought in its creative moment. For clearly there is nothing haphazard or transitory about the designation. It was not coined for the slang or commerce of any age. Rather it is akin to one of the ultimate elements into which ancient philosophers resolved the universe. It is not a description so much as a simple statement of truth and of mystery.

Neil M. Gunn *Whisky and Scotland*

It is said that beer drinkers are slow, and a little stupid; that they have an ox-like placidity not quite favourable to any brilliant intellectual display. But there are times when this placidity is what the labouring brain most needs. After the agitation of too active thinking there is safety in a tankard of ale. The wine drinkers are agile, but they are excitable; the beer drinkers are heavy, but in their heaviness is peace.

Philip G. Hamerton *The Intellectual Life*

To an offer of a last glass of whiskey: 'You might make that a double.'

Neville Heath q. in *Famous Last Words by Jonathon Green* 1979

Here's to good old Whiskey
So amber and clear
'Tis not as sweet as woman's lips
But a damned sight more sincere.

Lewis C. Henry (ed.) *Toasts for All Occasions*

Absinthe makes the parts grow stronger.

Jack Hibberd *Odyssey of a Prostitute* 1983

(Whisky) sloweth age, it strengtheneth youthe; it helpeth digestion; it cutteth fleume; it abandoneth melancholie; it relisheth the harte; it lighteneth the mind; it quickeneth the spirits; it cureth the hydropsie; it healeth the strangury; it pounceth the stone; it reppelleth grauel; it puffeth awaie ventositie; it kepyth and preserveth the head from whyrling – the eyes from dazelyng – the tongue from lispyng – the mouth from snaffelyng – the teethe from chatteryng – the throte from ratlyng – the weason from stieflyng – the stomach from wamblyng – the harte from swellyng – the guts from rumblyng – the hands from shiueryng . . . truly it is a soueraigne liquor.

Raphael Holinshed *Chronicles of England, Ireland and Scotland* 1577

IF WINE tells the truth – and so have said the wise – It makes me laugh to think how brandy lies!

Oliver Wendell Holmes *The Banker's Secret*

Say, for what were hopyards meant,
Or why was Burton built on Trent?
Oh many a peer of England brews
Livelier liquor than the Muse,
Malt does more than Milton can
To justify God's ways to man.
Ale, man, ale's the stuff to drink
For fellows whom it hurts to think:
Look into the pewter pot
To see the world as the world's not.

A. E. Housman *A Shropshire Lad* 1896

CLARET is the liquor for boys, port for men; but he who aspires to be a hero must drink brandy. In the first place, the flavour of brandy is most grateful to the palate; and then brandy will do soonest for a man what drinking can do for him. There are, indeed, few who are able to drink brandy. This is a power rather to be wished for than attained.

Dr Samuel Johnson
q. in *The Life of Samuel Johnson* by James Boswell 1791

Usquebaugh, n: (an Irish or Erse word which signifies the water of life.) It is a compounded distilled spirit, being drawn on aromaticks: and the Irish sort is particularly distinguished for its pleasant and mild flavour. The Highland sort is somewhat hotter, and by corruption in Scotch they call it whisky.

Samuel Johnson *Dictionary* 1755

. . . there are very few great moments in a man's lifetime – when he's born and when he dies and when he passes his son his first beer. It's not an event to be lightly passed over and so I wish you health and I wish you wealth and I wish you happiness.

Peter Kenna *Listen Closely* 1972

EDWIN LAW told me an infallible receipt for warming cold and wet feet on a journey. Pour half a glass of brandy into each boot. Also he often carries a large pair of stockings with him to wear over boots and trousers. He has been a long time in Nova Scotia.

Rev. Francis Kilvert *Kilvert's Diary* New Year's Eve, 1874

When the clergyman's daughter drinks nothing but water, she's certain to finish on gin.

Rudyard Kipling 1886

A mixture of brandy and water spoils two good things.

Charles Lamb 1823

Cocktails have all the disagreeability without the utility of a disinfectant.

Shane Leslie q. in *The Observer* 1939

No soldier can properly fight unless he is properly fed on beef and beer.

Duke of Marlborough (attrib.)

Oh some are fond of red wines, and some are fond of white,
And some are all for dancing by the pale moonlight;
But rum alone's the tipple, and the heart's delight . . .

John Masefield *Captain Stratton's Fancy*

As far as beers go in terms of 'this' beer or 'that' beer you can drink day and night, night and day, you can search the wide world over, and still not find the perfect beer. The reason for that is simple: beer is just an approximation . . . like a good cigar it can only hint at the possibly better, find that one and it'll point you towards the possibly best but you know what? There's no such thing!

Richard Meltzer *Gulcher* 1972

Tequila . . . the effect is you're lying on your back constantly spinning in both directions if not all seven, at the same time all the time. It's when you try to switch directions that the spatial flashes hit, and you can't catch up with yourself even if you're the great Paavo Nurmi. You're always at least a step ahead of yourself, and it's a track meet from start to finish, very much like the vaunted lysergic.

Richard Meltzer *Gulcher* 1972

Ale . . . to Beef what Eve was to Adam.

George Meredith *Evan Harrington* 1861

Absinthe makes the heart grow fonder. (cf: Drummond)

Addison Mizner 1901

What makes the cider blow its cork
With such a merry din?
What makes those little bubbles rise
And dance like harlequin?
It is the fatal apple, boys
The fruit of human sin.

Christopher Morley *A Glee upon Cider*

Gie me the real Glenlivet and I weel believe I could mak' drinking toddy oot o' sea-water. The human mind never tires o' Glenlivet, any mair than o' caller air. If a body could just find oot the exact proportion and quantity that ought to be drunk every day, and keep to that, I verily trow that he might leeve for ever, without dying at a', and that doctors and kirkyards would go oot o' fashion.

Christopher North (Prof. John Wilson) *Noctes Ambrosianae* 1822-1835

Who comes here?
A grenadier.
What do you want?
A pot of beer.
Where is your money?
I forgot.
Get you gone
You drunken sot!

Nursery Rhymes in *Namby Pamby* by Henry Carey

He found that learnin', fame,
Gas, philanthropy and steam,
Logic, loyalty, gude name,
Were a' mere shams;
The source o' joy below,
And the antidote to woe,
And the only proper go,
Was drinkin' drams.

George Outram *Drinkin' Drams*

It's lonesome away from your kindred and all,
By the campfire at night where the wild dingoes call,
But there's nothing so lonesome so morbid or drear
Than to stand in the bar of a Pub With No Beer.

Gordon Parsons *A Pub with No Beer*

All drinks stand cap in hand,
In presence of old Sherry.
Then let us drink old Sack, old Sack, boys
Which makes us blithe and merry.

Pasquil *Palinodia* 1619

The Honourable Edward Russel, Commander in Chief of the English forces . . .
had a mighty bowl of punch made at his house on October 25th, 1694. It was made
in a fountain in the garden . . . in the fountain were four hogsheads of brandy,
eight hogsheads of water, twenty-five thousand lemons, twenty gallons of lime
juice, thirteen hundred weight of fine Lisbon sugar, five pounds of grated
nutmegs, three hundred toasted biscuits and a pipe of Mountain malaga. And

there was built on purpose a little boat, in which was a boy who rowed round the fountain and filled the cups of the company, who exceeded six thousand in number.

Reuben & Sholto Percy *The Percy Anecdotes*

The joy of bourbon drinking is not the pharmacological effect of C_2H_5OH on the cortex, but rather the instant of the whiskey being knocked back and the little explosion of Kentucky, USA sunshine in the cavity of the nasopharynx and the hot bosky bits of Tennessee summertime – aesthetic considerations, to which the effect of the alcohol is, if not dispensable, at least secondary. By contrast Scotch: drinking Scotch is like looking at a picture of Noel Coward. The whisky assaults the nasopharynx with all the excitement of paregoric.

Walker Percy *Esquire* December 1975

M AN IS SO SKILFUL in flattering his vices, that he has even found means to render water poisonous and intoxicating.

Pliny *Natural History* 79 BC

Sir John Barleycorn is the strongest knight.

John Ray *Complete Collection of English Proverbs* 1670

Bring me Absinthe and let me whirl in a green Heaven with wings as light as a butterfly.

Jean Richepin q. in *Through the Wine-Glass* by H. Warner Allen 1954

C IDER is to be drunk when you are thirsty, after a long walk or ride along a dusty road. Its pleasant sharpness drives away thirst, its deceptively imperceptible strength overcomes fatigue, the natural virtue of the fruit restores the elasticity of tired muscles. It is a splendid refresher between meals, but it makes a deplorable mesalliance with delicate foods.

Vivian Rowe *Return to Normandy* 1951

You will meet, as I have done, the Englishman who turns up his nose at Norman cider as thin sour stuff not worth the trouble of drinking, then you will know he has been brought up on the fabricated, gassy stuff, all but tasteless and non-alcoholic, which all too often goes by the name of cider in England and which appeals to the palates of those who have never passed beyond a teenage appreciation of sugared and aerated liquids prepared by commercial laboratories . . . Do not laugh him to scorn or hold him up to contempt, but rather lead him quietly to a more mature appreciation. By doing so you will probably add years to his life and greatly increase the pleasure he derives from it.

Vivian Rowe *Return to Normandy* 1951

Whiskey . . . a torchlight procession marching down your throat.

Hon. G. W. E. Russell *Collections and Recollections*

ALL ALCOHOLIC DRINKS, rightly used, are good for body and soul alike, but as a restorative of both there is nothing like brandy.

George Saintsbury *Notes on a Cellar-book* 1920

Everybody knows that rum and water is sovereign for a cold, but perhaps everybody does not know exactly how the remedy should be applied . . . You must take it in bed: premature consumption merely wastes the good creature. It should be made in a large rummer-glass, as hot as you can drink it . . . not too sweet, but so strong that you sink back at once on the pillow, resigning the glass to the ready hands of a sympathising bedside attendant, preferably feminine. If you do not wake the next morning, possibly with a slight headache, but otherwise restored, there must be something really the matter with you.

George Saintsbury *Notes on a Cellar-book* 1920

Nor have I ever disdained the humble and much reviled liquid which is the most specially English of all spirits; which . . . you used to be able to procure at its best for much more than half a crown a bottle . . . I have always been sorry for gin.

George Saintsbury *Notes on a Cellar-book* 1920

LIQUEURS . . . are, save occasionally for medicinal purposes, the most positive of superfluities and extravagances. They are also, being as a rule both too strong and too sweet, the most questionably wholesome; and excess in them results in sufferings the most unpleasant of all such sufferings. Nor do they possess the natural grace and charm – the almost intellectual as well as sensual interest – of the best wine. On the other hand they are for the most part very pleasant to the taste; they are frequently very pretty to look at; and if there be any truth as to the connection between the wills and wishes of womankind and the Deity, they cannot be hateful to God.

George Saintsbury *Notes on a Cellar-book* 1920

I suppose (though I cannot say that it ever did me any) that absinthe has done a great deal of harm. Its principle is too potent, not to say too poisonous, to be let loose indiscriminately and intensively in the human frame. It was . . . as a rule made fearfully strong, and nobody but the kind of lunatic whom it was supposed to produce, and who may be thought to have been destined to lunacy, would drink it 'neat'. A person who drinks absinthe neat deserves his fate whatever it may be. The flavour is concentrated to repulsiveness; the spirit burns 'like a torchlight procession' . . . Moreover, you lose all the ceremonial and etiquette which make the proper fashion of drinking it delightful to a man of taste.

George Saintsbury *Notes on a Cellar-book* 1920

Bundaberg rum, overproof rum,
Will tan your insides and grow hair on your bum.
Let the blue-ribbon beat on his empty old drum
Or his water-logged belly, we'll stick to our rum.

Bill Scott
q. in *The Dictionary of Australian Quotations* ed. S. Murray-Smith 1984

If I had a thousand sons the first human principle I would teach them should be to forswear thin potations and to addict themselves to sack.

William Shakespeare *Henry IV Part 2* c. 1598

For a quart of ale is a dish for a king.

William Shakespeare *The Winter's Tale* c. 1610

As IN THE CASE of man, whose character is formed, strengthened and often mellowed by the process of time, so the flavour and bouquet of Brandy will acquire strength and softness as it loses by evaporation some of its youthful vigour. Brandy, like man, should gain rather than lose in character with age, but its birth and upbringing determine its characteristics.

André Simon *Wine and Food* 1936

Fifteen men on a dead man's chest –
Yo-ho-ho and a bottle of rum.
Drink and the Devil have done for the rest –
Yo-ho-ho and a bottle of rum.

Robert Louis Stevenson *Treasure Island* 1883

I had companions, I had friends,
I had of whisky various blends.
The whisky was all drunk; and lo!
The friends were gone for ever mo!

Robert Louis Stevenson *Rhyme to Henley*

I cannot eat but littyl meate,
My stomach is not goode
But sure I thinke that I can drinke
With him that wears a hood.
Though I go bare, take ye no care,
I nothing am a-cold;
I stuff my skin so full within
Of jolly goode ale and olde.
Back and side go bare, go bare,
Both foot and hand go cold;
But Belly, God send thee good ale enough,
Whether it be new or old!

John Still (attrib.) *Gammer Gurton's Needle* 1566
(also attrib. **William Stevenson** (1530?-1575) in ODQ)

It is not brandy, it is not wine,
It is Jameson's Irish Whiskey:
It fills the heart with joy divine,
And makes the fancy frisky.
All other spirits are vile resorts,
Except its own Scotch first cousin;
And as for your Clarets and Sherries and Ports,
A naggin is worth a dozen.

James Thomson *Sunday up the River* 1869

SCOTCH WHISKY to a Scotsman is as innocent as milk is to the rest of the human race.

Mark Twain

Beer is chiefly to be desired in the Summer, and it is a drink (believe me) for all constitutions, but especially for the cholerick and melancholick most wholesome.

Tobias Venner *Via recta ad Vitam Longam* 1620

BEER is acceptable very late at night at the end of a party. It has many valuable functions but I cannot help think that it has been a little over-praised by poets of the school of Chesterton and Belloc. It is a fine honest staple rather than a theme for poetry.

Evelyn Waugh *Wine in Peace and War* 1937

Cider and tinned salmon are the staple diet of the agricultural classes.

Evelyn Waugh *Scoop* 1938

Absinthe has a wonderful colour, la couleur verte. Il faut maintenant boire des choses vertes. A glass of absinthe is as poetical as anything in the world. Quelle différence y a-t-il entre un verre d'absinthe et un coucher de soleil . . . the soul is never liberated except by drunkenness in one form or another.

Oscar Wilde *The New Age*

After the first glass of absinthe you see things as you wish they were. After the second you see them as they are not. Finally you see things as they really are, and that is the most horrible thing in the world.

Oscar Wilde

My brain ceased to reel. I saw it all. 'Have you been having a drink?' 'I have. As you advised. Unpleasant stuff. Like medicine. Burns your throat too, and makes one as thirsty as the dickens. How anyone can mop it up, as you do, for pleasure beats me. Still, I would be the last to deny that it tunes up the system. I could bite a tiger.' 'What did you have?' 'Whisky. At least that was the label on the decanter . . .'

P. G. Wodehouse *Right Ho, Jeeves* 1934

He was white and shaken, like a dry martini.

P. G. Wodehouse *Cocktail Time* 1958

B REWED a vessel of strong Beer today. My two large Piggs . . . got so amazingly drunk by it, that they were not able to stand and appeared like dead things almost, and so remained all night from dinner-time today. I never saw Piggs so drunk in my life, I slit their ears for them without feeling. April 16th: My 2 Piggs are still unable to walk yet, but they are better than they were yesterday. They tumble about the yard and can by no means stand at all steady yet. In the afternoon my 2 Piggs were tolerably sober.

James Woodforde *Diary of a Country Parson* April 15th, 1778

My Boy Jack had another touch of the Ague about noon. I gave him a dram of gin at the beginning of the fit and pushed him headlong into one of my Ponds and ordered him to bed immediately and he was better after it and had nothing of the cold fit after, but was very hot . . .

James Woodforde *Diary of a Country Parson* May 22, 1779

CHAPTER SEVEN

THE
FLOWING BOWL

Wine throws a Man out of himself, and infuses Qualities into the Mind which she is a Stranger to in her sober Moments. The Person you converse with, after the third Bottle, is not the same Man who first sat down at Table with you.

Joseph Addison in *Spectator*

The water-wagon is the place for me!
Last night my feelings were immense;
Today I feel like thirty cents!
No time for mirth, no time for laughter –
The cold grey dawn of the morning after.

George Ade *The Sultan of Sulu* 1902

If all be true that I do think,
There are five good reasons why we should drink;
Good wine – a friend – or being dry –
Or lest we should be, by and by –
Or any other reason why!

Henry Aldrich *Five Reasons for Drinking* 1705

Drink and be merry, for our time on earth is short, and death lasts for ever.

Amphis *Fragment* BC 330

He that drinks well, does sleep well;
He that sleeps well, doth think well;
He that drinks well, doth do well;
He that doth well must drink well.

Anonymous *The Loyal Garland* 1686

One thousand drink themselves to death before one dies of thirst.

Anonymous *German proverb*

No man is drunk so long as he can lie on the floor without holding on.
Anonymous
q. in *H. L. Mencken's Dictionary of Quotations* 1942

We cold water girls and boys,
Freely renounce the treacherous joys
Of brandy, whiskey, rum and gin;
The serpent's lure to death and sin.

Anonymous *American temperance anthem* 1840

Beware of the man who does not drink.
Anonymous *Italian proverb*

They speak of my drinking, but never think of my thirst.

Anonymous *Scottish proverb*

The horse and mule live 30 years
And nothing know of wines and beers.
The goat and sheep at 20 die
And never taste of Scotch or Rye.
The cow drinks water by the ton
And at 18 is mostly done.
The dog at 15 cashes in
Without the aid of rum or gin.
The cat in milk and water soaks
And then in 12 short years it croaks.

The modest, sober, bone-dry hen
Lays eggs for nogs, then dies at 10.
All animals are strictly dry:
They sinless live and swiftly die;
But sinful, ginful, rum-soaked men
Survive for three score years and ten.
And some of them, a very few,
Stay pickled till they're 92.

Anonymous *Poor Beasts!*

There are several reasons for drinking,
And one has just entered my head;
If a man cannot drink when he's living
How the hell can he drink when he's dead.

Anonymous *Inscribed on a pint tankard*

Reality is a delusion created by an alcohol deficiency.

Anonymous on *BBC Radio 4* 1979

W HEN ONE IS ALONE, the bottle does come around so often.

Anonymous

Here's a health to all those we love,
Here's a health to all those that love us,
Here's a health to all those that love them that love those
That love them that love those that love us.

Anonymous *Toast* 1740

Tons of beef
Oceans of beer
A pretty girl
And a thousand a year!

Anonymous Toast q. in *Wine and Food* 1946

W HEN MEN DRINK wine they are rich, they are busy, they push lawsuits, they are happy, they help their friends.

Aristophanes *The Knights* 424 BC

Three cups of wine a prudent man may take:
The first of them for constitution sake;
The second to the girl he loves the best;
The third and last, to lull him to his rest –
Then home to bed. But if a fourth he pours,
That is the cup of folly, and not ours.
Loud noisy talking on the fifth attends;
The sixth breeds feuds and falling out of friends;
Seven beget blows, and faces stained with gore;
Eight, and the watch patrol breaks ope' the door;
Mad with the ninth, another cup goes round,
And the swilled sot drops senseless on the ground.

Athenaeus *The Deipnosophists* c. 200

Always be drunk. That is all: it is the question. You want to stop Time crushing your shoulders, bending you double, so get drunk – militantly. How? Use wine, poetry, or virtue, use your imagination, just get drunk.

Charles Baudelaire *Get Drunk*

Clink, clank! clink, clank! tingle, tangle! tingle, tangle! Are demons smiting ringing hammers into Mr Verdant Green's brain, or is the dreadful bell summoning him to rise for morning chapel? Oh, the shame and agony that Mr Verdant Green felt . . . the fever that throbbed his brain and parched his lips, that made him long to drink up Ocean; the eyes that felt like burning lead; the powerless hands that trembled like a weak old man's; the voice that came in faltering tones that jarred the brain at every word! How he despised himself; how he loathed the very idea of wine, how he resolved never, never to transgress so again! But perhaps (he) was not the only Oxford freshman who has made this resolution.

Cuthbert Bede
(Edward Bradley) *The Adventures of Mr Verdant Green* 1853-1857

Much is said about the prudent use of spirits, but we might as well speak of the prudent use of the plague – of fire handed prudently round among powder – of poison taken prudently every day.

Lyman Beecher *Six Sermons*

D O YOU REALISE that those martinis that you keep drinking are slow poison? Benchley: I'm in no hurry.

Robert Benchley (attr.)

Drinking makes such fools of people, and people are such fools to begin with, that it's compounding a felony.

Robert Benchley

Let us eat and drink, for tomorrow we shall die.

The Bible *Isaiah XII, 13* 700 BC

A MAN HATH no better thing under the sun than to eat, and to drink, and to be merry.

The Bible *Ecclesiastes I, 24* 200 BC

Wine is a mocker, strong drink is raging: and whosoever is deceived thereby is not wise.

The Bible *Proverbs X, 1* 350 BC

Who hath woe? Who hath sorrow? Who hath contentions? Who hath babbling? Who hath wounds without cause? Who hath redness of eyes? They that tarry long at the wine; they that go to seek mixed wine.

The Bible *Proverbs XIII, 29-30* 350 BC

L OOK NOT UPON the wine when it is red, when it giveth his colour in the cup, when it moveth itself aright. At the last it biteth like a serpent, and stingeth like an adder. Thine eyes shall behold strange women, and thine heart shall utter perverse things.

The Bible *Proverbs XIII, 31-33* 350 BC

Alcohol, n: (Arabic al kohl, a paint for the eyes.) The essential principle of all such liquids as give a man a black eye.

Ambrose Bierce *The Devil's Dictionary* 1911

Carouse, v: to celebrate with appropriate ceremonies the birth of a noble headache.

Ambrose Bierce *The Devil's Dictionary* 1911

F EAST, n: a festival. A religious celebration usually signalised by gluttony and drunkenness, frequently in honour of some holy person distinguished for abstemiousness.

Ambrose Bierce *The Devil's Dictionary* 1911

Potable, adj: suitable for drinking. Water is said to be potable; indeed, some declare it our natural beverage, although even they find it palatable only when suffering from the recurrent disorder known as thirst, for which it is a medicine. Upon nothing as has so great and diligent ingenuity been brought to bear . . . as upon the invention of substitutes for water.

Ambrose Bierce *The Devil's Dictionary* 1911

Empty wine bottles have a bad opinion of women.

Ambrose Bierce 1900

Drunk, adj: Boozy, fuddled, corned, tipsy, mellow, soaken, full, groggy, tired, top-heavy, glorious, overcome, swipy, elevated, overtaken, screwed, raddled, lushy, nappy, muzzy, maudlin, pious, floppy, loppy, happy, etc.

Ambrose Bierce *The Devil's Dictionary* 1911

Red wine for children, champagne for men, and brandy for soldiers.

Otto von Bismarck

The trouble with the world is that everybody in it is three drinks behind.

Humphrey Bogart q. in *Esquire* magazine 1964

There is substantial internal evidence to point to the affinity between art and alcohol and the Alcoholist has become a formidable figure of our time. The creative Alcoholist is an individual persuaded, by cultural conditions, to regard drink as (at best) an aid to creativity and (at worst) an occupational hazard . . . The danger, of course, is that drinking will become a surrogate for creativity.

Alan Bold *Drink to Me Only* 1982

IT CANNOT BE DENIED that by far the greatest part of mankind have in all ages been fond of drinking . . . Does it not proclaim the truth of what the gloomy but noble-minded philosopher Maupertuis observes, that all mankind are agreed in this 'de chercher des remèdes au mal de vivre – to endeavour to find remedies for the pain of existence.'

James Boswell in *London Magazine* 1780

Drinking is in reality an occupation which employs a considerable portion of the time of many people; and to conduct it in the most rational and agreeable manner is one of the great arts of living.

James Boswell *Journals* 1775

A DRUNKARD . . . is a spectacle of deformity and a shame of humanity, a view of sin and a grief of nature. He is the annoyance of modesty and the trouble of civility, the spoil of wealth and the spite of reason. He is only the brewer's agent and the ale-house's benefactor, the beggar's companion and the constable's trouble. He is his wife's woe, his children's sorrow, his neighbours' scoff and his own shame. In short, he is a tub of swill, a spirit of sleep, a picture of a beast and a monster of a man.

Nicholas Breton *The Good and the Bad* 1616

Alcohol is the prince of liquids, and carries the palate to its highest pitch of exaltation.

Jean-Anthelme Brillat-Savarin *La Physiologie du goût* 1825

No churchman am I for to rail and to write,
No statesman nor soldier to plot or to fight
No sly man of business contriving a snare –
For a big-belly'd bottle's the whole of my care.
The peer I don't envy, I give his bow;
I scorn not the peasant, tho' ever so low;
But a club of good fellows, like those that are here,
And a bottle like this, are my glory and care.

Robert Burns *The Cure for All Care* 1784

BUT SEE THE MISCHIEF: many men, knowing that merry company is the only medicine against melancholy, will therefore neglect their business, and spend all their day among good fellows in a tavern . . . in drinking. Flourishing wits and men of good parts, good fashion, and good worth . . . drown their wits, seethe their brains in ale . . . weaken their temperatures, contract filthy diseases, rheumes, dropsies, calentures, tremors, get swoln jugulars, pimpled red-faces, sore eyes, &c: heat their livers, alter their complexions, spoil their stomachs, overthrow their bodies for drink.

Robert Burton *The Anatomy of Melancholy* 1621

There should be asylums for habitual teetotallers, but they would probably relapse into teatotalism as soon as they came out.

Samuel Butler *Notebooks* 1902

The human intellect owes its superiority over that of the lower animals in great measure to the stimulus which alcohol has given to imagination.

Samuel Butler *Notebooks* 1902

Man being reasonable must get drunk
The best of life is but intoxication
Glory, the grape, love, gold – in these are sunk
The hopes of all men and of every nation.

George Gordon, Lord Byron *Don Juan* 1819

What's drinking?
A mere pause from thinking.

George Gordon, Lord Byron *The Deformed Transformed* 1824

Let us have wine and women, mirth and laughter
Sermons and soda-water the day after.

George Gordon, Lord Byron *Don Juan* 1819

For if my pure libations exceed three
I feel my heart becomes so sympathetic,
That I must have recourse to black Bohee;
'Tis pity wine should be so deleterious,
For tea and coffee leave us much more serious.
Unless when qualified with thee, Cognac!
Sweet Naiad of the Phlegethonic rill!
Ah! why the liver wilt thou thus attack,
And make, like other nymphs, thy lovers ill?

George Gordon, Lord Byron *Don Juan* 1819

Drunkenness is a joy reserved for the gods: so men do partake of it impiously, and
so they are very properly punished for their audacity.

James Branch Cabell *Jurgen* 1919

People are entitled to shout when they are drunk. That is not being disorderly.

Mr Campbell q. in *Geoffrey Madan's Notebooks* 1981

I THINK A MAN ought to get drunk at least twice a year just on principle, so he
won't let himself get snotty about it.

Raymond Chandler *Selected Letters* ed. Frank McShane 1981

Drunkenness is the very sepulchre
Of man's wit and his discretion.

Geoffrey Chaucer *The Canterbury Tales* c. 1386

You must allow that drunkenness, which is equally destructive to body and mind, is a fine pleasure.

Philip Stanhope, Fourth Earl of Chesterfield
Letter to his son, October 9th, 1746

The rolling English drunkard made the rolling English road.

G. K. Chesterton *The Rolling English Road*

T HE DIPSOMANIAC and the abstainer both make the same mistake: they both regard wine as a drug and not as a drink.

G. K. Chesterton

I hear many cry when deplorable excesses happen 'Would there were no wine!' Oh folly!, oh madness! Is it the wine that causes this abuse? No, it is the intemperance of those who take an evil delight in it. Cry rather: 'Would to God there were no drunkenness, no luxury.' If you say 'Would there were no wine' because of the drunkards, then you must say 'Would there were no steel,' because of the murderers, 'Would there were no night,' because of the thieves, 'Would there were no light,' because of the informers, and 'Would there were no women,' because of adultery.

St John Chrysostom *Homilies* c. 388

W HEN I WAS YOUNGER, I made it a rule never to take strong drink before lunch. It is now my rule never to do so before breakfast.

Winston Churchill q. in *The Wit of Sir Winston* 1965

There is nothing wrong with sobriety in moderation.

John Ciardi in *Saturday Review* 1966

Ha! see where the wild-blazing Grog-Shop appears,
As the red waves of wretchedness swell.
How it burns on the code of tempestuous years,
The horrible Light-House of Hell!

M'Donald Clarke *The Rum Hole*

For a bad hangover, take the juice of two quarts of whiskey.

Eddie Condon   q. in *Jam Session* by Ralph J. Gleason

To drink is a Christian diversion,
Unknown to the Turk or the Persian:
Let Mahometan fools
Live by heathenish rules,
And be damned over teacups and coffee,
But let British lads sing,
Crown a health to the king,
And a fig for your sultan and sophy!

William Congreve   *The Way of the World* 1700

A night of good drinking
Is worth a year's thinking.

Charles Cotton   *Chanson à Boire* c. 1665

Nothing in Nature's sober found,
But an eternal health goes round.
Fill up the bowl then, fill it high,
Find all the glasses there, for why
Should every creature drink but I,
Why, man of morals, tell me why?

Abraham Cowley   *Anacreontiques* 1656

The gentle fair on nervous tea relied,
Champagne the courtier drinks, the spleen to chase,
The colonel Burgundy, and Port his Grace;
Turtle and 'rrack the city rules charm,
Ale and content the labouring peasants warm.

George Crabbe   *Inebriety* 1810

Then trust me there's nothing like drinking,
So pleasant on this side of the grave;
It keeps the unhappy from thinking,
And makes e'en the valiant more brave.

Charles Dibdin   *Nothing Like Grog* c. 1780

I like best the wine drunk at the cost of others.

Diogenes the Cynic 300 BC

Be sober; let the loved one drink.

Norman Douglas *Venus in the Kitchen* 1952

There is wan thing, an' on'y wan thing to be said in favour iv drink, and that is that it has caused manny a lady to be loved that otherwise might've died single.

Finlay Peter Dunne *Mr Dooley Says* 1910

THE SECRET of drunkenness is, that it insulates us in thought, whilst it unites us in feeling.

Ralph Waldo Emerson *Journals* 1857

The peculiar charm of alcohol lies in the sense of careless well-being and bodily and mental comfort which it creates. It unburdens the individual of his cares and his fears . . . Under such conditions it is easy to laugh or to weep, to love or to hate, not wisely but too well.

Dr Haven Emerson *Alcohol and Man*

Liquor is not a necessity. It is a means of momentarily side-stepping necessity.

Clifton Fadiman *Selected Writings* 1955

WE FREQUENTLY hear of people dying from too much drinking. That this happens is a matter of record. But the blame is always placed on whiskey. Why this should be I could never understand. You can die from drinking too much of anything – coffee, water, milk, soft drinks and all such stuff as that. And so long as the presence of death lurks with anyone who goes through the simple act of swallowing, I will make mine whiskey.

W. C. Fields

Drink! for you know not whence you came, nor why:
Drink! for you know not why you go, nor where.

Edward Fitzgerald
The Rubaiyat of Omar Khayyam c. 1100, translated 1857

Come landlord, fill a flowing bowl until it does run over,
Tonight we'll all merry be – tomorrow we'll get sober.

John Fletcher & Ben Jonson *The Bloody Brother* c. 1616

Maybe alcohol picks you up a little bit, but it sure lets you down in a hurry.

Betty Ford

There are more old drunkards than old doctors.

Benjamin Franklin *Poor Richard's Almanac* 1740

Let the drunkard alone, and by and by he'll fall of himself.

Thomas Fuller MD *Gnomologia* 1732

What key will unlock the door to hell? Whis-key.

J. C. Furnas *The Life and Times of the Late Demon Rum*

Water is the gift of God, whisky and beer are the concoctions of the Devil. Come and have a drink of water.
John Furphy *inscription on water-carts* c. 1873

DRUNKENNESS is never anything but a substitute for happiness. It amounts to buying the dream of a thing when you haven't money enough to buy the dreamed-of thing materially.

André Gide *Journals* 1896

A lush can always find a reason if he's thirsty. Listen. If he's happy, he takes a couple of shots to celebrate his happiness. Sad, he needs them to drown his sorrow. Low, to pick him up, excited, to calm him down. Sick for his health and healthy, it can't hurt him . . . a lush just can't lose.

Ivan Goff & Ben Roberts *Come Fill the Cup* Warner Bros. 1951

Call things by their right names . . . Glass of brandy and water! That is the current but not the appropriate name: ask for a glass of liquid fire and distilled damnation.

Rev. Robert Hall q. in *Life of Robert Hall* by Gregory 1910

Two things show little wit:
The full or empty cup.
If full, then empty it;
If empty, fill it up.

Kenneth Hare
q. in *A Wine and Food Bedside Book* ed. C. Morny 1972

TEETOTALLERS seem to die the same as others, so what's the use of knocking off the beer?

A. P. Herbert q. in *How to Cook a Wolf* by M. F. K. Fisher 1951

Drink not the third glass, which thou canst not tame,
When once it is within thee; but before
Mayst rule it, as thou list; and pour the shame
Which it would pour on thee, upon the floor.

George Herbert *The Temple* 1634

The rummers were seized, the wine poured out . . . This was the finishing blow to three of us. Hector fell on the floor; his lordship sunk in his chair; and I, after a hurrah and a hiccup, began to "cast the cat"; an Oxford phrase for what usually happens to a man after taking an emetic. Happily I had not far to go, and the fellow and the master of arts had just sense enough to help me to my chamber, where at daylight next morning I found myself, on the hearth, with my head resting against the fender, the pain of which awakened me.

Thomas Holcroft *Hugh Trevor* 1794

Drunkenness . . . makes man a beast; it drowns noble reason, their eyes swim, they hiccup in their talk, they gabble and blur their words, they stagger and fall and deal themselves dishonourable wounds, their faces grow blotched and bloated, scorpions are in their mind, they see devils and frightful sights.

Gerard Manley Hopkins
q. in *Gerard Manley Hopkins* by Paddy Kitchen 1978

No poems can please nor live long which are written by water drinkers. Ever since Bacchus enrolled poets, as half-crazed, amongst his Satyrs and Fauns, the sweet Muses have usually smelt of wine in the morning . . . poets never cease to rival each other in drinking by night and continuing to drink by day.

Horace *Epistles* 50 BC

THE FLOWING BOWL – whom has it not made eloquent? Whom has it not made free, even amid pinching poverty?

Horace *Epistles* 50 BC

What does drunkenness not accomplish? It unlocks secrets, confirms our hopes, urges the indolent into battle, lifts the burden from anxious minds, teaches new arts.

Horace (Q. Horatius Flaccus) *Epistles* 50 BC

Alcoholic psychosis is nothin' more or less'n ole DTs in a dinner suit.

Frank McKinney 'Kin' Hubbard *Abe Martin's Broadcast* 1905

Oh, I was down by Manly Pier
Drinking tubes of ice-cold beer
With a bucket full of prawns upon me knee.
But when I'd swallowed the last prawn
I had a Technicolour yawn
And I chundered in the old Pacific sea.

Barry Humphries *Chunder Down Under* 1964

To tell the truth, I'm as full as a fairy's phonebook. I'm as full as a state school hat-rack. I'm as full as two race trains. I'm as full as a seaside shithouse on Boxing Day. Awh, I'm sorry again, ladies. Please forgive me. That's a rotten thing to say in mixed company. I'm as low as the basic wage for talking like that. That's bloody parliamentary language. I'm that low I could parachute out of a snake's arsehole – and still free-fall. Are you with me?

Barry Humphries as *Sir Les Patterson* 1978

The sway of alcohol over mankind is unquestionably due to its power to stimulate the mystic faculties of human nature, usually crushed to earth by the cold facts and dry criticisms of the sober hour. Sobriety diminishes, discriminates and says No; drunkenness expands, unites and says Yes. It is in fact the great exciter of the Yes function in man. It brings its votary from the chill periphery of things to the radiant core. It makes him for the moment one with truth.

William James q. in *New York Times* 1948

*W*INE *is the first weapon that devils use in attacking the young.*

St Jerome *The Virgin's Profession* c. 420

In the bottle discontent seeks for comfort, cowardice for courage, and bashfulness for confidence.

Dr Samuel Johnson
Lives of the Poets 1779-1781

There are some sluggish men who are improved by drinking, as there are fruits that are not good until they are rotten.

Dr Samuel Johnson
quoted in *The Life of Samuel Johnson* by James Boswell 1791

Drink to me only with thine eyes,
And I will pledge with mine;
Or leave a kiss but in the cup,
And I'll not look for wine.

Ben Jonson *To Celia* 1616

A DRINKER shouldn't drink on his own, because he can't get high on his own, only lower.

James Kennaway *Some Gorgeous Accident* 1967

The pleasure of drinking is one of a small group that can be fully enjoyed only in congenial company and it is essentially social as no other art is.

Henry Herbert Knox
q. in *A Wine and Food Bedside Book* ed. C. Morny 1972

Dehortations from the use of strong liquors have been the favourite topic of sober declaimers in all ages, and have been received with abundance of applause by water-drinking critics. But with the patient himself, the man that has to be cured, unfortunately their sound has seldom prevailed. Yet the evil is acknowledged, the remedy simple. Abstain. No force can oblige the man to raise the glass to his head against his will. 'Tis as easy as not to steal, as not to tell lies . . .

Charles Lamb *Confessions of a Drunkard* 1823

A man takes a drink, the drink takes another, and the drink takes the man.

Sinclair Lewis *in conversation . . .*

Touch the goblet no more!
It will make thy very heart sore
To its very core!
Its perfume is the breath
Of the Angel of Death,
And the light that within it lies
Is the flash of his evil eyes.
Beware, oh beware!
For sickness, sorrow and care
Are all there!

Henry Wadsworth Longfellow
The Golden Legend 1851

Whatsoever is in the heart of the sober man is in the mouth of the drunkard.

John Lyly *Euphues* 1578

COMING OF a temperance family, drunkenness had always been for me a symbol of freedom. It was a kicking overboard of the lumber of puritan ethics; it was a quick road to fantasy; it achieved a communion among those whom sobriety divided. I heard a temperance lecturer explain that alcohol impairs the mind through weakening the synapses of the brain, and I was willing to believe this; we have more mind than is comfortable anyway, the same again and to hell with the synapses.

Louis MacNeice *The Strings Are False*

Nothing is more destructive, either in regard to the Health or the Vigilance and Industry of the Poor than the infamous Liquor . . . Intoxicating Gin, that charms the Unactive, the desperate and crazy of either Sex, and makes the starving Sot behold his Rags and Nakedness with stupid Insolence, or banter both in Senseless Laughter, and more insipid Jests. It is a Fiery Lake that sets the Brain in Flame, Burns up the Entrails and scorches every part within; and at the same time a Lethe of Oblivion, in which the Wretch immers'd drowns his most pinching Cares, and with his Reason all anxious reflection on Brats that cry for Food, hard Winter Frosts, and horrid Empty Home.

Bernard de Mandeville
The Fable of the Bees, or, Private Vices, Public Benefits 1714

IF I MUST DIE, let me die drinking in an inn.

Walter Map *De nugis curialum* c. 1200

Drink helps us to penetrate the veil; it gives us glimpses of the Magi of creation where they sit weaving their spells and sowing their seeds of incantation to the flowing mind.

Don Marquis *The Almost Perfect State*

An old stomach
Reforms more whiskey drinkers
Than a new resolve.

Don Marquis *Archy Does His Part* 1835

Good people all, of every degree,
I pray ye all be warned by me;
I advise ye all to pause and think,
And never more to taste strong drink.
Therefore, be warned, and think in time,
And don't drink any more whisky, rum or wine.
But go at once – make no delay,
And join the Blue Ribbon Army without dismay,
And rally round to Mr Murphy, and make a bold stand,
And help drive the Bane of Society from our land.

William McGonagall
A Tribute to Mr Murphy and the Blue Ribbon Army

Oh, thou Demon Drink, thou fell destroyer,
The curse of society and its greatest annoyer,
What hast thou done to society, let me think?
I answer thou has caused most of the ills, thou Demon Drink.

William McGonagall *The Demon Drink*

And when you wanna loosen up rather than introspect or perceive like a sonofagun, booze has it over dope going away. Not just the way the Beach Boys have it over Tommy James, but the way God has it over an apartment house.

Richard Meltzer *Gulcher* 1972

A PROHIBITIONIST is the sort of man one wouldn't care to drink with – even if he drank.

H. L. Mencken 1920

There ain't gonna be no whiskey; there ain't gonna be no gin;
There ain't gonna be no highball, to put the whiskey in;
There ain't gonna be no cigarettes to make folks pale and thin;
But you can't take away that tendency to sin, sin, sin.

Vaughan Miller
There Ain't Gonna Be No Whiskey, a popular Prohibition-era song, 1919

It is, of course, true that we can be intemperate in eating as well as in drinking, but the results of the intemperance would appear to be different. After a fifth helping of rice-pudding one does not become over-familiar with strangers, nor does an extra slice of ham inspire a man to beat his wife.

A. A. Milne *Not That It Matters*

'It is true, the blushful Hippocrene.' To tell oneself this is to pardon everything. However unpleasant a drunken man may seem at first sight, as soon as one realizes that he has merely been putting away a blushful Hippocrene, one ceases to be angry with him . . . If only the poets had praised over-eating rather than over-drinking, how much pleasanter the streets would be on festival nights.

A. A. Milne *Not That It Matters*

Soon as the potion works, their human countenance,
Th' express resemblance of the gods, is chang'd
Into some brutish form of wolf or bear,
Or ounce or tiger, hog or bearded goat,
All other parts remaining as they were;
And they, so perfect is their misery,
Not once perceive their foul disfigurement.

John Milton *Comus* 1634

Friend of my soul, this goblet sip,
'Twill chase that pensive tear;
'Tis not so sweet as woman's lip,
But, oh! 'tis more sincere.
Like her delusive beam,
'Twill steal away thy mind;
But, truer than love's dream,
It leaves no sting behind.

Thomas Moore *Anacreontic* 1800

O NE DRINK OF WINE and you act like a monkey; two drinks and you strut like a peacock; three drinks and you roar like a lion; and four drinks – you behave like a pig.

Henry V. Morton *In the Steps of St Paul*

Candy is dandy
But liquor is quicker.

Ogden Nash *Reflections on Ice-breaking*

Nor have we one or two kinds of drunkards only, but eight kinds. The first is ape drunk, and he leaps and sings and hollows and danceth for the heavens: the second is lion drunk, and he flings the pots about the house, calls his hostess whore, breaks the glass windows with his dagger, and is apt to quarrel with any man that speaks to him: the third is swine drunk, heavy, lumpish and sleepy, and cries for a little more drink, and a few more clothes: the fourth is sheep drunk, wise in his own conceit, when he cannot bring forth a right word: the fifth is maudlin drunk, when a fellow will weep for kindness in the midst of his ale, and kiss you, saying; By God Captain, I love thee, go thy ways, thou dost not think so of me as I do of thee; I would (if it pleased God) could I not love thee so well as I do, and then he puts his finger in his eye, and cries: the sixth is martin drunk, when a man is drunk and drinks himself sober ere he stir: the seventh is goat drunk, when in his drunkenness he hath no mind but on lechery: the eighth is fox drunk, when he is crafty drunk, as many of the Dutch men be, will never bargain but when they are drunk.

Thomas Nashe *Pierce Pennilesse* 1592

I only drink to make other people seem more interesting.

George Jean Nathan
inscribed beneath his portrait in *Charley O's* bar, New York City 1958
(also attributed to Don Marquis)

AFTERNOON TEAS in Australian homes are for women and teetotallers. You will notice that your host leaves his chair frequently and goes away for a minute or two. You are wrong if you think he has a weak bladder. He is going out to the garage. Follow him. That's where the grog will be.

John O'Grady *Aussie Etiket* 1971

One more drink and I'll be under the host.

Dorothy Parker
q. in *You Might As Well Live* by John Keats 1970

Drink and dance and laugh and lie,
Love, the reeling midnight through,
For tomorrow we shall die!
(But, alas, we never do.)

Dorothy Parker *The Flaw in Paganism* 1931

There are two reasons for drinking: one is, when you are thirsty, to cure it; the other, when you are not thirsty, to prevent it.

Thomas Love Peacock *Melincourt* 1817

Not drunk is he who from the floor
Can rise alone and still drink more;
But drunk is he who prostrate lies
Without the power to move or rise.

Thomas Love Peacock
The Misfortunes of Elphin 1829

A TEETOTALLER! Well! He is the true Heautontimorumenos, the self-punisher, with a jug of toast-and-water for his Christmas wassail. So far his folly is merely pitiable, but his intolerance makes it offensive. He cannot enjoy his own tipple unless he can deprive me of mine.

Thomas Love Peacock *Gryll Grange* 1861

At first, a man will think it no shame to get drunk once a year, on his birthday; he marries, and lest he should be thought to pay less regard to the birthday of his wife than his own, gets drunk on that day also; he becomes a father, and as if children brought nothing but cares with them, he drowns the remembrance of every addition to his family in wine. Then there are friends' birthdays and great men's birthdays, and great public occasions, all of which he must assist in celebrating; till at length, there is scarcely a day in the year which does not furnish its apology for an anniversary debauch. What was an occasional indulgence becomes a uniform habit . . . its paroxysms returning till its victim is destroyed.

Reuben & Sholto Percy *The Percy Anecdotes*

IN THE NAME of all drunkards, in the name of all tipplers, in the name of all fools, in the name of all clowns, in the name of all want-wits, in the name of all vodkas, in the name of all wines, in the name of all beers, in the name of all flasks, in the name of all pots, in the name of all barrels, in the name of all buckets, in the name of all mugs, in the name of all glasses and cups, in the name of all cards, dice and spillikins, in the name of all tobaccos and taverns, for there is the dwelling of our father, Bacchus.

Peter the Great *Bacchus*

A hot drink is as good as an overcoat.

Gaius Petronius *Satyricon* 70

Thou sparkling bowl! thou sparkling bowl!
Though lips of bards thy rim may press . . .
I will not touch thee; for there clings
A scorpion to thy side, that stings!

John Pierpont *The Sparkling Bowl*

It's all right to drink like a fish – if you drink what a fish drinks.

Mary Pettibone Poole *A Glass Eye at the Keyhole* 1938

I wet, I humect, I moisten my gullet, I drink, all for fear of dying. Drink always, and you shall never die.

François Rabelais *Gargantua* 1535

When I drink, I think; and when I think, I drink.

François Rabelais 1534

TAKE ESPECIAL CARE that you delight not in wine, for there never was any man that came to honour or preferment that loved it. For it transforms a man into a beast, decays health, poisons the breath, destroys natural heat, brings a man's stomach to an artificial heat, deforms the face, rots the teeth, and to conclude makes a man contemptible . . . It were better for a man to be subject to any vice than to this. For all other vanities and sins are recovered, but a drunkard will never shake off the delight of beastliness.

Sir Walter Raleigh *Instructions to His Son* 1632

Oh! That second Bottle is the Sincerest, Wisest, and most Impartial, Downright Friend we have; tells us truth of ourselves, and forces us to speak Truths of Others; banishes Flattery from our Tongues, and distrust from our Hearts; sets us above the mean Policy of Court Prudence; which makes us lie to one another all Day, for fear of being betrayed by one another at Night. And . . . I believe, the errantest Villain breathing, is honest as long as that Bottle lives.

John Wilmot, 2nd Earl of Rochester *Familiar Letters* 1685

Drunks are rarely amusing unless they know some good songs and lose a lot at poker.

Karyl Roosevelt q. in *New York Times* 1975

Drunkenness is temporary suicide: the happiness that it brings is merely negative, a momentary cessation of unhappiness.

Bertrand Russell *The Conquest of Happiness* 1930

Pure water is the best of gifts that man to man can bring,
But who am I that I should have the best of anything?
Let princes revel at the pump, let peers with ponds make free;
Whiskey or wine or even beer is good enough for me.

Hon. G. W. E. Russell *Collections and Recollections*

THERE IS ABSOLUTELY no scientific proof, of a trustworthy kind, that moderate consumption of sound alcoholic liquor does a healthy body any harm at all; while on the other hand it is the unbroken testimony of all history that alcoholic liquors have been used by the strongest, wisest, handsomest and in every way best races of all times.

George Saintsbury *Notes on a Cellar-book* 1920

There is no money . . . of the expenditure of which I am less ashamed, or which gave me better value in return, than the price of the liquids chronicled in this book. When they were good they pleased my senses, cheered my spirits, improved my moral and intellectual powers, besides enabling me to confer the same benefits on other people.

George Saintsbury *Notes on a Cellar-book* 1920

All fanatics and all faddists are dishonest. A.M.D.G. is only the exaltation to a blasphemous superlative of their invariable and indeed constitutive state of mind. But it is a question whether the most Jesuitical Jesuit of the most heated Protestant imagination has ever outdone a thorough-going temperance advocate in the endless doggings and windings, suppressions and suggestions of his method.

George Saintsbury *Notes on a Cellar-book* 1920

One may boldly say . . . that for every evil deed that fact or fancy or the unscrupulous exaggeration of partisans can charge on alcohol, it has prompted a hundred good and kind ones; that for every life it has destroyed or spoiled it has made thousands happy; that much of the best imaginative work of the world has been due to its influence.

George Saintsbury *Notes on a Cellar-book* 1920

THE HUMAN BODY is perfectly suited for the ingestion of alcohol, and for its rapid utilization. In that sense we are not unlike alcohol lamps. Endless is our eagerness to devour alcohol . . . Along the way it bathes the brain with happiness, lifting the inhibitory cortex off the primal swamp of the id and permitting to surface all sorts of delicious urges such as the one to walk into people's houses wearing your wife's hat.

Richard Selzer *The Drinking Man's Liver* 1974

It should be unequivocally affirmed that he is no gentleman, in fact a very milksop, of no bringing up, that will not drink. He is fit for no company, for it is a credit to have a strong brain and to carry one's liquor well.

Richard Selzer *The Drinking Man's Liver* 1974

Drunkenness is simply voluntary insanity.

Lucius Annaeus Seneca *Epistulae morales ad Lucilium*

Porter: . . . drink, sir, is a great provoker of three things . . . nose-painting, sleep and urine. Lechery, sir, it provokes and unprovokes: it provoketh the desire, but it takes away the performance. Therefore much drink may be said to be an equivocator with lechery; it makes him, and it mars him; it sets him on, and it takes him off; it persuades him, and disheartens him; makes him stand to, and not stand to; in conclusion, equivocates him in a sleep, and, giving him the lie, leaves him.

William Shakespeare *Macbeth* 1605

I'm only a beer teetotaller, not a champagne teetotaller.

George Bernard Shaw *Candida* 1904

If a man has a bit of conscience, it always takes him when he's sober; and then it makes him low-spirited. A drop of booze just takes that off and makes him happy.

George Bernard Shaw *Pygmalion* 1912

A bumper of good liquor
Will end a contest quicker
Than justice, judge or vicar.

Richard B. Sheridan *The Duenna* 1775

Anybody that can't get drunk by midnight ain't trying.

Toots Shor 1950

D RINK IS THE LAW OF LIFE. To live all must drink, man and beast, young and old, large and small. It was ever thus . . .

André Simon *The Concise Encyclopedia of Gastronomy* 1952

We believe that the best plan is to let people drink what they like, and wear what they like; to make no sumptuary laws either for the belly or for the back . . . laws against rum and water are made by men who can change a wet coat for a dry one whenever they choose, and who do not often work up to their knees in mud and water; and, in the next place, if this stimulus did all the mischief it is thought to do by the wise men of claret, its cheapness and plenty would rather lessen than increase the avidity with which it is at present sought for.

Sidney Smith
in *The Works of the Rev. Sydney Smith* 1869

I don't think alcohol is the Devil in solution, but it causes a great deal of misery. It's no use saying that it's all right in moderation. Shall we have arsenic in moderation and murder in moderation? Wine is the juice of the grape gone bad.

Lord Soper

I'm not so think as you drunk I am.

Sir John Squire

No woman should marry a teetotaller, or a man who does not smoke.

Robert Louis Stevenson *Virginibus Puerisque* 1881

. . . A man once drunk with wine or strong drink rather resembleth a brute than a Christian man. For do not his eyes begin to stare and to be red, fiery and bleared, blubbering forth seas of tears? Doth he not foam and froth at the mouth like a boar? Doth not his tongue falter and stammer in his mouth? . . . Are not his wits and spirits, as it were, drowned? Is not his understanding altogether decayed? Do not his hands, and all his body vibrate, quaver and shake, as it were, with a quotidian fever . . . The drunkard, in his drunkenness, killeth his friend, revileth his lover, discloseth secrets, and regardeth no man.

Philip Stubbes *The Anatomie of Abuses* 1583

Up to the age of forty, eating is beneficial; after forty, drinking.
The Talmud 200 BC

T HERE ARE TWO THINGS that will be believed of any man whatsoever, and one of them is that he has taken to drink.

Booth Tarkington

An alcoholic is someone you don't like who drinks as much as you do.

Dylan Thomas

It is worse to be drunk with ale or beer than with wine; for the drunkenness endureth to the utter ruin of the brain and understanding, by reason that the fumes and vapours of ale or beer that ascend to the head are more gross, and therefore cannot be so soon resolved as those that rise up of wine.

Tobias Venner *Via recta ad Vitam Longam* 1620

I don't have a drink problem except when I can't get one.
Tom Waits in 1979

I have a partiality for drunkenness, though I never practised it: it is a reality: but what is sobriety, only the absence of drunkenness?

Horace Walpole letter to Mary & Agnes Berry, July 9th, 1789

A hair of the same dog next morning
Is best to quench our fev'rish burning.

Edward Ward *British Wonders* 1717

I have made an important discovery . . . that alcohol, taken in sufficient quantities, produces all the effects of intoxication.

Oscar Wilde

Don't get drunk before dinner, you can't really enjoy it.

Rev. Mr Wilkins q. in *Geoffrey Madan's Notebooks* 1981

A drinking man's someone who wants to forget he isn't still young an' believing.

Tennessee Williams
Cat on a Hot Tin Roof 1955

THE EFFECT was intense and gratifying. As he drained his first glass, it seemed to him that a torchlight procession, of whose existence he had hitherto not been aware, had begun to march down his throat and explore the recesses of his stomach. The second glass, though slightly too heavily charged with molten lava, was extremely palatable. It helped the torchlight procession along by adding to it a brass band of singular sweetness of tone. And with the third somebody began to touch off fireworks in his head.

P. G. Wodehouse *Meet Mr Mulliner* 1927

I ALWAYS SAY that if you've seen one Gentleman of the Press having delirium tremens, you've seen them all.

P. G. Wodehouse *Bachelors Anonymous* 1973

It was my Uncle George who discovered that alcohol was a food well in advance of modern medical thought.

P. G. Wodehouse *The Inimitable Jeeves* 1923

I have had occasion, I fancy, to speak before now of these pick-me-ups of Jeeves's, and their effect on a fellow who is hanging to life by a thread on the morning after. What they consist of, I couldn't tell you. He says some kind of sauce, the yolk of a raw egg, and a dash of red pepper, but nothing will convince me that the thing doesn't go much deeper than that. Be that as it may, however, the results of swallowing one are amazing. For perhaps the split part of a second nothing happens. It is as though all Nature waited breathless. Then suddenly, it is as if the Last Trump had sounded and Judgement set in with unusual severity. Bonfires burst out in all parts of the frame. The abdomen becomes heavily charged with lava. A great wind seems to blow through the world, and the subject is aware of something resembling a steam hammer striking the back of the head. During this phase, the ears ring loudly, the eyeballs rotate and there is a tingling about the brow. And then, just as you are feeling you ought to ring up your lawyer and see that your affairs are in order before it is too late, the whole situation seems to clarify. The wind drops. The ears cease to ring. Birds twitter. Brass bands start playing. The sun comes up over the horizon with a jerk. And a moment later all you are conscious of is a great peace.

P. G. Wodehouse *Right Ho, Jeeves* 1934

CHAPTER EIGHT

THE TRUE, THE BLUSHFUL HIPPOCRENE

In order named these are the hardest to control: Wine, Women and Song.

Franklin P. Adams *The Ancient Three*

The wines that one remembers best are not necessarily the finest that one has tasted, and the highest quality may fail to delight so much as some far more humble beverage drunk in more favourable circumstances.

H. Warner Allen *A Contemplation of Wine* 1950

THE POINT about white Burgundies is that I hate them myself. They so closely resemble a blend of cold chalk soup and alum cordial with an additive or two to bring it to the colour of children's pee.

Kingsley Amis *The Green Man* 1969

Good wine needs no bush.

Anonymous *English proverb*

Aristotle, that master of arts,
Had been but a dunce without wine,
And what we ascribe to his parts
Is but due to the juice of the vine.

Anonymous *Wine and Wisdom* 1710

By wine we are generous made;
It furnishes fancy with wings;
Without it we should ne'er have had
Philosophers, poets or kings.

Anonymous *Wine and Wisdom* 1710

Burgundy for kings, champagne for duchesses, and claret for gentlemen.

Anonymous *French proverb*

One barrel of wine can work more miracles than a church full of saints.

Anonymous *Italian proverb*

Wine has two defects: if you add water to it, you ruin it; if you do not, it ruins you.

Anonymous *Spanish proverb*

There is good wine and there is better wine, but there is no such thing as bad wine.

Anonymous q. in *A Wine and Food Bedside Book* ed. C. Morny 1972

WINE IS MAN'S most successful effort to translate the perishable into the permanent.

John Arlott *Wine* 1984

A vintage wine, one of the most perfect of nature's products – to those who can appreciate perfection.

H. E. Armstrong in *The Times* 1920

Port: the milk of donhood.

Max Beerbohm
q. in *Geoffrey Madan's Notebooks* 1981

To exalt, enthrone, establish and defend,
To welcome home mankind's mysterious friend:
Wine, true begetter of all arts that be;
Wine, privilege of the completely free;
Wine the recorder; wine the sagely strong;
Wine, bright avenger of sly-dealing wrong,
Awake, Ausonian Muse, and sing the vineyard song!

Hilaire Belloc *Heroic Poem in Praise of Wine* 1935

NEITHER DO MEN put new wine into old bottles; else the bottles break, and the wine runneth out and the bottles perish: but they put new wine into new bottles, and both are preserved.

The Bible *Matthew XI, 17* c. 75

1. Never drink claret in an East wind.
2. Take your pleasures singly, one by one.
3. Never sit on a hard chair after drinking port.

Rev. H. J. Bidder q. in *Geoffrey Madan's Notebooks* 1981

Wine, n: Fermented grape juice known to the Women's Christian Union as 'liquor', sometimes as 'rum'. Wine, madam, is God's next best gift to man.

Ambrose Bierce *The Devil's Dictionary* 1911

Drink wine in Winter for cold, and in Summer for heat.

H. G. Bohn *Handbook of Proverbs* 1855

Wine, if moderately drunken, do acuate and quicken a man's wits, comfort the heart, scour the liver; specially if it be white wine, it doth rejoice all the powers of man and nourish them; it doth engender good blood, comfort and nourish the brain and the body, it resolveth flegm; it engendreth heat, and is good against heaviness and pensifulness; it is full of agility; wherefore it is medicinable, specially white wine, for it doth mundify and cleanse wounds and sores.

Andrew Boorde
The Breviarie of Health 1598

C HOSE YOUR WYNE after this sorte; it must be fyne, fayre, and clene to the eye; it must be fragraunt and redolent, havynge a good odour and flavour in the nose; it must sprynckle (sparkle) in the cup when it is drawne or put out of the pot into the cup; it must be colde and pleasaunt in the mouthe; and it must be strong and subtyll of substaunce.

Andrew Boorde *The Breviarie of Health* 1598

T HE MAN WHO likes good wines is never a drunkard; his pleasure is the appreciation of quality, not the consumption of quantity, which lowers a human being to the level of a brute.

X. Marcel Boulestin *Simple French Cooking for English Homes* 1923

That little sentence 'have the chill taken off' has done more harm to good wine than it is possible to imagine.

X. Marcel Boulestin *Simple French Cooking for English Homes* 1923

W INE, the most delightful of drinks, whether we owe it to Noah, who planted the vine, or to Bacchus, who pressed juice from the grape, dates from the childhood of the world.

Jean-Anthelme Brillat-Savarin *La Physiologie du goût* 1825

Wine cheers the sad, revives the old, inspires
The young, makes weariness forget his toil,
And fears her danger; opens a new world
When this, the present, falls.

George Gordon, Lord Byron *Don Juan* 1819

An English autumn, though it hath no vines
Blushing with Baccant coronals along
The paths, o'er which the far festoon entwines
The red grape in the sunny lands of song,
Hath yet a purchased choice of choicest wines;
The claret light and the Madeira strong.
If Britain mourn her bleakness, we can tell her,
The very best of vineyards is the cellar.

George Gordon, Lord Byron *Don Juan* 1819-1821

And Noah he often said to his wife when he sat down to dine
'I don't care where the water goes if it doesn't get into the wine.'

G. K. Chesterton *The Flying Inn*

No man has a right to inflict the torture of bad wine upon his fellow creatures.

Marcus Clarke *The Peripatetic Philosopher* 1869

*D*RINK WINE *and have the gout; drink none and have it too.*

Thomas Cogan *The Haven of Health* 1588

Life and wine for the likeness of nature are most agreeable. And this is the cause as I think why men by nature so greedily covet wine; except some odde Abstemius, one among a thousand perchance, degenerate and is of a doggish nature; for dogges of nature do abhor wine.

Thomas Cogan *The Haven of Health* 1588

Fill the bowl with rosy wine,
Around our temples roses twine,
And let us cheerfully awhile,
Like the wine and roses, smile.

Abraham Cowley *Anacreontiques* 1656

'I rather like bad wine,' said Mr. Mountchesney; 'one gets so bored with good wine.'

Benjamin Disraeli *Sybil* 1845

Wine is a precarious aphrodisiac, and its fumes have blighted many a mating.

Norman Douglas *An Almanac*

A man will be eloquent if you give him good wine.

Ralph Waldo Emerson *Representative Men* 1850

When there is no wine, love perishes, and everything else that is pleasant to man.

Euripedes *The Bacchae* 410 BC

THE DRINKING OF WINE seems to have a moral edge over many pleasures and hobbies in that it promotes love of one's neighbour. As a general thing it is not a lone occupation. A bottle of wine begs to be shared; I have never met a miserly wine lover.

Clifton Fadiman *Any Number Can Play* 1957

I wonder often what the vintners buy
One-half so precious as the stuff they sell.

Edward Fitzgerald *The Rubaiyat of Omar Khayyam* c. 1100, trans. 1857

Wine hath drowned more men than the sea.

Thomas Fuller MD *Gnomologia* 1732

Wine is a turn-coat; first a friend, and then an enemy.

Thomas Fuller MD *Gnomologia* 1732

Fill ev'ry glass, for wine inspires us,
And fires us
With courage, love and joy.
Women and wine should life employ.
Is there aught on earth desirous?

John Gay *The Beggar's Opera* 1728

Never have a small glass of port, my lad. It just goes wambling around looking for damage to do. Have a large glass. It settles down and does you good.

Lord Goddard (attr.)

Wine rejoices the heart of man, and joy is the mother of all virtue.

Johann Wolfgang von Goethe *Goetz von Berlichingen* 1771

Five qualities there are wine's praise advancing:
Strong, beautiful, fragrant, cool and dancing.

John Harington *The Englishman's Doctor* 1608

Red bordeaux is like the lawful wife: an excellent beverage that goes with every dish and enables one to enjoy one's food. But now and then a man wants a change, and champagne is the most complete and exhilarating change . . . it is like a woman of the streets: everyone that can afford it tries it sooner or later, but it has no real attraction. Moselle is like the girl of fourteen to eighteen: light, quick on the tongue, with an exquisite, evanescent perfume, but little body. It may be used constantly and in quantities, but must be taken young.

Frank Harris *My Life and Loves* 1925

WINE IS LIKE RAIN: when it falls on the mire it but makes it the fouler, But when it strikes the good soil, wakes it to beauty and bloom.

John Hay *Distichs* 1871

I am beauty and love;
I am friendship, the comforter;
I am that which forgives and forgets.
The Spirit of Wine.

W. E. Henley *The Spirit of Wine* 1888

God made the Vine,
Was it a sin
That Man made Wine
To drown trouble in?

Oliver Herford *A Plea* 1901

On thou drink of gods, and angels! Wine!

Robert Herrick *Hesperides* 1648

*W*INE . . . *is a food.*

Oliver Wendell Holmes
Address to the Massachussetts Medical Society, 1860

And wine can of their wits the wise beguile,
Make the sage frolic and the serious smile.

Homer *The Odyssey* 800 BC

God made only water, but man made wine.

Victor Hugo *Les Contemplations* 1856

One of the disadvantages of wine is that it makes a man mistake words for thoughts.

Dr Samuel Johnson

Wine gives a man nothing. It neither gives him knowledge nor wit; it only animates a man, and enables him to bring out what a dread of the company has repressed. This is one of the disadvantages of wine: it makes a man mistake words for thoughts.

Dr Samuel Johnson
q. in *The Life of Samuel Johnson* by James Boswell 1791

F EW PEOPLE HAD intellectual pleasures sufficient to forgo the pleasures of wine. They could not otherwise contrive how to fill the interval between dinner and supper.

Dr Samuel Johnson
q. in *The Life of Samuel Johnson* by James Boswell 1791

Wine makes a man better pleased with himself; I do not say it makes him more pleasing to others.

Dr Samuel Johnson
q. in *The Life of Samuel Johnson* by James Boswell 1791

Think, for a moment, of an almost paper-white glass of liquid, just shot with greeny-gold, just tart on your tongue, full of wild-flower scents and spring-water freshness. and think of a burnt-amber fluid, as smooth as syrup in the glass, as fat as butter to smell and sea-deep with strange flavours. Both are wine. Wine is grape-juice. Every drop of liquid filling so many bottles has been drawn out of the ground by the roots of a vine. All these different drinks have at one time been sap in a stick. It is the first of many strange and some . . . mysterious circumstances which go to make wine not only the most delicious, but the most fascinating drink in the world.

Hugh Johnson *Wine* 1974

O, for a draught of vintage! that hath been
Cool'd a long age in the deep-delv'd earth,
Tasting of Flora and the country-green,
Dance, and Provencal song, and sunburnt mirth!
Oh, for a beaker of the warm South,
Full of the true, the blushful Hippocrene,
With beaded bubbles winking at the brim,
And purple-stained mouth;
That I might drink and leave the world unseen,
And with thee fade away into the forest dim.

John Keats *Ode to a Nightingale* 1819

How I like claret! . . . It fills one's mouth with a gushing freshness, then goes down cool and feverless; then, you do not feel it quarrelling with one's liver. No; 'tis rather a peace-maker, and lies as quiet as it did in the grape. Then it is as fragrant as the Queen Bee, and the more ethereal part mounts into the brain, not assaulting the cerebral apartments, like a bully looking for his trull, and hurrying from door to door, bouncing against the wainscot, but rather walks like Aladdin about his enchanted palace, so gently that you do not feel his step.

John Keats letter, 1819

If Heaven did not love wine,
Then there would be no wine star in Heaven.
If Earth did not love wine
There would be no wine springs on earth –
Why then be ashamed before Heaven to love wine? . . .
Three cups, and one can perfectly understand the Great Tao;
A gallon, and one is in accord with all nature.

Li T'ai Po 740

SOME PEOPLE tell you you should not drink claret after strawberries. They are wrong.

Wiliam Maginn
The Maxims of Sir Morgan O'Doherty, Bart. 1849

Wine is like a woman – up to thirty years, fine, but beyond that . . .!

Henri Martin q. in *Esquire* January 1974

Port speaks the sentences of wisdom, Burgundy sings the inspired Ode.

George Meredith *The Egoist* 1879

HOCKS, TOO, have a compassed age. I have tasted senior Hocks. Their flavours are as of a brook of many voices; they have depth also. Senatorial Port! we say. We cannot say that of any other wine. Port is deep-sea deep. It is in its flavour deep; mark the difference. It is like a classic tragedy, organic in conception . . . Neither of Hermitage nor of Hock can you say that it is the blood of those long years, retaining the strength of youth with the wisdom of age. To Port for that! Port is our noblest legacy! . . . Port speaks in sentences of wisdom, Burgundy sings the inspired Ode. Or put it, that Port is the Homeric hexameter, Burgundy the Pindaric duthyramb.

George Meredith *The Egoist* 1879

Good wine makes good blood,
Good blood causeth good humours,
Good humours cause good thoughts,
Good thoughts bring forth good works,
Good works carry a man to heaven.
Ergo,
Good wine carrieth a man to heaven.

John Minsheu 1599

What though youth gave love and roses,
Age still leaves us friends and wine.

Thomas Moore

Wine has been to me a firm friend and a wise councillor. Often . . . wine has shown me matters in their true perspective, and has, as though by the touch of a magic wand, reduced great disasters to small inconveniences. Wine has lit up for me the pages of literature, and revealed in life romance lurking in the commonplace. Wine has made me bold but not foolish, has induced me to say silly things but not to do them. Under its influence words have often come too easily which had better not have been spoken, and letters written which had better not been sent. But if such small indiscretions standing in the debit column of wine's account were added up, they would amount to nothing in comparison with the vast accumulation on the credit side.

Viscount Norwich *Old Men Forget*

A friend and a bottle is all my design;
He has no room for treason that's top-full of wine.

John Oldham *The Careless Good Fellow* 1683

Wine is the most healthful and most hygenic of beverages.

Louis Pasteur

If I drink water while this doth last,
May I never again drink wine:
For how can a man, in his life of a span,
Do anything better than dine?
We'll dine and drink, and say if we think
That anything better can be;
And when we have dined, wish all mankind
May dine as well as we.

Thomas Love Peacock

The juice of the grape is the liquid quintessence of concentrated sunbeams. Man is exotic in this northern climate, and must be nourished like a hot-house plant by the perpetual adhibition of artificial heat.

Thomas Love Peacock q. in *Wine and Food* 1948

BOYS SHOULD abstain from the use of wine until their eighteenth year, for it is wrong to add fire to fire.

Plato *Laws* 360 BC

The great evil in wine is that it first seizes the feet; it is a crafty wrestler.

Titus Maccius Plautus *Pseudolus* 190 BC

In vino veritas (In wine there is truth).

Pliny the Elder *Natural History* 79 BC

Wine lets no lover unrewarded go.

Alexander Pope *The Wife of Bath* 1714

Wine can of their wits the wise beguile,
Make the sage frolic, and the serious smile.

Alexander Pope *trans. of Homer's Odyssey* (c. 800 BC) 1726

Wine is drunk for immediate pleasure first, and to attain after that a general feeling of well-being, in which the mind is placid but lively, the emotions are friendly, and the body calm and satisfied. In wine drinking, consequently, three faculties are involved: Sight, Smell, Taste . . .

Raymond Postgate *The Plain Man's Guide to Wine* 1951

It is difficult not to be lyrical over the bouquet of a good wine. Tokay smells like green grass and weeds, trampled underfoot in a lush meadow. A full burgundy has a scent so strong it may make you dizzy; in its compound of flavours you can imagine violets and blackberries. A hock or moselle smells like a large bouquet of midsummer flowers. A claret is usually more delicate: its scents seem (but this may be fanciful) to succeed one another, like a chorus mincing across the stage. Moreover, the bouquet, too, may be a warning as well as a pleasure. A nasty wine, such as a bad sherry, tells your nose before you taste it.

Raymond Postgate *The Plain Man's Guide to Wine* 1951

WINEMANSHIP . . . remember your mainstay is hypnotic suggestion. Suggest that some rubbishy sherry . . . is your special pride, and has a tremendously individual taste. Insist on getting it yourself 'from the cellar'. Take about four minutes uncorking it. Say 'I think decanting destroys it', if you have forgotten or are too bored, to decant it. Keep staring at the bottle before you pour it. When you have drawn the cork, look particularly hard at the cork, and, of course, smell it.

Stephen Potter *One-Upmanship* 1952

Notes on Tastemanship: Before drinking, or rather sipping, the wine, you smell it for bouquet. Not with a noisy sniff but silently and delicately, perhaps making a funnel of your hands to concentrate the essence . . . A good general rule is to state that the bouquet is better than the taste, and vice versa.

Stephen Potter *One-Upmanship* 1952

Wine is the milk of the old, the balm of adults and the vehicle of the gourmand.

Grimod de la Reynière *Almanach des Gourmands* 1804

If God forbade drinking, would He have made wine so good?

Armand, Cardinal Richelieu *Miramé* c. 1625

Port is incomparable when good . . . It strengthens while it gladdens as no other wine can do, and there is something in port which must have been created in pre-established harmony with the best English character.

George Saintsbury *Notes on a Cellar-book* 1920

He drank it as port should be drunk – a trial of the bouquet; a slow sip; a rather larger and slightly less slow one, and so on; but never a gulp; and during the drinking his face exchanged its usual bluff and almost brusque aspect for the peculiar blandness . . . which good wine gives to worthy countenances.

George Saintsbury *Notes on a Cellar-book* 1920

WINE INVENTS nothing; it only tattles.

Johan Christoff von Schiller *The Piccolomini* 1799

A glass of good wine is a gracious creature, and reconciles poor mortality to itself, and that is what few things can do.

Sir Walter Scott *Journal* 1825-1832

Give me a bowl of wine;
In this I bury all unkindness.

William Shakespeare *Julius Caesar* 1599

O thou invisible spirit of wine, if thou hast no name to be known by, let us call thee Devil!

William Shakespeare *Othello* 1604

What man can pretend to be a believer in love who is an abjurer of wine?

Richard B. Sheridan *The School for Scandal* 1777

Water, like air, is indispensable; wine is not, but it is desirable. Wherever men have chosen to settle and live, they have first of all made quite sure that there was a supply of water, but whenever they have attained a higher measure of civilisation or culture, they have always spent a good deal of their time, labour and hard-earned money that they and theirs might drink wine.

André Simon *How to Enjoy Wine* 1952

The chief appeal which wine has always had and still has for all intelligent people is due to its specific action upon the nervous system; wine is both soothing and stimulating; it is a joy and solace; it may become a habit, but never a craving.

André Simon *How to Enjoy Wine* 1952

Wine is best because it is the safest, pleasantest and most wholesome of all beverages. It is safer than water or milk, you cannot get typhoid or T.B. from any wine, be it old or young, cheap and nasty, or rare and costly . . . Wine is a 'good familiar creature' as Shakespeare puts it . . . Wine is a gentle stimulant, a good counseller, a true friend, who neither bores nor irritates us: it does not send us to sleep, nor does it keep us awake; it never becomes a craving or a tyrant; it is always ready to cheer, to help but not to bully us.

André Simon *A Wine Primer* 1946

There are as many types of wine as there are types of men and women in the world, a few are very good, some are very bad, but the great majority are neither good nor bad, just 'ordinaires'. Some are long lived, they are the exception; some are short lived; some are sound and others are sick, but all must die.

André Simon *The Concise Encyclopedia of Gastronomy* 1952

What! shall a man be invited to a feast? shall he don his white tie with care and take his way through the inclement weather to his friend's home, determined, though weary and jaded with his daily toil, to shine at his best, and repay with the blithest company his friend's entertainment and shall he be offered lemonade to drink? It is enough to curdle the milk of human kindness in his breast for ever . . . The man is neither a wine-bibber nor a sot. But he is accustomed to drink his glass of wine, even as he is accustomed to eat his dinner, and one is as necessary to him as the other. Well, we do not imagine that he dines with him twice!

Spectator

Wine is bottled poetry.

Robert Louis Stevenson

It's a Naive Domestic Burgundy, Without any Breeding. But I think you'll be Amused by its Presumption.

James Thurber caption to *New Yorker* cartoon, 1943

W INE BY ITS MOISTURE quencheth my thirst, whether I consider it or not . . . To consider it is to drink it spiritually. To rejoice in its diffusion is to be of a public mind. And to take pleasure in all the benefits it doth to all is Heavenly, for so they do in Heaven.

Thomas Traherne q. in *Wine and Food* 1948

A meal without wine is a day without sunshine.

Louis Vaudable
q. in *Life* magazine 1966

Who loves not wine, women and song
Remains a fool his whole life long.

J. H. Voss
Musenalmanack ascribed to Martin Luther 1777

Sebastian had found a book on wine-tasting, and we followed its instructions in detail. We warmed the glass slightly at a candle, filled it a third high, swirled the wine around, nursed it in our hands, held it to the light, breathed it, sipped it, filled our mouths with it, and rolled it over the tongue, ringing it down the palate like a coin on a counter, tilted our heads back and let it trickle down the throat. Then we talked of it and nibbled Bath Oliver biscuits, and passed on to another wine; then back to the first, then on to another, until all three were in circulation and the order of glasses got confused, and we fell out over which was which, and we passed the glasses to and fro between us until there were six glasses, some of them with mixed wines in them which we had filled from the wrong bottle, till we were obliged to start again with three clean glasses each and the bottles were empty and our praise of them wilder and more exotic. 'It is a little, shy wine like a gazelle.' 'Like a leprechaun.' 'Dappled, in a tapestry meadow.' 'Like a flute by still water.' 'And this is a wise old wine.' 'A prophet in a cave.' 'Ought we to be drunk every night?' Sebastian asked one morning. 'Yes, I think so.' 'I think so too.'

Evelyn Waugh *Brideshead Revisited* 1945

Wine is a bride who brings a great dowry to the man who woos her persistently and gracefully; she turns her back on a rough approach.

Evelyn Waugh *Wine in Peace and War* 1937

All port tastes the same after lunch.

C. M. Wells
q. in *Geoffrey Madan's Notebooks* 1981

Wine has a drastic, an astringent taste. I cannot help wincing as I drink. Ascent of flowers, radiance and heat, are distilled here to a fiery, yellow liquid. Just behind my shoulder-blades some dry thing, wide-eyed, gently closes, gradually lulls itself to sleep. This is rapture. This is relief.

Virginia Woolf *The Waves* 1931

WINE GIVES you joy; love, grief and tortures, besides surgeons. Wine makes us witty; love, only sots. Wine makes us sleep; love breaks it.

William Wycherley *The Country Wife* 1673

CHAPTER NINE

A MATTER OF TASTE

No animal eats such variety of food as man. He claims, more justly than any other creature, the title of omnivorous . . . Man – all-devouring man, will embrace the whole range of the creation . . . With the lion and the wolf he will eat of fresh slain animals; with the dogs and the vulture he will feed on putrid flesh (every person knows in what a putrid state game is often eaten), with the ox and the guinea-pig he will devour raw vegetables . . . with the squirrel and the mouse he will feast on nuts and grain, with birds of prey he feeds on fowl of almost every species; with fishes he feeds on fish; and with insects and reptiles he sometimes lives on insects and reptiles. . . . there exists a material difference between the gourmand, or epicure, and the glutton. The first seeks for peculiar delicacy and distinct flavour in the various dishes presented to the judgement and enjoyment of his discerning palate; while the other lays aside nearly all that relates to the rational pleasures of creating or stimulating an appetite . . . and merely looks to quantity; this, has his stomach in view, and tries how heavy it may be laden, without endangering his health.

Frederick Accum 1821

As long as a person who pursues a right habit of life, eats and drinks no more than his stomach calls for and will bear, without occasioning uneasiness of any kind to himself, he may be said to live temperate. The stomach revolts against the reverse of it; indeed, the stomach is the grand organ of the human system, it is the conscience of the body, and like that, will become uneasy if all is not right within; it speaks pretty plainly to those who lead an intemperate life.

Frederick Accum *Cookbook* 1821

THE BEST OF ALL sauces is hunger engendered by exercise in the open air, and, equally, the best of digestives is pleasant company.

St Ange

You can't eat your cake and have it.

Anonymous *English proverb*

Jack Sprat could eat no fat,
His wife could eat no lean,
And so between the two of them
They licked the platter clean.

Anonymous *Nursery Rhyme* c. 1639

A glutton digs his grave with his teeth.

Anonymous *French Proverb*

The stomach . . . is a very hospitable gentleman, who is unfashionable enough to live in a sunk storey, as his ancestors have always done before him since the memory of man. The palate is the footman, whose duty it is to receive all strangers at the top of the stairs, and to announce their rank and quality before they are suffered to descend to the apartments of his master. The latter is occasionally rather irritable and choleric, and, in such humours, scruples not to kick out his guests, when their company is disagreeable, who rush past the astonished footman at the landing-place and make their exit with far less ceremony than precipitation.

Anonymous *Memoirs of a Stomach* c. 1833

ON NE MANGE bien que chez soi. (One only eats well at home.)

Anonymous *French saying*

From watching the way in which a person eats, one can learn a great deal about the way in which he loves himself and, consequently, about the way he will probably love or hate his neighbour. The behaviour towards others of the gobbler will be different from that of the pecker, of the person who eats his tidbit first from the person who leaves his to the last.

W. H. Auden
introduction to *The Art of Eating* by M. F. K. Fisher 1963

THE JOYS of the table are superior to all other pleasures, notably those of personal adornment, of drinking and of love, and those procured by perfumes and by music.

Hassan el Baghdadi *Kitabe el-tabih* 1226

An empty stomach produces an empty brain; our mind, independent as it may appear to be, respects the laws of digestion, and we may say with as much justice as La Rochefoucauld of the heart, that good thoughts proceed from the stomach.

Honoré de Balzac q. in *Pleasures of the Table* by G. Ellwanger 1903

A gourmet who thinks of calories is like a tart who looks at her watch.

James Beard
quoted beneath his portrait in *Charley O's* bar, New York City.

All food is the gift of the gods and has something of the miraculous, the egg no less than the truffle.

Sybille Bedford
q. in *Writers' Favourite Recipes* ed. G. Vincent 1978

'Oh my friends be warned by me,
That breakfast, dinner, lunch and tea
Are all the human frame requires . . .'
With that, the wretched child expires.

Hilaire Belloc *Cautionary Tales* 1908

Pure men like pure food which gives true health, balanced mentality, sustaining strength, life long enough to search. Pure food which has delicate taste, soothes, nourishes and brings them joy. Pure food that promotes the knowledge of God.

Bhagavad Gita

Edible: Good to eat and wholesome to digest, as a worm to a toad, a toad to a snake, a snake to a pig, a pig to a man and a man to a worm.

Ambrose Bierce *The Devil's Dictionary* 1911

APPETITE, n: an instinct thoughtfully implanted by Providence as a solution to the labour question.

Ambrose Bierce *The Devil's Dictionary* 1911

Abdomen, n: The temple of the god Stomach, in whose worship, with sacrificial rights, all true men engage . . . the one deity that men really adore.

Ambrose Bierce *The Devil's Dictionary* 1911

Glutton, n: a person who escapes the evils of moderation by committing dyspepsia.

Ambrose Bierce *The Devil's Dictionary* 1911

A KISS IS BUT a modified bite, and a fond mother, when she says her babe is 'almost good enough to eat', merely shows that she is herself only a trifle too good to eat it.

Ambrose Bierce *Tangential Views*

DO NOT BE AFRAID to talk about food. Food which is worth eating is worth discussing. And there is the occult power of words which somehow will develop its qualities.

X. Marcel Boulestin
Simple French Cooking for English Homes 1923

Two things should be avoided in life: bad temper and indigestion.

X. Marcel Boulestin *What Shall We Have Today?* 1931

Eats first, morals after.

Bertolt Brecht *The Threepenny Opera* 1928

Tell me what you eat and I will tell you who you are.

Jean-Anthelme Brillat-Savarin *La Physiologie du goût* 1825

Gastronomy rules all life: the newborn baby's tears demand the nurse's breast, and the dying man receives, with some pleasure, the last cooling drink.

Jean-Anthelme Brillat-Savarin *La Physiologie du goût* 1825

GOURMETS . . . have broad faces, sparkling eyes, small foreheads, short noses, full lips and round chins. The females are plump, rather pretty than handsome, with a tendency to embonpoint. It is under this exterior that the pleasantest guests are to be found: they accept all that is offered, eat slowly and taste with reflection. They never hurry away from the places where they have been well treated; and you are sure of them for the evening, because they know all the games and pastimes which form the ordinary accessories of a gastronomic meeting.

Jean-Anthelme Brillat-Savarin
La Physiologie du goût 1825

Animals feed; man eats: only the man of intellect knows how to eat.

Jean-Anthelme Brillat-Savarin *La Physiologie du goût* 1825

Gourmandism is an act of judgement, by which we give preference to things which are agreeable to our taste over those which are not.

Jean-Anthelme Brillat-Savarin *La Physiologie du goût* 1825

The pleasure of eating is the only one which, enjoyed in moderation, is not followed by weariness.

Jean-Anthelme Brillat-Savarin *La Physiologie du goût* 1825

GOURMANDISM is an impassioned, reasoned, and habitual preference for everything which gratifies the organ of taste. Gourmandism is the enemy of excess; indigestion and drunkenness are offences which render the offender liable to be struck off the rolls . . . it shows implicit obedience to the commands of the Creator who, when he ordered us to eat in order to live, gave us the inducement of appetite, the encouragement of savour and the reward of pleasure . . . gourmandism is the common bond which unites the nations of the world.

Jean-Anthelme Brillat-Savarin
La Physiologie du goût 1825

There are neither raptures nor ecstasies, nor transports of bliss in the pleasures of the table, but they make up in duration what they lack in intensity, and are distinguished above all by the merit of inclining us towards all the other pleasures of life, or at least consoling us for the loss of them. In short, at the end of a good dinner, body and soul both enjoy a remarkable sense of well-being.

Jean-Anthelme Brillat-Savarin *La Physiologie du goût* 1825

THOSE . . . to whom nature has refused an aptitude for the enjoyments of taste have long faces, long noses and large eyes; whatever their height, they have always in their tournure a character of elongation. They have black and straight hair, and are, above all, deficient in embonpoint: it is they who invented trousers. The women whom nature has afflicted with the same misfortune are angular, get tired at table and live on tea and scandal.

Jean-Anthelme Brillat-Savarin *La Physiologie du goût* 1825

Food for all is a necessity. Food should not be a merchandise, to be bought and sold as jewels are bought and sold by those who have the money to buy. Food is a human necessity like water and air, and it should be available.

Pearl S. Buck *To My Daughters, With Love* 1967

Some hae meat, and canna eat,
And some wad eat that want it;
But we hae meat and we can eat,
And sae the Lord be thankit.

Robert Burns *The Selkirk Grace*

Man is the only animal that can remain on friendly terms with the victims he intends to eat until he eats them.

Samuel Butler *Notebooks* 1902

All eating is a kind of proselytising – a kind of dogmatising – a maintaining that the eater's way of looking at things is better than the eatee's.

Samuel Butler *Notebooks* 1902

Sometimes when I am in the mood
I can eat any kind of food
H. sapiens is omnivorous
And so, Good Lord, deliver us
From qualms on eating flesh or fish
When served in an attractive dish.

Bruce Campbell
q. in *Writers' Favourite Recipes* ed. G. Vincent 1978

Always get up from the table feeling as if you could still eat a penny bun.

Sir Hugh Casson & Joyce Grenfell
Nanny Says 1972

IT IS A DIFFICULT matter, my fellow citizens, to argue with the belly, since it has no ears.

Marcus Porcius Cato 200 BC

There's no sauce in the world like hunger.

Miguel de Cervantes *Don Quixote* 1605-1615

To care for oneself by drinking excellent wines and by eating excellent dishes – that is the proper, the true medication.

M. Chatillon-Plessis
q. in *Pleasures of the Table* by G. Ellwanger 1903

O gluttony, full of cursedness,
O cause first of our confusion,
O original of our damnation.

Geoffrey Chaucer *The Canterbury Tales* 1387

A voracious sense of smell leans forward on its nostrils like a glutton eating with his elbows on the table.

Malcolm de Chazal *Sens Plastique* 1949

J UST ENOUGH food and drink should be taken to restore our strength, and not to overburden it.

Marcus Tullius Cicero *De Senectute* c. 50 BC

I have been a great observer and I can truly say that I have never known a man 'fond of good eating and drinking' as it is called; that I have never known such a man (and hundreds I have known) who was not worthy of respect.

William Cobbett *Advice to Young Men* 1829

Strange how one's thoughts turn to food when there is nothing else to think of.

John Colton & Clemence Rudolph *Rain*

Probably some of everyone's most dismal nursery memories are connected with food. One might come to accept the stewed prunes, the hateful greens, even the tapioca pudding . . . The miseries of fish days were harder to overcome because the food looked so terrifying even before it was put on your plate. Egg sauce didn't do much to compensate for the black skin and monstrous head of boiled cod; fish pudding, a few spiteful bones inevitably lying in wait in that viscous mass, and whitings biting their own tails were frightening dishes for children . . . black mackintosh skin . . . the empty eye-socket and accusing stare . . .

Elizabeth David *French Provincial Cooking* 1960

A big man is always accused of gluttony, whereas a wizened or osseous man can eat like a refugee at every meal, and no-one notices his greed.

Robertson Davies *The Table Talk of Samuel Marchbanks* 1949

It's a very odd thing –
As odd as can be –
That whatever Miss T eats
Turns into Miss T.
Porridge and apples,
Mince, muffins and mutton,
Jam, junket and jumbles –
Not a rap, not a button
It matters; the moment
They're out of her plate . . .
Whatever Miss T eats
Turns into Miss T.

Walter de la Mare *Miss T*

Oliver Twist has asked for more!

Charles Dickens *Oliver Twist* 1837-1838

If only it were as easy to banish hunger by rubbing the belly as it is to masturbate.

Diogenes the Cynic
q. in *Lives & Opinions of Eminent Philosophers* by Diogenes Laertius 200 BC

A GOOD EATER must be a good man; for a good eater must have a good digestion, and a good digestion depends upon a good conscience.

Benjamin Disraeli *The Young Duke* 1831

Beware of gross feeders. They are a menace to their fellow creatures. Will they not act, on occasion, even as they feed? Assuredly they will. Everybody acts as he feeds.

Norman Douglas *Alone*

A man's worst enemy is his own empty stomach.

Norman Douglas *Venus in the Kitchen* 1952

TO EAT UNDERSTANDINGLY and to drink understandingly are two arts that may not be learned from the day to the morrow.

Alexandre Dumas (père) *Grand Dictionnaire de Cuisine* 1873

Taking food and drink is a great enjoyment for healthy people, and those who do not enjoy eating seldom have much capacity for enjoyment or usefulness of any sort.

Charles W. Eliot *The Happy Life*

We only eat to live when we do not understand how to live to eat.

George Ellwanger *Pleasures of the Table* 1903
(but q. as a 'trivial axiom' by A. Soyer in *The Pantropheon* 1853)

LET THE STOICS say what they please, we do not eat for the good of living, but because the meat is savoury and the appetite is keen.

Ralph Waldo Emerson *Essays* 1844

The way to a man's heart is through his stomach.

Fanny Fern *Willis Parton*

When a man is small, he loves and hates food with a ferocity which soon dims. At six years old his very bowels will heave when such a dish as creamed carrots or cold tapioca appears before him. His throat will close, and spots of nausea and rage swim in his vision. It is hard, later, to remember why, but at the time there is no pose in his disgust. He cannot eat; he says 'To hell with it!'

M. F. K. Fisher *Serve It Forth* 1937

Between the ages of twenty and fifty, John Doe spends some twenty thousand hours chewing and swallowing food, more than eight hundred days and nights of steady eating. The mere contemplation of this fact is upsetting enough.

M. F. K. Fisher *Serve It Forth* 1937

Once at least in the life of every human, whether he be brute or trembling daffodil, comes a moment of complete gastronomic satisfaction. It is, I am sure, as much a matter of spirit as of body. Everything is right; nothing jars. There is a kind of harmony, with every sensation and emotion melted into one chord of well-being. Oddly enough, it is hard for people to describe these moments. They have sunk beatifically into the past or have been ignored or forgotten in the harsh rush of the present.

M. F. K. Fisher *Serve It Forth* 1937

The ability to choose what food you must eat, and knowingly, will make you able to choose other less transitory things with courage and finesse.

M. F. K. Fisher *How to Cook a Wolf* 1951

A complete lack of caution is perhaps one of the true signs of a real gourmet: he has no need for it, being filled as he is with a God-given and intelligently self-cultivated sense of gastronomical freedom.

M. F. K. Fisher *An Alphabet for Gourmets* 1949

IN GENERAL, I think, human beings are happiest at table when they are very young, very much in love or very lone.

M. F. K. Fisher *An Alphabet for Gourmets* 1949

PROBABLY NO strychnine has sent as many husbands into their graves as mealtime scolding has, and nothing has driven more men into the arms of other women as the sound of a shrill whine at table.

M. F. K. Fisher *An Alphabet for Gourmets* 1949

WHEN I HEAR of a gourmet with exquisite taste I assume . . . that there is something exaggeratedly elaborate, and even languidly perverted about his gourmandism. I do not think simply of an exquisitely laid table and an exquisite meal. Instead I see his silver carved in subtly erotic patterns, and his courses following one another in cabalistic design, half pain, half pleasure. I take it for granted . . . that rare volumes on witchcraft have equal place with Escoffier in his kitchen library . . .

M. F. K. Fisher *An Alphabet for Gourmets* 1949

It is a curious fact that no man likes to call himself a glutton, and yet each of us has in him a trace of gluttony, potential or actual. I cannot believe that there exists a single coherent human being who will not confess, at least to himself, that once or twice he has stuffed himself to bursting point on anything from quail financière to flapjacks, for no other reason than the beastlike satisfaction of his belly.

M. F. K. Fisher *An Alphabet for Gourmets* 1949

J is for Juvenile Dining . . . and the mistakenness of adults who think that the pappy pabulum stuffed down their children's gullets is swallowed, when and if it is swallowed, with anything more than weak helplessness and a bitter, if still subconscious acceptance, of the hard fact that they must eat to survive.

M. F. K. Fisher *An Alphabet for Gourmets* 1949

Eat not to dullness, drink not to elevation.

Benjamin Franklin *Rules for His Own Conduct* c. 1730

'What I like about gluttony,' a bishop I once knew used to say, 'is that it doesn't hurt anyone else.'

Monica Furlong *Christian Uncertainties* 1950

*T*HERE IS *poetry in a pork chop to a hungry man.*

Philip Gibbs q. in *New York Times* 1951

Food is the most primitive form of comfort.

Sheila Graham *A State of Heat*

Great food is like great sex – the more you have the more you want.

Gael Greene quoted 1979

A gourmet is just a glutton with brains.

Philip W. Haberman, Jr q. in *Vogue* magazine 1961

MAN HAS TO EAT to live; and to this primary condition of life he raises no particular objection. Man, indeed, eats and drinks with gusto – and not unfrequently, let it be confessed, without actual necessity.

Frederick W. Hackwood *Good Cheer* 1911

Eating does not consist in putting cold, greasy animal food into one's mouth. Eating consists of putting into the mouth – chewing, enjoying the flavour, and swallowing, of course – warm, juicy, thinnish or thickish, fat or lean, morsels of properly prepared food precisely at the nick of time.

Frederick W. Hackwood *Good Cheer* 1911

The difference between a gourmet and a gourmand we take to be this: a gourmet is he who selects, for his nice and learned delectation, the most choice delicacies, prepared in the most scientific manner; whereas the gourmand bears a closer analogy to that class of great eaters ill-naturedly (we dare say) denominated, or classed with, aldermen.

Abraham Hayward *The Art of Dining* 1852

A true gastronome is as insensible to suffering as a conqueror.

Abraham Hayward *The Art of Dining* 1852

Love and business and family and religion and art and patriotism are nothing but shadows of words when a man's starving.

O. Henry (William Sydney Porter) *Heart of the West* 1907

All things require skill but an appetite.

George Herbert *Outlandish Proverbs* 1640

Conversation is the enemy of food and good wine.

Alfred Hitchcock q. in *Time* magazine 1978

THE GUZZLER is one who is to be found haunting kitchens and larders where leftovers may be found – steak-and-kidney pies grown cold with the gravy solidified into splendid jelly, spaghetti bolognese grown glutinous so that pasta and sauce may be picked up together, quiches firmly set that may be cut off in thin slices again and again. There are always bits inaccessible to the carving knife that may be picked off the carcase of a bird by knowledgeable fingers, while hacking at a joint yields treasure and there is always the marrow to be had from the mutton bone.

David Holloway
q. in *Writers' Favourite Recipes* ed. G. Vincent 1978

A hungry stomach will not allow its owner to forget it, whatever his cares and sorrows.

Homer *The Odyssey* 800 BC

To pretend that food is an art, or even a high art, is pretentious gluttony. La nouvelle cuisine is vegetables arranged to look like something other than vegetables on a side plate, small helpings, a big bill, and long boring descriptions of what you are going to eat from the menu, or worse, the proprietor.

Philip Howard *The Times* 14.12. 1984

I F YOU ARE EVER at a loss to support a flagging conversation, introduce the subject of eating.
Leigh Hunt q. in *Geoffrey Madan's Notebooks* 1981

SOME PHYSIOLOGISTS will have it that the stomach is a mill; others, that it is a fermenting-vat; others again, that it is a stew-pan; but in my opinion, gentlemen, it is neither a mill, nor a ferment-vat nor a stew-pan; but a stomach, gentlemen, a stomach!

John Hunter

What was one day a sheep's hind leg and a handful of spinach was, the next, part of the hand that wrote, the brain that conceived the slow movement of the Jupiter Symphony.

Aldous Huxley *Point Counter Point* 1928

The whole of nature, as has been said, is a conjugation of the verb to eat, in the active and passive.
Dean William Inge *Outspoken Essays* second series, 1922

Statistics show that of those who contract the habit of eating, very few survive.

William Wallace Irwin q. in *Food* by Waverley Root 1980

Women never dine alone. When they dine alone they don't dine.

Henry James *The Given Case*

Some people have a foolish way of not minding, or pretending not to mind, what they eat. For my part, I mind my belly very studiously and very carefully, for I look upon it that he who does not mind his belly will hardly mind anything else.

Dr Samuel Johnson
in *The Life of Samuel Johnson* by James Boswell 1791

To eat is a necessity, but to eat intelligently is an art.
La Rochefoucauld *Maxims* 1665

On being asked 'Have you finished all that port (three bottles) without assistance?' 'No – not quite that – I had the assistance of a bottle of Madeira.'

Sir Hercules Langrishe
q. in *The Art of Dining* by Abraham Hayward 1852

I have not, hitherto, taken much interest in (horticulture). I am aware that God, having arranged that the earth should bring forth grass, the herb yielding seed, and the fruit tree yielding fruit after his kind, saw that it was good, and had I been present at the time I would have raised no objection, particularly since I would have only had to wait another couple of days for the bit about the fowls of the earth going forth and multiplying, presumably in order to ensure a regular supply of Père Bise's poularde braisée à la crème d'estragon.

Bernard Levin *Taking Sides* 1979

I AM GLUTTONY. My parents are all dead, and the devil a penny they have left me, but a bare pension, and that is thirty meals a day – a small trifle to suffice Nature. I come of a royal parentage! My grandfather was a gammon of bacon and my grandmother a hogshead of claret wine.

Christopher Marlowe *Dr Faustus* 1604

To be without a sense of taste is to be deficient in an exquisite faculty, that of appreciating the qualities of food, just as a person may lack the faculty of appreciating the quality of a book or a work of art. It is to want a vital sense, one of the elements of human superiority.

Guy de Maupassant

One should eat to live, not live to eat.

Molière (Jean-Baptiste Poquelin) *L'Avare* 1668

A gourmet is a being pleasing to heaven.

Charles Monselet *Lettres gourmandes* 1974

A TRUE GASTRONOME should always be ready to eat as a soldier should always be ready to fight.

Charles Monselet *Lettres gourmandes* 1974

The present . . . takes pride in its ability to produce ever larger quantities of food – pasteurized, homogenized, sterilized, frozen or otherwise reduced to an infant's standard of tastelessness.

Lewis Mumford q. in *Food* by Waverley Root 1980

Gluttony is ranked with the deadly sins; it should be honoured with the cardinal virtues. For the glutton, duty and amusement go hand in hand. Mind and body alike are satisfied. The good of a pleasantly planned dinner outbalances the evil of daily trials and tribulations. By artistic gluttony, beauty is increased, if not actually created. Rejoice in the knowledge that gluttony is the best cosmetic. Gross are they who see in eating and drinking nought but grossness. Gluttony is a vice only when it leads to stupid, inartistic excess.

Elizabeth Robins Pennell *The Feasts of Autolycus* 1896

For a gourmand there is no need to produce complicated dishes with fancy names. Prepare for him raw materials of good quality. Transform them as little as possible and accompany them with suitable sauces and you will have produced a meal which is just right. The gourmand is always happy and cheerful. He is always in a state of pleasant well-being. Not surprising, since what he has eaten has been assimilated and absorbed into his individual being. The gourmand is in harmony with the outside world. He is in fact a normal person.

Edouard de Pomiane *Cooking with Pomiane* 1962

The non-gourmand is afraid of eating this and that as he will not be able to digest them. When he has finished eating he will be out of sorts. He is out of step with the world and, in fact, abnormal. That is why he is unhappy, embittered, pessimistic, disagreeable, and even dangerous for those around him.

Edouard de Pomiane
Cooking with Pomiane 1962

Peter was ill during the evening, in consequence of overeating himself. His mother put him to bed and gave him a dose of camomile tea, but Flopsy, Mopsy and Cottontail had bread and milk and blackberries for supper.

Beatrix Potter *The Tale of Peter Rabbit* 1902

PERMANENT TASTES are acquired very easily at this time of life. As a rule, children dislike foods which are said to be good for them, or are forced on them, and they take strong fancies to foods which they are not allowed to eat; advantage should be taken of these tendencies.

Eric Pritchard *Infant Education* 1907

Man, embroidering on the primitive act of eating, has eventually created a comprehensive function, a ceremony significant in a variety of ways, illustrative of culture or decadence and so revealing that the table metamorphosed becomes a stage on which both poets and emperors appear, the scene of endless productions . . . Thus 'all the world's a stage', and the table, besides providing entrances and exits, supplies a very valuable key to the history of Civilisation.

Nancy Quennell *The Epicure's Anthology* 1936

Dyspepsy is the ruin of most things: empires, expeditions and everything else.

Thomas de Quincey q. in *Food* by Waverley Root 1980

Eat slowly; only men in rags
and gluttons old in sin
Mistake themselves for carpet-bags
And tumble victuals in.

Sir Walter Raleigh *Instructions to His Son* 1632

The Gourmand is not only the being whom nature has endowed with an excellent stomach and a vast appetite . . . but also he who adds to these advantages an enlightened taste, whose first characteristic resides in a singularly delicate palate cultivated by long experience. With him all the senses should be in constant accord with that of the taste, inasmuch as he should criticise his dishes even before they approach his lips. It is sufficient to say that his vision should be penetrating, his ear alert, his touch fine and his tongue capable.

Grimod de la Reynière *Almanach des Gourmands* 1804

Digestion is the business of the stomach and indigestion that of the doctors.

Grimod de la Reynière *Almanach des Gourmands* 1804

LIFE IS SO BRIEF that we should not glance either too far backwards or forwards in order to be happy. Let us therefore study how to fix our happiness in our glass and on our plate.

Grimod de la Reynière *Almanach des Gourmands* 1804

True gastronomy is making the most of what is available, however modest.

Claudia Roden *Picnic* 1981

The phenomenon of taste is . . . an artificial phenomenon acquired by education . . . The infant is born with . . . unprejudiced taste buds, which at first transmit to the brain a message about the taste of whatever is being eaten without making any judgement about whether that taste is good or bad. The child learns quickly how to convert the measurable chemical and physical stimuli reaching it from the exterior into an aesthetic estimate of quality – the transfiguration of mathematics into emotion. It discovers what it likes and what it does not like . . . Once learned, these judgements harden into prejudices.

Waverley Root *Food* 1980

EVER SINCE EVE started it all by offering Adam the apple, woman's punishment has been to have to supply a man with food and then suffer the consequences when it disagrees with him.

Helen Rowland *A Guide to Men*

There is nothing to which men, while they have food and drink, cannot reconcile themselves.

George Santayana *Interpretations of Poetry and Religion* 1900

The ravenous stomach . . . It is the least refined of organs, a fetid, rank and gaseous trough that knows but the pressure of fullness, the cavernous echo of emptiness – a pink, moist, hairless creature whose call is a belch, and who responds to its ingesta with delirious contractions and metallic bleeping. It is, all in all, an uncouth performance. Devoid of dream and imagination, lacking the lambent finesse of the heart, ignorant of the sweet language of the sex organs, the stomach sweats and steams and grunts most happily.

Richard Selzer *The Belly* 1975

MASTER OF DECEPTION, the stomach is the archetype of the enemy within. Slung athwart the upper abdomen like a slowly fattening worm . . . the stomach dwells, grinding its cud in blunt rumination. Is the world undone? A retarded serf, the stomach simply pursues its banality. Does the sun fall from the sky? The stomach cares not a fig. Quakes the earth? Ho hum. The stomach's contentment bears only on its content, from moment to moment. Yet interrupt for a time the care and feeding of this sack of appetite, do it insult with no matter how imagined a slight, then turns the worm to serpent that poisons the intellect for thought, the soul for poetry, the heart for love.

Richard Selzer *The Belly* 1975

Appetite, a universal wolf.

William Shakespeare

The most important activity in human life is eating. As any community progresses, its diet is the most salient guide to its refinement.

A. H. Sharar
Lucknow: the last phase of an oriental culture 1975

T HERE IS NO LOVE sincerer than the love of food.

George Bernard Shaw *Man and Superman* 1903

Our dependence upon Gaster-the-Belly is universally acknowledged, in spite of which . . . Gastronomy, that is the proper understanding of our own inner regions, is much less honoured than Astronomy. This is probably mainly due to the widespread idea that so long as the fires are kept burning, all must be well, and that any fuel is food to the furnace that is Gaster-the-Belly. But Gaster-the-Belly is not at all like a coke oven: it is a temperamental furnace, one that may refuse one day what it accepted the day before, one that has likes and dislikes that must not be disregarded if we are to enjoy the best of health.

André Simon *The Concise Encyclopedia of Gastronomy* 1952

Gastronomes are not the slaves but the masters of Gaster-the-Belly, intelligent and kindly masters, who realize that a good servant is a friend in need and that he deserves to be well treated, listened to and at times humoured; no good service can be possibly expected from a starving servant any more than a drunken one.

André Simon *The Concise Encyclopedia of Gastronomy* 1952

Of course, like all other senses, smell and taste can be educated or trained and become a source of real artistic pleasure or sensual joy. The difference is that whilst the occasions to enjoy fine pictures or great music are very rare for the majority of people, Gastronomes are given not once, but twice or thrice, on every day of their lives, the chance to use critically their senses of taste and smell, and to train them to recognise that which is good, better and best.

André Simon *The Concise Encyclopedia of Gastronomy* 1952

G OURMAND IS THE GREEDY fellow who does not mind very much about quality so long as he gets a lot: even when he is not asking, he is hoping for more. Gourmet is the 'choosey' eater, with definite likes and dislikes of his own, who prefers quality to quantity. Gastronome is the cultured and knowledgeable gourmet: his approach to all that is best to eat and drink is that of the epicurean philosopher who recognises the ethical value of the amenities of a gracious way of living; it is not that of the materialist whose chief concern is merely sensual gratification . . . The greater number of gastronomes there will be in the world, the happier world it will be.

André Simon
q. in *A Wine and Food Bedside Book* ed. C. Morny 1972

Food without wine is a corpse; wine without food is a ghost; united and well matched they are as body and soul, living partners.

André Simon
q. in *A Wine and Food Bedside Book* ed. C. Morny 1972

T HE GREEDY MAN has ever accomplished, I apprehend, more good in this world than all those sinister individuals put together who openly boast, lean and sallow men that they are, how they do not care what they eat so long as it comes out of a tin.

Osbert Sitwell
introduction to *Lady Sysonby's Cookbook* 1935

I am convinced that digestion is the great secret of life and that character, talents, virtues and qualities are powerfully affected by beef, mutton, pie-crust and rich soups.

Sydney Smith
q. in *The Smith of Smiths* by Hesketh Pearson 1934

Old friendships are destroyed by toasted cheese, and hard salted meat has led to suicide. Unpleasant feelings of the body produce corresponding sensations of the mind, and a great sense of wretchedness is sketched out by a morsel of indigestible, misguided food.

Sydney Smith q. in *The Smith of Smiths* by Hesketh Pearson 1934

I T MATTERS NOT how simple the food – a chop, steak, or a plain boiled or roast joint, but let it be of good quality and properly cooked, and every one who partakes of it will enjoy it.

Alexis Soyer *The Modern Housewife* 1851

Man began at first by satisfying the imperious necessities of his stomach; he then ate to live and all was good to him. Experience by degrees gave rise to eclecticism – choice. It was then discovered that a coarse and solid food might be replaced by a delicate and savoury alimentation; joyous appetite, and sensuality, its effeminate companion, took the place of hunger, and this happy couple gave birth to the more amiable of fairies, who, under the name of Gastronomy, was soon to govern the world and prescribe to it imperishable laws.

Alexis Soyer *The Pantropheon* 1853

T HE APPETITE – indispensable basis, on which will always rest the culinary exegesis (has) three degrees of intensity: The bold appetite . . . is that which is felt when fasting. It reflects but very little; is not squeamish about viands, and loses all reserve at the sight of a very indifferent ragout. The indolent appetite requires to be encouraged. It must be enticed, pressed, irritated. At first nothing moves it, but after having tasted a succulent dish it rouses, it is astonished . . . The eclectic appetite . . . is the child of art. Happy, thrice happy, the skilful cook to whom it says 'Thou art my father'. But how difficult is this creation, how rare. It is the work of genius.

Alexis Soyer *The Pantropheon* 1853

And by his side rode loathsome Gluttony,
Deformed creature on a filthy swine.
His belly was upblown with luxury,
And eke with fatness swollen was his eyne.
Full of diseases was his carcass blew,
And a dry Dropsie through his flesh did flow,
Which by misdiet daily greater grew;
Such one was gluttony, the second of that crew.

Edmund Spenser
The Faerie Queene 1589-1596

If there were no such thing as eating, we would have to invent it to save man from despairing.

Dr Wilhelm Stekhel *The Depths of the Soul*

N O MAN ABSTAINS from the pleasures of the table, unless forced to do so by some constitutional defect . . . If the stomach be unsound, the heart which is lodged in it must be corrupted: it therefore follows that all abstemious people are persons of bad heart. You sober people . . . are cold in manners as in constitution, and are envious and malignant.

Lancelot Sturgeon *Essays on Good Living*

He was an ingenious man that first found out eating and drinking.

Jonathan Swift *Polite Conversation* 1738

In eating, a third of the stomach should be filled with food, a third with drink, and the rest left empty.

The Talmud *200*

Seeing is deceiving. It's eating that's believing.

James Thurber *Further Fables for Our Time* 1956

Nicolas Wood . . . did with ease eat a whole Sheep . . . and that raw, at one meal; at another time he ate 30 dozens of Pidgeons . . . at Lord Wootton's, in Kent, he ate at one meal fourscore and four Rabbits; he suddenly devoured 18 yards of black pudding, and when at once he had 60 lb. weight of Cherries, he said they were but wash-meat; he made an end of an whole Hog once, and after it for fruit swallowed three pecks of Damsons . . . After having broken his fast with . . . one bottle of Milk, one bottle of Pottage, with bread, butter and cheese, he ate . . . six penny wheaten loaves, 3 sixpenny veal pies, one pound of sweet Butter, one good dish of Thornback, and a shiver off a peck household loaf of an inch thick, and all this in the space of an hour, the House yielding no more, he departed unsatisfied.

William Turner *The Wonders of Nature* 1697

To eat is human, to digest divine.

Mark Twain

P ART OF THE SECRET of success in life is to eat what you like and let the food fight it out inside.

Mark Twain

Food is better than power . . . If a man abstain from food for ten days, though he live, he would not be able to see, hear, perceive, think, act and understand. But when he obtains food, he is able to see, hear, perceive, think, act and understand.

Upanishads

The fate of a nation has often depended upon the good or bad digestion of a prime minister.

Voltaire *Philosophical Dictionary* 1764

Gluttony is an emotional escape, a sign that something is eating us.

Peter de Vries
Comfort Me with Apples 1956

Content the stomach and the stomach will content you.

Thomas Walker *The Original* 1835

A food is not necessarily essential just because your child hates it.

Katherine Whitehorn *How to Survive Children*

We in our skool are proud of our maners which makyth us the weeds we are and when grabber shoot peas from peashooter at the deaf master we are much shoked i do not think. Nor do we makes lakes of treacle in the poridge or rivers of gravy through the mashed potatoes perish the thort.

Geoffrey Willans and Ronald Searle *The Compleet Molesworth* 1958

An egg of one hour old, bread of one day, a goat of one month, wine of six months, flesh of a year, fish of ten years and a wife of twenty years, a friend among a hundred, are the best of all number.

John Wodroephe *Spared Hours* 1623

CHAPTER TEN

THE SOUL
OF COOKING

IN MEAT, we've got a product not only subject to easy contamination but extremely amenable to adulteration and to concealment of adulteration. Partially spoiled meat can be subjected to cooking and curing operations and chemicals that make it look fine.

U.S. Department of Agriculture q. in *Food* by Waverley Root 1980

First a roasted kid, a yearling,
With its innards firmly strung,
And upon it, well to season,
Tarragon and mint are hung . . .
Lemons too, with nadd (a mixture of perfumes) besprinkled,
Scented well with ambergris,
And, for garnishing the slices,
Shreds of appetizing cheese . . .

Mahmud ibn al-Husain al-Kushajim
q. in *The Islamic Culture* by A. J. Arberry 1939

Beefsteaks and porter are good belly mortar.

Anonymous *Scottish Proverb*

The nearer the bone, the sweeter the meat.

Anonymous *English Proverb*

It is a poor roast that gives no dripping.

Anonymous *Danish proverb*

SAUERKRAUT and bacon drive all care away.

Anonymous *Pennsylvania German proverb*

Useless during life, and only valuable when deprived of it, the pig has sometimes been compared to a miser, whose hoarded treasures are of little value till death has deprived them of their rapacious owner.

Evelyn Bach *Recipes from Hungary* 1938

Of all wild or domesticated animals . . . the lamb is . . . without exception the most useful to man as food.

Mrs Isabella Beeton *The Book of Household Management* 1861

In the latter times some shall depart from the faith, giving heed to seducing spirits, and doctrines of devils . . . commanding to abstain from meats, which God hath created to be received with thanksgiving of them which believe and know the truth.

The Bible *Timothy IV, 1-3* c. 60

Every moving thing that liveth shall be meat for you; even as the green herb have I given you all things.

The Bible *Genesis* 1000 BC

THE SWINE, because it parts the hoof and is cloven-footed but does not chew the cud is unclean to you; of their flesh you shall not eat, and their carcases you shall not touch.

The Bible *Leviticus* I:4 1000 BC

Carnivorous, adj: addicted to the cruelty of devouring the timorous vegetarian, his heirs and assigns.

Ambrose Bierce   *The Devil's Dictionary* 1911

As for the leg of mutton, it is truly wonderful; nothing so good had I ever tasted in the shape of a leg of mutton. The leg of mutton in Wales beats the leg of mutton of any other country, and I had never tasted a Welsh leg of mutton before. Certainly I shall never forget the first Welsh leg of mutton which I tasted, rich but delicate, replete with juices deprived from the aromatic herbs of the noble Berwyn, cooked to a turn and weighing just four pounds.

George Borrow   *Wild Wales* 1862

A DAUBE COOKED gently in an earthenware stew pot of venerable age, for three whole days, the three days required, and seasoned as it should be, a daube of succulent and well-basted meats, is surely the greatest of all treasures! Should I decide to swallow it, it is only when I have savoured it with the most sensitive parts of my mouth that I can distinguish the sharpness of the pepper, the virtues of the garlic, the fineness of the pork fat, the mildness of the onion and the exquisiteness of the thyme, all melted with the steam from the liquid seasoned with little pinches of salt.

Henri Bosco

Meat is a natural nourishment of man because his stomach is too small to deal with the bulk of food he would have to consume if his diet was restricted to fruit and vegetables.

Jean-Anthelme Brillat-Savarin   *La Physiologie du goût* 1825

The best of remedies is a beef-steak
Against sea-sickness.

George Gordon, Lord Byron   *Don Juan* 1819

Beef is the soul of cooking.

Antonin Carème   *Le Cuisinier Parisien* 1828

NOW PORK CHOPS are not particularly difficult to cook. I can cook them myself. You cook them in their own fat, they bring with them everything that is necessary except salt and pepper.

Raymond Chandler   *Selected Letters* ed. Frank McShane 1981

Doctor, do you think it could have been the sausage?

Paul Claudel last words, 1955

CASSOULET . . . that sumptuous amalgamation of haricot beans, sausage, pork, mutton, and preserved goose, aromatically spiced with garlic and herbs, is cooked at great length in an earthenware pot, emerging with a golden crust which conceals an interior of gently bubbling, creamy beans and uniquely savoury meats.

Elizabeth David *French Provincial Cooking* 1960

A skilful, experienced butcher treats his meat almost as a tailor does his cloth. If it is stretched out of shape, if there are seams in the wrong places, if he has to make up a respectable-looking joint by adding a piece here, skewering in some fat there, he knows that as soon as the meat is exposed to violent heat it will contract; unnaturally stretched muscles will spring back into place; it will cook unevenly; it will end up looking like a parcel damaged in the Christmas mails. No wonder people say that the cheaper cuts are a false economy.

Elizabeth David *French Provincial Cooking* 1960

Tongue: well that's a werry good thing when it ain't a woman's.

Charles Dickens
The Pickwick Papers 1836-1837

To see the butcher slap the steak before he laid it on the block, and give his knife a sharpening, was to forget breakfast instantly. It was agreeable too – it really was – to see him cut it off so smooth and juicy. There was nothing savage in the act, although the knife was large and keen; it was a piece of art, high art; there was delicacy of touch, clearness of tone, skilful handling of the subject, fine shading. It was the triumph of mind over matter; quite.

Charles Dickens *Martin Chuzzlewit* 1843

The still hissing bacon and eggs that looked like tufts of primroses.

Benjamin Disraeli
Coningsby 1844

Without (the pig) there were, in truth, an aching void and an empty cuisine, – no lard, no hams, no bacon, no sausages, no sparerib, no larded fillets and game; no truffles and no scientifically blended pâtés; no souse, no headcheese . . . His ways are ways of fatness and all his paths are progressive. He not only seeks to instruct, like Virgil, but seeks to please, like Theocritus. Civilisation radiates from him as light from a prism. With his increase culture advances, wealth accumulates, and cookery improves . . . His unctuous Lardship! the very fat and marrow of the stock-exchange, the grease of the commercial wheel.

George Ellwanger *Pleasures of the Table* 1903

There are several different kind of stews. A stew can be a sweat or welter in hot close atmosphere or, according to the English dictionaries, a saaa. It can be a tank or pond for storing live fish. It can be a brothel. It can be something cooked by long simmering in a closed vessel with a little liquid in it.

M. F. K. Fisher *Consider the Oyster* 1941

THE SAUSAGE . . . here is no delicacy of high purport, here is no food for the gods, here's nothing sacrificial, nothing knightly or hieratic, no tragic actor was ever garlanded by a sausage, no-one was ever poisoned by it except accidentally, no-one was ever smacked over the face by it without reviving; added to those fundamentals of nourishment – bread and wine – it changes their nature and converts them into a snack. Debarred from villainy by its composition, and from heroism by its shape, it has always sought safety in humour . . . Rolling, tumbling, waddling, looking over its shoulder without turning round, it diverts attention from its infirmity by cracking jokes . . . It is the plebian of the breakfast table.

E. M. Forster
q. in *A Wine and Food Bedside Book* ed. C. Morny 1972

Veal is the quintessential Lonely Guy meat. There's something pale and lonely about it, especially if it doesn't have any veins. It's so wan and Kierkegaardian. You just know it's not going to hurt you.

Bruce Jay Friedman *The Lonely Guy Cookbook* 1976

Boeuf à la Bourguignonne (Beef in the Burgundy style): This is the stew of stews, an apotheosis of stew, which has nothing whatsoever to do with the watery, stringy mixture served up in British institutions. It's a rich, carefully cooked recipe which is served up on special occasions in French homes, and which appears without shame on the menus of high-class restaurants.

Jane Grigson *The Mushroom Feast* 1975

One good oxtail is worth a thousand words . . . I'm in favour of rice and Burgundy with it, especially when writing a novel of sex and violence.

Alex Hamilton q. in *Writers' Favourite Recipes* ed. G. Vincent 1978

APRIL: We are still on the threshold of Spring. The jolly lambkin, whose younger brothers leapt so artlessly onto our table in March, now gambols a hint more sedately, but his flesh is nearly as delicious. Grass will give him a new flavour, and nowhere in the world is better grass lamb to be found than in England . . . May: Ducklings and Spring Chickens greet us in an ecstatic chorus, eager for their funereal couch of green peas.

Ambrose Heath *Good Food* 1932

A little meat best fits a little belly,
As sweetly, Lady, give me leave to tell ye,
This little pipkin fits this little jelly.

Robert Herrick *Hesperides* 1648

O, scent of the daubes of my childhood . . . my grandmother's dark kitchen . . . was lit by a ray of sunshine in which the dust and the flies were dancing, and there was a sound like a little bubbling spring. It was daube, which since midday had been murmuring gently on the stove, giving out sweet smells which brought tears to your eyes. Thyme, rosemary, bay leaves, spices, the wine of the marinade, and the fumet of the meat were becoming transformed under the magic wand which is the fire, into a delicious whole, which was served at about seven o'clock in the evening, so well cooked and so tender that it was carved with a spoon.

Pierre Huguenin *Les Meilleures Recettes de ma pauvre mère* 1936

I think that I could never spy
A poem as lovely as a pie
A banquet in a single course
Blushing with rich tomato sauce
A pie whose crust is oven kissed
Whose gravy scalds the eater's wrist
The pastie and the sausage roll
Have not thy brown mysterious soul
The dark hued aborigine
Is less indigenous than thee;
As round and rich as Zara
As tasteful as Patrick White
With a glass of purple para
You're the great Australian bite.

Barry Humphries
unpublished poem q. in *The Dictionary of Australian Quotations* 1984

Your butcher breathes an atmosphere of good living. The beef mingles kindly with his animal nature. He grows fat with the best of it, perhaps with inhaling its very essence; and has no time to grow spare, theoretical and hypochondriacal.

Leigh Hunt *The Seer* c. 1840

There is no meat this side of paradise as supremely satisfying as a good, hefty mutton chop properly prepared . . . when it is a deep burgundy red beneath a scorched exterior, steams with its own sealed-in juices at the touch of a fork, and has a full-bodied flavour with which that of no red meat, the finest steaks included, can compare.

Jay Jacobs *The Gourmet*

Any of us would rather kill a cow than not have beef.
Dr Samuel Johnson 1760

IT TAKES A CERTAIN kind of mind to see beauty in a hamburger bun. Yet is it any more unusual to find grace in the texture and softly carved silhouette of a bun than to reflect lovingly on the hackles of a fishing fly? Or the arrangements and textures on a butterfly's wing? Not if you are a MacDonald's man.

Ray Kroc *Grinding It Out* 1978

(The pig) hath a fair sepulchre in the grateful stomach of the judicious epicure – and for such a tomb might be content to die.

Charles Lamb *Dissertation upon Roast Pig* 1823

There is no flavour comparable, I will contend, to that of the crisp, tawny, well-matched, not over-roasted crackling, as it is well called – the very teeth are invited to their share of the pleasure at this banquet in overcoming the coy, brittle resistance – with the adhesive oleaginous – oh, call it not fat! but an indefinable sweetness growing up to it – the tender blossoming of fat – fat cropped in the bud – taken in the shoot – in the first innocence – the cream and quintessence of the child pig's yet pure food – the lean, no lean, but a kind of animal manna – or rather fat and lean so blended and running into each other, that both together make one ambrosian result, or common substance.

Charles Lamb *Dissertation upon Roast Pig* 1823

Pig – let me speak his praise – is no less provocative of the appetite than he is satisfactory to the criticalness of the censorious palate. The strong man may batten on him, and the weakling refuseth not his mild juices.

Charles Lamb *Dissertation on Roast Pig* 1823

I CAN SEE A PIG – a pig of 180 pounds – classical in all the tints of its marble freshness. It sheds its internal graces in an excellent and cleanly market. With deft execution the white-aproned purveyor removes a spare-rib from a side. Then in front of the site of the spare-rib there remains an area of unequalled promise – a tract of the most delightsome possibilities . . . No poem ever stirred the human heart, no slab of tesselated pavement ever fired the archeologist, with respectful interest to that evoked by this entrancing esculent.

Charles Lamb *Dissertation on Roast Pig* 1823

THE PIG HAS LIVED only to eat, he eats only to die . . . He eats everything his gluttonous snout touches, he will be eaten completely . . . he eats all the time, he will be eaten all the time . . . The pig is nothing but an enormous dish which walks while waiting to be served . . . In a sort of photograph of his future destiny, everything announces that he will be eaten, but eaten in such a fashion that there will remain of him not the smallest bone, not a hair, not an atom.

Charles Monselet *Lettres gourmandes* 1974

The mountain sheep are sweeter,
But the valley sheep are fatter,
Therefore we deemed it meeter,
To carry off the latter.

Thomas Love Peacock
The War-Song of Dinas Vawr

I think I could eat one of Bellamy's veal pies.

William Pitt the Younger supposed last words 1806

Let us eat flesh, but only for hunger not for wantonness. Let us kill an animal; but let us do it with sorrow and pity and not abusing it, or tormenting it.

Plutarch c. 75

Of birth renowned, entitled well to boast,
And reared with care, the little pig is dead:
We sorrow, but we scent the savoury roast,
And mix a bumper while our tears we shed.
Regret not, little pig, thine early fate:
Honours are thine beyond the fattening sty, –
We eat thee, brother, and incorporate
Thy substance, thus, in our humanity.

M. Pouvoisin *La Mort du Goret*

MEAT IS A STATUS dish in which the sizzle counts for more than the intrinsic nutritional worth.

Magnus Pyke quoted 1978

Pig. This is the king of unclean beasts; whose empire is most universal, whose qualities are least in question: no pig, no lard, and consequently no cooking, no ham, no sausages, no andouilles, no black puddings, and finally no pork-butchers. Ungrateful doctors! you have condemned the pig; he is, as regards indigestion, one of the finest feathers in your cap.

Grimod de la Reynière *Calendrier Gastronomique*

Man's ingratitude towards the pig has basely reviled the name of an animal that is the most useful to the human race when he is no more. He is treated as the Abbé Geoffroy treats Voltaire: his memory is defamed while his flesh is being savoured, and he is repaid with ironical contempt for the ineffable pleasures he procures for us.

Grimod de la Reynière *Almanach des Gourmands* 1804

A hamburger is warm and fragrant and juicy. A hamburger is soft and non-threatening. It personifies the Great Mother herself who has nourished us from the beginning. A hamburger is an icon of layered circles, the circle being at once the most spiritual and the most sensual of shapes. A hamburger is companionable and faintly erotic. The nipple of the Goddess, the bountiful belly-ball of Eve. You are what you think you eat.

Tom Robbins *Esquire* December 1983

The knightly sirloin, and the noble baron of beef.

Sir Walter Scott *Old Mortality* 1816

GIVE THEM GREAT meals of beef and iron and steel, they will eat like wolves and fight like devils.

William Shakespeare *King Henry V* 1600

It is only by softening and disguising dead flesh by culinary preparation that it is rendered susceptible of mastication or digestion; and that the sight of its bloody juices and raw horror does not excite intolerable loathing and disgust.

Percy Bysshe Shelley *Queen Mab* 1813

Good beef dripping, spread upon some rather thick freshly made toast, then put under the grill until it melts into the toast, a little salt on it – and a large mug of mulled ale with it – will keep cold and wet out, and keep peace and good will within.

André Simon *A Concise Encyclopedia of Gastronomy* 1952

Sausage: a name that covers a multitude of tasty little 'bags of mystery', mostly finely chopped and highly-seasoned meat encased in hog or sheep gut or some other non-edible but non-poisonous container.

André Simon *A Concise Encyclopedia of Gastronomy* 1952

PORK – no animal is more used for nourishment and none more indispensable in the kitchen; employed either fresh or salt, all is useful, even to its bristles and its blood; it is the superfluous riches of the farmer, and helps to pay the rent of the cottager.

Alexis Soyer *The Modern Housewife* 1851

If intelligence, strength, or graceful beauty of form were to decide what rank this numerous class of animals – which has contributed its quota to the triumphs of the culinary art – the pig, with its vile and stupid ugliness, its depraved habits, and its waddling obesity, would be banished for ever more from the farmyard and the larder in every civilised nation of the world.

Alexis Soyer *The Pantropheon* 1853

NATURE has created the pig for man's palate; he is good only to be eaten; and life appears to have been given to him merely as a sort of salt to prevent his corrupting.

Alexis Soyer *The Pantropheon* 1853

Gently stir and blow the fire,
Lay the mutton down to roast,
Dress it quickly, I desire,
In the dripping put a toast,
That I hunger may remove –
Mutton is the meat I love.
On the dresser see it lie;
Oh, the charming white and red;
Finer meat ne'er met the eye,
On the sweetest grass it fed:
Let the jack go swiftly round,
Let me have it nicely brown'd.
On the table spread the cloth,
Let the knives be sharp and clean,
Pickles get and salad both,
Let them each be fresh and green.
With small beer, good ale and wine,
Oh ye gods! how I shall dine.

Jonathan Swift
q. in *The Cook's Oracle* by Dr Kitchiner 1820
(also attrib. to Sidney Smith by G. Ellwanger *Pleasures of the Table* 1903)

. . . a mighty porterhouse steak an inch and a half thick, hot and sputtering from the griddle; dusted with fragrant pepper; enriched with little melting bits of butter of the most unimpeachable freshness and genuineness; the precious juices of the meat trickling out and joining the gravy, archipelagoed with mushrooms; a township or two of tender, yellowish fat gracing an outlying district of this ample country of beefsteak; the long white bone which divides the sirloin from the tenderloin still in place.

Mark Twain *A Tramp Abroad* 1894

Nothing helps scenery like bacon and eggs.

Mark Twain 1890

Steak tartare . . . not only one of the glories of great eating, but a possible cure-all for lethargy, obesity, hangovers and maybe even sexual impotence.

Jim Villas *Esquire* November 1975

One fat Sir Loin possesses more sublime
Than all the airy castles built by rhyme.

John Wolcot *Bozzy and Piozzi* 1786

CHAPTER ELEVEN

EAT YOUR HEART OUT

Fair fa your honest sonsie face,
Great chieftain o' the puddin' – race!
Aboon them a ye tak your place,
Painch, tripe or thairm
Weel are ye wordy o' a grace
As lang's my arm.

Robert Burns *To a Haggis*

One way to horrify eight out of ten Anglo-Saxons is to suggest their eating anything but the actual red fibrous meat of a beast. A heart or a kidney or even a sweetbread is anathema. It is too bad, since there are so many nutritious and entertaining ways to prepare the various livers and lights. They can become gastronomic pleasures, instead of dogged voodoo . . .

M. F. K. Fisher *How to Cook a Wolf* 1951

The best thing about liver is how virtuous it makes you feel after you've eaten some.

Bruce Jay Friedman *The Lonely Guy Cookbook* 1976

O N EATING calf's liver with sauté mushrooms: I've always wondered what it would be like to eat a baby. I think it would taste like this.

Gael Greene

Mr Leopold Bloom ate with relish the inner organs of beasts and fowls. He liked thick giblet soup, nutty gizzards, a stuffed roast heart, liver slices fried with crustcrumbs, fried hencod's roes. Most of all he liked grilled mutton kidneys which gave to his palate a fine tang of faintly scented urine.

James Joyce *Ulysses* 1922

The world of tripery is barred to the well-bred, except for an occasional exposure to an expurgated version of 'tripes à la mode de Caen'. They have never seen 'gras-double' (tripe cooked with vegetables, principally onions) or 'pieds et paquets' (sheep's tripe and calves' feet with salt pork).

A. J. Liebling *Between Meals* 1962

The poorer sort (in China) go to the shambles and take the raw liver as soon as it is drawn from the beasts; then they chop it up small, put it in garlic sauce and eat it there and then. And they do likewise with every other kind of flesh. The gentry also eat their meat raw.

Marco Polo
Travels ed. R. Latham 1958

T RIPE'S GOOD meat if it be well wiped.

John Ray *English Proverbs* 1670

On an outing . . . I once cored an apple, saw to my astonishment (and with the aid of my obsession) what it looked like, and ran off into the woods to fall upon the orifice of the fruit, pretending that the cool and mealy hole was actually between the legs of that mythical being who always called me Big Boy when she pleaded for what no girl in all recorded history ever had. 'Oh shove it in me, Big Boy,' cried the cored apple that I banged silly on that picnic . . . 'Come, Big Boy, come,' screamed the maddened piece of liver that, in my own insanity, I bought one afternoon at a butcher shop and, believe it or not, violated behind a billboard on the way to a bar mitzvah lesson.

Philip Roth *Portnoy's Complaint* 1969

A S A RULE ONE does not attempt to make a haggis; one just buys a haggis and does not enquire too closely as to how it was made.

André Simon *A Concise Encyclopedia of Gastronomy* 1952

What is the size of a pumpernickel, has the shape of Diana's helmet, and crouches like a thundercloud above its bellymates, turgid with nourishment? What has the industry of an insect, the regenerative powers of a starfish, yet is turned to a mass of fatty globules by a double martini . . . It is . . . the liver, doted upon by the French, assaulted by the Irish, disdained by the Americans and chopped up with egg, onion and chicken fat by the Jews.

Richard Selzer *The Drinking Man's Liver* 1974

CHAPTER TWELVE

THE GAME'S THE THING

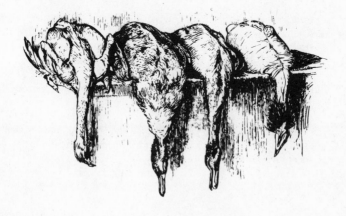

It is difficult to imagine a happier conjunction that the blending of the symbols when the arms of a sportsman are quartered with those of a cook. The tints of the autumnal woods reflected in the plumage of mature and lusty game are types of rich experiences and genial sentiments which flit about the sportsman's board and linger at his hearth with as gracious a fitness as that which diffuses a faint blush through the russet of a well-cooked mallard's breast, and with a zest equal to the relish which lurks within a woodcock's thigh.

John Aldergrove q. in *Pleasures of the Table* by G. Ellwanger 1903

Few people know how to eat a small (game) bird; here is the method . . .: Take a plump little bird by the beak, sprinkle him with a little salt, remove the gizzard, thrust him boldly into your mouth, bite him off close to your fingers, and chew hard; this will produce enough juice to wet the whole organ and you will taste a delight unknown to the common herd.

Jean-Anthelme Brillat-Savarin *La Physiologie du goût* 1825

The quail is of all game the most delicate and the most agreeable. A good, fat quail pleases equally by its taste, its shape and its colour. You show your ignorance whenever you serve it otherwise than roasted or en papillote, for its savour is extremely volatile and every time the animal is put in contact with liquid, it dissolves, evaporates and perishes.

Jean-Anthelme Brillat-Savarin *La Physiologie du goût* 1825

When preparing a sheep or calf's head, or a rabbit or hare, I advise you always to remove the jaws and eyes, as these have a deplorable effect on a table. The sight of them can make the soundest persons feel sick; and how really horrible is the sinister gaze of those hollow sockets, and those mangled, moist, sad eyes!

Clarisse q. in *A Concise Encyclopedia of Gastronomy* by A. Simon 1952

F ESAUNT exceedeth all foules in sweetnesse and wholesomenesse, and is equal to a capon in nourishing . . . It is meate for Princes and great estates, and for poor Schollers when they can get it.

Thomas Cogan *Haven of Health* 1588

Pygeons be easily dygested and are very holsome to them which are fleumatike or pure melancholy.

Elyot's Castel of Health 1539

Of the wealth of aliments bestowed on man by a bountiful Providence for his sustenance and delectation, none lends a greater grace or ministers more to the variety of the table than game. The offspring of wild nature, nursed upon its fruits, its mast, and its vegetation, and exhaling the very essence of its most secluded recesses, it sheds an added lustre even upon the most elaborate repast.

George Ellwanger *Pleasures of the Table* 1903

About one thing the Englishman has a particularly strict code. If a bird says 'Cluk bik bik bik bik' and 'caw' you may kill it, eat it or ask Fortnums to pickle it in Napoleon brandy with wild strawberries. If it says 'tweet' it is a dear and precious friend and you'd better lay off it if you want to remain a member of Boodles.

Clement Freud
Freud on Food 1978

The hare has always been game, not an adjunct of feudal economy, and highly regarded as a richly flavoured food. That's really the difference – the hare rich and gamey in flavour, the rabbit (good wild rabbit) fresh and succulent. The hare makes one think of port, burgundy, redcurrant jelly, spices and cream; the rabbit needs onions, mustard, white wine, dry cider and thyme.

Jane Grigson *Good Things* 1971

LET US SAY it at once: game birds are never so good as when shot just right, hung just right, plucked just right and roasted just right. Done to a turn, as they say, and . . . served with the original toast on which their delectable drippings have fallen.

Ambrose Heath
q. in *A Wine and Food Bedside Book* ed. C. Morny 1972

A popular lunch when stalking deer is one or two fried egg and bacon sandwiches. The bacon should be fatty so that the mouth does not become dry (much drinking of water is bad for climbing hills). The sandwich should be made with thick toast for structural strength, as otherwise a bag of greasy crumbs may be all that is left after a lengthy crawl – a poor reward after a hopefully successful stalk.

Sir Ian Mactaggart *Picnic* by Claudia Roden 1981

Whether woodcock or partridge what does it signify, if the taste is the same? But the partridge is dearer, and therefore thought preferable.

Martial *Epigrams XIII* c. 80

An olive, stoned, inside a warbler;
The warbler inside an ortolan;
The ortolan inside a lark;
The lark inside a thrush;
The thrush inside a quail;
The quail, in vine-leaves, in a golden plover;
The plover inside a lapwing;
The lapwing inside a partridge;
The partridge inside a woodcock;
The woodcock inside a teal;
The teal inside a guinea-fowl;
The guinea-fowl, well larded, inside a duck;
The duck inside a pheasant;
The pheasant inside a goose;
The goose inside a turkey;
The turkey inside a swan;
The swan inside a bustard.

Robert Nye
q. in *Writers' Favourite Recipes* ed. G. Vincent 1978

The distinctive flavour of grouse is not easily abated by other subtleties, so that, however you dress your bird, whether as soup or braise or pie, the dominant flavour is always grouse, and short of violence with a clove of garlic or a curry that would make coke palatable, it is impossible to cover it.

Major Hugh Pollard
The Sportsman's Cookery Book 1926

For a steady diet no meat tastes better or is more nourishing than elk venison . . . elk tongues are most delicious eating, being juicy, tender and well flavoured; they are excellent to take out as a lunch on a long hunting trip.

Theodore Roosevelt
Big Game Hunting in the Rockies and on the Great Plains 1899

THE FLESH of the moose is very good, though some deem it coarse. Old hunters, who always like rich, greasy food, rank a moose's nose with a beaver's tail, as the chief of backwood delicacies . . .

Theodore Roosevelt
Big Game Hunting in the Rockies and on the Great Plains 1899

I do not suppose that this is the primary function of the rabbit, but it can serve as a touchstone to separate food snobs from those earthy characters who really like to eat. Hare is respectable, even distinguished; rabbit is common and vulgar, and it is good form to turn up the nose at it.

Waverley Root *Food 1980*

T HE FLESH of the eland has been very much over-estimated . . . and is not to be compared for flavour to that of the buffalo, giraffe, hippopotamus or white rhinocerous, supposing, of course, that the animals are all fat and in good condition.

Frederick Selous *A Hunter's Wanderings in Africa* 1890

Whilst there are both fish in the sea and plants in the field that are distinctly poisonous, there does not appear to be any poisonous bird, so that a complete list of 'edible' birds would include every known species of bird. Such a list . . . would have been quite misleading, since the majority of the names included would have been of rare birds inhabiting inaccessible mountains or forests, and of others so rank and so tough that none but starving, shipwrecked sailors would ever think of eating them.

André Simon *The Concise Encyclopedia of Gastronomy* 1952

If there is a pure and elevated pleasure in this world, it is that of roast pheasant and bread sauce; – barn-door fowls for dissenters, but for the real churchman, the thirty-nine times articles clerk – the pheasant, the pheasant!

Sydney Smith letter to R. H. Barham, c. 1842

More than any other food, game spells true gourmandise; there is no more perfect luncheon or supper for any day of the year than a cold roast bird and a bottle of wine.

Nika Standen
A Concise Encyclopedia of Gastronomy by André Simon 1952

CHAPTER THIRTEEN

IT TAKES
ALL SORTS

Take a Saracen, young and fat,
In haste let the thief be slayne,
Opened, and his skin off flayne,
And sodded full hastily,
With powder and spicery,
And saffron of good colour.

Anonymous
The Romance of Richard Coeur de Lion c. 1350

There are those who have tried the Bat and found it tastes like a housemouse,
only mousier.

Anonymous   *The Spectator* 6th June 1894

Rats are not a dainty dish to set before a king
But for a really hungry man they're just the very thing;
Wrap each rat in bacon fat, roast slow before the fire,
Take him down and serve him brown, you've all you can desire.

Anonymous   q. in *Australian Brewing and Wine Journal* 1943

Cannibal: a gastronome of the old school.

Ambrose Bierce   *The Devil's Dictionary* 1911

CAMEL MEAT has a distinctive taste which shows up in a peculiar way. While you're eating it it tastes just like rather ordinary beef or relatively tasty veal (depending on age), but when you've finished and run your tongue around your mouth, you suddenly discover a slightly sweetish aftertaste, like horse but not quite so much so, very faint, but definite.

Dr Lloyd Cabot Briggs   q. in *Food* by Waverley Root 1980

STUFFED with a simple stuffing made of breadcrumbs, a sprinkling of sweet herbs, and a little pepper and salt, mixed with the liver and heart of the rat, and roasted for a few minutes in a hot oven, it proved to be a delicious dish not unlike a snipe in flavour. Young rats may also be made into pies, if meat stock, consommé or a piece of beef be added to provide the gravy.

Captain L. C. Cameron
q. in *The Concise Encyclopedia of Gastronomy* by André Simon 1952

HORSEMEAT is delicious when you are in the condition to appreciate it . . . and as to rat meat, it approaches in delicacy the taste of roast pig.

Auguste Escoffier
q. in *Great Cooks and their Recipes* by A. Willan 1977

. . . he brightened up
And thought himself in luck
When close before him what he saw
Looked something like a duck!
Still cautious grown, but, to be sure,
His brain he set to rack;
At length he turned to one behind,
And pointing, cried 'Quack, quack?'
The Chinese gravely shook his head,
Next made a reverend bow;
And then expressed what dish it was,
By uttering "Bow-wow-wow!"

W. C. Hunter
An Old Resident *The 'Fan Kwae' at Canton, before Treaty days* 1911

A cat is something between a rabbit and a squirrel with a flavour of its own. It is delicious. Don't drown your kittens, eat 'em.

Henry Labouchère

Spaniel, like lamb; Poodle far the best; Bulldog coarse and tasteless.

Henry Labouchère

The horse is a noble animal. This opinion is widely shared in Anglo-Saxon countries where it is felt that it is an ignoble action to eat a noble animal, and one which is an intimate friend of man, on the same principle which forbade Alice, in *Through the Looking Glass*, to sink her knife into a leg of mutton to which she had just been formally introduced.

Waverley Root *Esquire* January 1974

Skool Food, or the Piece of Cod which Passeth Understanding.

Geoffrey Willans and Ronald Searle *The Compleet Molesworth* 1958

ELEPHANT'S HEART, roasted on a forked stick over the ashes . . . one of the greatest delicacies that an African hunter is likely to enjoy. The meat from the thick part of the trunk and from the cavity above the eye is also very well tasted, but needs much stewing to make it tender; the foot I consider tasteless and insipid.

Frederick Selous *A Hunter's Wanderings in Africa* 1890

GIRAFFE ARE SPLENDID eating, and in good condition and fat are a luxury that no one can properly appreciate till he has lived for a time on nothing but the dry meat of the smaller antelopes.

Frederick Selous *A Hunter's Wanderings in Africa* 1890

Now it may be that the Iguana is no pleasant object to look at. Its small eyes, pail-shaped snout and shark-like, jaws, lined with a saw's teeth of steel are, I know, repellent to many. Even the reptile's best friends, indeed, will be obliged to admit it presents at first sight a somewhat case-hardened exterior, and that its saurian countenance bears an unpleasing expression, both sarcastic and ferocious, but it is good, very good to eat; and its cost does not amount to more than the equivalent of a shilling: two facts which must tell in its favour.

Osbert Sitwell
in *Wine and Food* xxxiv 1942

A young fox, fattened on grapes, and roasted on the spit, is a tidbit for a king during the autumn. Such was the idea of the Roman peasants, but we must be allowed, however, to differ from their opinion.

Alexis Soyer *The Pantropheon* 1853

I HAVE BEEN assured by a very knowing American . . . that a young healthy child, well nursed, is at a year old a most delicious, nourishing and wholesome food, whether stewed, roasted, baked or boiled; and I make no doubt that it will equally serve in a fricassee or a ragout.

Jonathan Swift *A Modest Proposal* 1729

CHAPTER FOURTEEN

THE STAFF OF LIFE

Without wishing in the slightest degree to disparage the skill and labour of breadmakers by trade, truth compels us to assert our conviction of the superior wholesomeness of bread made in our own homes.

Eliza Acton *Modern Cookery for Private Families* 1855

Bread always falls on its buttered side.

Anonymous *English proverb*

He who cannot cut the bread evenly cannot get on well with people.

Anonymous *Czech proverb*

B READ IS AN emotive substance. Shortage of it has traditionally been a sign of dangerous irritation among those prone to riot.

Anonymous *Daily Telegraph* 1978

God grant me bread with eyes and cheese without them; and wine that leaps up to the eyes.

Anonymous *French saying*

A meal without rice is like a pretty girl with only one eye.

Anonymous *Chinese proverb*

PASTRY-MAKING . . . is one of the most important branches of the culinary science. It unceasingly occupies itself with ministering pleasure to the sight as well as the taste.

Mrs Isabella Beeton *The Book of Household Management* 1880

Man doth not live by bread only.

The Bible *Deuteronomy III, 4* 650 BC

The history of man from the beginning has been the history of his struggle for his daily bread.

Josue de Castro q. in *Food* by Waverley Root 1980

As to toast, it may fairly be pronounced a contrivance for consuming bread, butter, firing and time.

Esther Copley *The Complete Cottage Cookery* 1849

Acceptable, adequate – chill words to describe our daily bread, our companion of life. Even so, applied to the British factory loaf they seem to me much exaggerated.

Elizabeth David *English Bread and Yeast Cookery* 1977

ALL BREAD baked in the old manner, without tins, is known as 'crusty', because the loaves have an all-round crust, so that while to journalists and cookery writers the term 'crusty' in association with bread is an evocative or emotive word, to bakers it signifies just a method of baking, which by no means always lives up to the promise seemingly implied by the name.

Elizabeth David *English Bread and Yeast Cookery* 1977

Tea: that much despised and rare feast . . . let us imagine summer, a green lawn, or a sandy beach will do, with exquisitely thin cucumber sandwiches straight out of *The Importance of Being Earnest*, followed by plates of equally thin bread and butter and Gentleman's Relish, topped by tiny iced cakes, pretty pastel shades, and fragrant Earl Gray, with slices of lemon. And winter, with snow and roaring winds outside, a fire brightly burning one's toes, with delicious toasted crumpets, soaked in butter which drips down one's cheeks, Ceylon tea this time, with rich, fruity, home-made cake.

Kay Dick q. in *Writers' Favourite Recipes* ed. G. Vincent 1978

Plain fare gives as much pleasure as a costly diet, while bread and water confer the highest possible pleasure when they are brought to hungry lips.

Epicurus *Letter to Menoeceus*

There is an inevitable ritual about serving and eating spaghetti . . . eaten as it should be, in varying degrees of longness and a fine uniformity of writhing limpness and buttery richness and accompanying noisy sounds.

M. F. K. Fisher *An Alphabet for Gourmets* 1949

THE BASE (of the wedding cake) was formed of a cube of blue paste-board representing a temple with a portico, colonnades and statuettes of white plaster with stars of gold paper. Above this was a castle made of Savoy cake, surrounded by tiny battlements of angelica, almonds, raisins and oranges cut into quarters. Finally, at the very top, which depicted a green meadow complete with rocks, lakes composed of jam and little boats made of nut shells, was a small Cupid balancing himself on a chocolate swing, the two uprights of which were topped with natural rosebuds by way of finials.

Gustave Flaubert *Madame Bovary* 1856

The bagel, an unsweetened doughnut with rigor mortis.

Beatrice & Ira Freeman q. in *New York Times* 1960

Not only does the white loaf do no good, it is actually harmful to the body. Every encouragement should be given to the abolition of this foul food . . . the white loaf is not even fit to be given away.

Maurice Frohn in *Daily Telegraph* 1973

THE COMESTIBLE known as the Bath Bun, and now sold everywhere throughout the kingdom . . . is a sweet bun of a somewhat stodgy type, and is popularly supposed to constitute, with a little milk, the average form of luncheon taken by curates.

Frederick Hackwood *Good Cheer* 1911

Better is half a loaf than no bread.

John Heywood *Proverbs* 1546

Soya Beans are one of the few basic food materials which have survived the severe test of milleniums on a large scale natural experiment, involving today nearly one half of the world's population, and are endorsed by modern science as well.

A. A. Horvath
q. in *A Concise Encyclopedia of Gastronomy* by A. Simon 1952

Bread, milk and butter are of venerable antiquity. They taste of the morning of the world.

Leigh Hunt *The Seer* c. 1840

My objections to the sandwich are two: (i) the amount of bread is out of all proportion to the amount of meat; (ii) the fact that it is disguised by bread enables the preparer of the sandwich to use in it inferior meat . . . if I had my way I would make the provision of sandwiches a penal offence.

C. E. M. Joad *Wine and Food* 1939

OATS: a grain which in England is generally given to horses, but which in Scotland supports the people.

Samuel Johnson *Dictionary of the English Language* 1755

Inhabitants of underdeveloped nations and victims of natural disasters are the only people who have ever been happy to see soybeans.

Fran Lebowitz *Metropolitan Life* 1978

There is good dripping toast by the fire in the evening. Good jelly dripping and crusty, home-baked bread, with the mealy savour of ripe wheat roundly in your mouth and under your teeth, roasted sweet and crisp and deep brown, and covered with little pockets where the dripping will hide and melt and shine in the light, deep down inside, ready to run when your teeth bite in.

Richard Llewellyn
How Green Was My Valley 1939

Si le peuple n'as pas de pain, qu'il mange la brioche. (If the people have no bread, let them eat cake.)
(Although generally accepted as Marie's fatal one-liner, Rousseau's *Confessions* (1737-41) attribute it to an unnamed 'grande princesse'.)

Marie Antoinette 1789

There will be no beans in the Almost Perfect State.

Don Marquis *The Almost Perfect State*

IF PALE BEANS bubble for you in a red earthenware pot, you can often decline the dinners of sumptuous hosts.

Martial *Epigrams* c. 80

What is the matter with Mary Jane?
She's perfectly well and she hasn't a pain,
And it's lovely rice pudding for dinner again,
What is the matter with Mary Jane.

A. A. Milne *Rice Pudding*

No man is lonely while eating spaghetti.

Robert Morley

How important bread is to a nation and how utterly are we betrayed in this country. If Mother's proud she must be the only one.

Robert Morley
Morley Marvels 1976

W HAT IS MORE delicious than fresh hot-buttered toast, with or without the addition of bloaterpaste? . . . And well-made porridge with brown sugar and cream is a dish fit for a king.

Iris Murdoch *The Sea, The Sea*

The lion and the unicorn
Were fighting for the crown;
The lion beat the unicorn
All round the town.
Some gave them white bread,
And some gave them brown;
And some gave them plum-cake,
And sent them out of town.

Nursery Rhymes
in *Useful Transactions in Philosophy* by William King 1708-1709

Little Tommy Tucker
Sings for his supper;
What shall we give him?
White bread and butter.

Nursery Rhymes *Tom Thumb's Pretty Song Book* c. 1744

Pat-a-cake, pat-a-cake, baker's man,
Bake me a cake as fast as you can;
Pat it and prick it and mark it with B,
Put it in the oven for baby and me.

Nursery Rhymes q. in *The Campaigners* by Tom D'Urfey 1698

I never had a piece of toast
Particularly long and wide,
But fell upon the sanded floor,
And always on the buttered side.

James Payn in *Chambers Journal* 1884

The taste was that of the little crumb of madeleine which on Sunday mornings at Combray . . . when I used to say good-day to her in her bedroom, my aunt Leonie used to give me, dipping it first in her own cup of real or limeflower tea.

Marcel Proust *A la Recherche du Temps Perdu*

They that have no other meat
Bread and butter are glad to eat.

John Ray *English Proverbs* 1670

Making toast by the fireside
Nurse fell in the grate and died.
And what makes it ten times worse,
All the toast was burnt with nurse.

Rhymes for Heartless Homes
q. in *A Wine and Food Bedside Book* ed. C. Morny 1972

The oat is the Horatio Alger of cereals, which progressed, if not from rags to riches, at least from weed to health food.

Waverley Root *Food* 1980

I've got brown sandwiches and green sandwiches . . . it's either very new cheese or very old meat.

Neil Simon *The Odd Couple* Paramount 1968

Bread, Wine and Oil, that blessed trinity of the kindly fruits of the earth, have been, since Biblical times, the symbol of peace – and plenty, the reward promised by angels in heaven to men of goodwill upon earth.

André Simon *The Concise Encyclopedia of Gastronomy* 1952

B EANS ARE HIGHLY nutritious and satisfying, they can also be delicious if and when properly prepared, and they possess over all vegetables the great advantage of being just as good, if not better, when kept waiting, an advantage in the case of people whose disposition or occupation makes it difficult for them to be punctual at mealtime.

André Simon *The Concise Encyclopedia of Gastronomy* 1952

The art of pastry-cook . . . is a most important branch of the culinary science; unceasingly occupied with flattering the sight as much as the taste, it raises graceful monuments, delicious fortresses, seductive ramparts, which as soon as they are on all sides attacked, totter, crumble and no longer present anything but glorious and ephemeral ruins, like every other work of man – all pass away whether they be temples, columns, pyramids or pies.

Alexis Soyer *The Pantropheon* 1853

Bread is the staff of life; in which is contained, inclusive, the quintessence of beef, mutton, veal, venison, partridge, plum-pudding and custard: and to render all complete, there is intermingled a due quantity of water, whose crudities are also corrected by yeast or barm, through which it means it becomes a wholesome fermented liquor, diffused through the mass of the bread.

Jonathan Swift *A Tale of a Tub* 1704

A TEA TABLE without a big cake in the country in England would look very bare and penurious. The ideal table should include some sort of hot buttered toast or scone, one or two sorts of sandwiches, a plate of small light cakes and our friend the luncheon cake. Add a pot of jam or honey, and plate of brown and white bread and butter – which I implore my readers not to cut too thin – and every eye will sparkle, and all those wishing to follow the fashionable craze of slimming will groan in despair.

Lady Sysonby *Lady Sysonby's Cookbook* 1935

CHAPTER FIFTEEN

CHEAP & CHEERFUL

No fruit tree has exerted so profound an influence on the growth of civilisation as the olive. It has provided the sustenance, the means for survival, in all the countries in which it grows. The rich, oily fruits have shaped the whole character of the Mediterranean, and the distinctive flavour of its food.

Anonymous *Gourmet* magazine 1969

Rarebit, n: a Welsh rabbit, in the speech of the humourless, who point out that it is not a rabbit. To whom it may be solemnly explained that the comestible known as toad-in-the-hole is really not a toad, and that 'riz-de-veau à la financière' is not the smile of a calf prepared after the recipe of a she banker.

Ambrose Bierce *The Devil's Dictionary* 1911

The whole Mediterranean, the sculpture, the palms, the gold beads, the bearded heroes, the wine, the ideas, the ships, the moonlight, the winged gorgons, the bronze men, the philosophers – all of it seems to rise in the sour, pungent taste of these black olives between the teeth. A taste older than meat, older than wine. A taste as old as cold water.

Lawrence Durrell *Prospero's Cell*

GOOD OIL, like good wine, is a gift from the gods. The grape and the olive are among the priceless benefactions of the soil, and were destined, each in its way, to promote the welfare of man.

George Ellwanger *Pleasures of the Table* 1903

Cooking on skewers . . . this primitive form of cooking, is still among the easiest and most savoury, though too few of us attempt it in our homes. Angels on horseback – those snugly blanketed darlings – are perhaps the nearest we get to it, they and their cousins, the devils, though the oyster rides more cosily in its fragile bacon rasher than the stuffed prune, I always think.

Ambrose Heath *Good Food* 1932

The possibility of . . . the disappearance of meals altogether into the unending snack, an undistinguishable population indistinguishably nibbling, rabbits in a national park. Already large sections of the public, absent-mindedly munching, must find it difficult to say at any given moment whether they are enjoying elevenses, lunch, tea or some chance, additional makeshift.

Arnold Palmer *Moveable Feasts* 1952

EXCEPT THE VINE, there is no plant which bears a fruit of as great an importance as the olive.

Pliny *Historia Naturalis* 79 BC

No man in the world has more courage than the man who can stop after eating one peanut.

Channing Pollock

Mmmmmmmmmmmmmmmmmm. These are nice. Little Roquefort cheese morsels rolled in crushed nuts. Very tasty. Very subtle. It's the way the dry sackiness of the nuts tiptoes up against the dour savour of the cheese that is so nice, so subtle. Wonder what the Black Panthers eat here on the hors-d'oeuvre trail? Do the Panthers like little Roquefort cheese morsels rolled in crushed nuts this way, and asparagus tips in mayonnaise dabs, and meatballs petites au Coq Hardi, all of which are at this very moment being offered to them on gadrooned silver platters by maids in black uniforms with hand-ironed white aprons . . .

Tom Wolfe *Radical Chic* 1970

CHAPTER SIXTEEN

EAT YOUR GREENS

Spinach is the broom of the stomach.

Anonymous *French proverb*

An accident happened to my brother Jim
When somebody threw a tomato at him –
Tomatoes are juicy and don't hurt the skin,
But this one was specially packed in a tin.

Anonymous

*C*ABBAGE, *n: A familiar kitchen-garden vegetable about as large and wise as a man's head.*

Ambrose Bierce *The Devil's Dictionary* 1911

Salad refreshes without weakening and comforts without irritating.

Jean-Anthelme Brillat-Savarin *La Physiologie du goût* 1825

I appreciate the potato only as a protection against famine, except for that I know of nothing more eminently tasteless.

Jean-Anthelme Brillat-Savarin *La Physiologie du goût* 1825

Of the many gifts that Europe owes to Asia none . . . have been more welcome, or have done more to reconcile man to a life of poverty than the Vine and Onion family.

E. A. Bunyard in *Wine and Food* 1935

God made the wicked Grocer
For a mystery and a sign,
That men might shun the awful shop
And go to inns to dine . . .
The righteous minds of innkeepers
induce them now and then
To crack a bottle with a friend
Or treat unmoneyed men,
But who hath seen the grocer
Treat housemaids to his teas
Or crack a bottle of fish-sauce
or stand a man a cheese?

G. K. Chesterton *A Song Against Grocers*

Life is too short to stuff a mushroom.

Shirley Conran *Superwoman* 1978

Petit pois are like children – you have to understand them.

James de Coquet in *Le Figaro*

Persons living entirely on vegetables are seldom of a plump and succulent habit.

William Cullen
First Lines of the Practice of Physic 1774

Because lettuces are owned by the moon, they cool and moisten what heat and dryness Mars causeth. The juice of the lettuce mixed or boiled with oil of roses and applied to the forehead and temples, procureth sleep, and easeth the Headache proceeding of an hot cause.

Nicholas Culpeper *The Complete Herbal* 1653

The pasty taste, the natural insipidity, the unhealthy quality of (the potato), which is flatulent and indigestible, has caused it to be rejected from refined households and returned to the people, whose coarse palates and stronger stomachs are satisfied with anything capable of appeasing hunger.

Legrand d'Aussy *Histoire de la vie privée des Français* 1783

I DON'T ALTOGETHER agree that a plain green salad ever becomes a bore – not, that is, if it's made with fresh, well-drained crisp greenstuff and a properly seasoned dressing of good-quality olive oil and a sound wine vinegar. But I do agree that all this talk about 'tossed salads' is a bore; it seems to me that a salad and its dressing are things we should take more or less for granted at a meal, like bread and salt; and not carry on about them.

Elizabeth David *The Spectator* 1961

A world devoid of tomato soup, tomato sauce, tomato ketchup and tomato paste is hard to visualize. Could the tin and processed food industries have got where they have without the benefit of the tomato compounds which colour, flavour, thicken and conceal so many deficiencies? How did the Italians eat spaghetti before the advent of the tomato? Was there such a thing as a tomato-less Neapolitan pizza? What were English salads like before there were tomatoes to mix with lettuce? Did Provençal cooking exist . . .? Without it would the British landlady's and railway dining-car breakfast ever have become what it is? How many people would accept baked beans innocent of tomato sauce?

Elizabeth David
An Omelette and a Glass of Wine 1984

WHATEVER dressing one gives to mushrooms, to whatever sauces our Apiciuses put them, they are not really good but to be sent back to the dungheap where they are born.

Denis Diderot *L'Encyclopedie* 1728

This root, no matter how much you prepare it, is tasteless and floury. It cannot pass for an agreeable food; but it supplies a food sufficiently abundant and sufficiently healthy for men who ask only to sustain themselves. The potato is criticised with reason for being windy, but what matters windiness for the vigorous organisms of peasants and labourers?

Denis Diderot *L'Encyclopedie* 1728

Most vigitaryans I iver see looked enough like their food to be classed as cannybals.

Finlay Peter Dunne *Mr Dooley's Philosophy* 1900

T O REMEMBER a successful salad is generally to remember a successful dinner; at all events, the perfect dinner necessarily includes the perfect salad. The mere process of salad-making is among the most simple . . . yet an unexceptionable salad is as rare in the average household as a piece of old Gubbio or a fine old Ghiordes prayer-rug.

George Ellwanger *Pleasures of the Table* 1903

Be very careful that your greens be nicely picked and washed, and when so done, always lay them in a clean pan, for fear of sand or dirt, which are apt to hang around wooden vessels. Boil all your greens in well-tinned copper saucepan by themselves, and be sure to let them have plenty of water. Boil no kind of meat with them as that discolour them; and use no iron pans, such as being very improper for the purpose . . . Numbers of cooks spoil their garden stuffs by boiling them too much: all kinds of vegetables should have a little crispness; for if you boil them too much, you will deprive them both of their sweetness and beauty.

John Farley
The London Art of Cookery and Housekeepers Complete Assistant 1783

There are many ways to love a vegetable. The most sensible way is to love it well-treated. Then you can eat it with the comfortable knowledge that you will be a better man for it, in your spirit and your body too . . .

M. F. K. Fisher *How to Cook a Wolf* 1951

To see cucumbers in a dream denotes that you will speedily fall in love. Or, if you are in love, then you will marry the object of your affection. To dream that you are eating garlic denotes that you will discover hidden secrets and meet with some domestic jar. To dream that there is garlic in the house is lucky. To dream of lettuces is said to portend trouble . . . to dream of mushrooms denotes fleeting happiness, to dream you are gathering them, fickleness in a lover or consort. To dream of olives portends concord, liberty and dignity . . . parsley portends that you will be crossed in love . . . if you are eating it you will shortly hear good news. To dream of pumpkins is a very bad omen.

Richard Folkard *Plant Lore* 1884

Mushrooms are like men – the bad most closely counterfeit the good.

Gavarni
q. in *Pleasures of the Table* by G. Ellwanger 1903

Let us be many-sided! Turnips are good, but they are best mixed with chestnuts. And these two noble products of the earth grow far apart.

Johann Wolfgang von Goethe
Prose Maxims

JERUSALEM artichokes . . . are dressed divers wayes, some boile them in water . . . others bake them in pies . . . others some other way as they are led by their skill in Cookerie. But in my judgment, which way soever they be drest and eaten they stir up and cause a filthie loathesome stinking winde within the body, thereby causing the belly to be much pained and tormented, and are a meat more fit for swine than men.

John Goodyer q. in *Food* by Waverley Root 1980

The artichoke above all is the vegetable expression of civilised living, of the long view, of increasing delight by anticipation and crescendo. No wonder it was once regarded as an aphrodisiac. It had no place in the troll's world of instant gratification. It makes no appeal to the meat-and-two-veg. mentality.

Jane Grigson
Jane Grigson's Vegetable Book 1978

Cabbage as a food has problems. It is easy to grow, a useful source of greenery for much of the year. Yet as a vegetable it has original sin, and needs improvement. It can smell foul in the pot, linger through the house with pertinacity, and ruin a meal with its wet flab. Cabbage also has a nasty history of being good for you.

Jane Grigson *Jane Grigson's Vegetable Book* 1978

Jerusalem artichokes . . . are none the worse for not being artichokes and having nothing at all to do with Jerusalem.

Jane Grigson *Jane Grigson's Vegetable Book* 1978

I have to declare my interest in the matter of deep-fried potatoes. They are most unsuitable for making in the ordinary family kitchen. The telephone rings, a child crawls round your feet, the cat demands his supper with a paw, and your attention is diverted.

Jane Grigson *Jane Grigson's Vegetable Book* 1978

WHEN BUYING spinach, assess its liveliness. It should have a bouncing, bright appearance. As you stuff it into your basket or string bag, it should crunch and squeak.

Jane Grigson *Jane Grigson's Vegetable Book* 1978

A number of leafy vegetables are referred to loosely as 'greens'. 'Eat up your greens. Finish your greens.' Greens were never asparagus or tiny French beans or sugar peas, but the nastier aspects of the cabbage clan.

Jane Grigson *Jane Grigson's Vegetable Book* 1978

A number of rare or newly experienced foods have been claimed to be aphrodisiacs. At one time this quality was even ascribed to the tomato. Reflect on that when you are next preparing the family salad.

Jane Grigson *The Mushroom Feast* 1975

ACCORDING TO THE Spanish proverb, four persons are wanted to make a good salad: a spendthrift for oil, a miser for vinegar, a counsellor for salt, and a madman to stir it all up.

Abraham Hayward *The Art of Dining* 1852

Cauliflower perks up this month (June). He suffers from an inferiority complex, because he has never had a chance to be, and look, anything but plain and dull. But there are so many pretty ways of dressing him, that we might give him a little sympathy . . .

Ambrose Heath *Good Food* 1932

The potato is one of nature's best-designed products; it is born in a sturdy package, with a wonderful shelf-life. Yet we haul it from field to factory, peel it and slice it by machine, cook it in hot grease, dose it with additives, wrap it in a petroleum or natural-gas derivative, freeze it, store it in a frozen warehouse, haul it across the country in a diesel refrigerated truck, store it in another frozen warehouse, deliver it in a reefer truck to a supermarket freezer, move it to a kitchen freezer, and, eventually, we reheat it.

John & Karen Hess *Viva* magazine 1978

V EGETARIANISM is harmless enough, though it is apt to fill a man with wind and self-righteousness.

Sir Robert Hutchinson
q. in *The Wit of Medicine* ed. L. & M. Cowan 1972

In the vegetable world there is nothing so innocent, so confiding in its expression, as the small green face of the freshly shelled spring pea. Asparagus is pushing and bossy, lettuce is loud and blowsy, radishes are gay and playful, but the little green pea is so helpless and friendly that it makes really sensitive stomachs suffer to see the way he is treated in the average home. Fling him in the water and let him boil – and that's that.

William Wallace Irwin *The Garrulous Gourmet*

The fennel is beyond every other vegetable, delicious. It greatly resembles in appearance the largest size celery, perfectly white, and there is no vegetable equals it in flavour. It is eaten at dessert, crude, and with, or without dry salt, indeed I preferred it to every other vegetable, or to any fruit.

Thomas Jefferson
Garden Book

A cucumber should be well sliced, and dressed with pepper and vinegar, and then thrown out as good for nothing.

Dr Samuel Johnson *Boswell's Tour to the Hebrides* 1773

Large, naked, raw carrots are acceptable as food only to those who live in hutches eagerly awaiting Easter.

Fran Lebowitz *Metropolitan Life* 1978

Vegetables are interesting but lack a sense of purpose when unaccompanied by a good cut of meat.

Fran Lebowitz *Metropolitan Life* 1978

Potato: bland, amiable, and homely, an honest vegetable, giving honour where honour is due – in an honest soup.

Della Lutes *The Country Kitchen* 1938

Cabbage: so revered by the Egyptians for its stimulating qualities as to warrant a temple built in its honour.

Della Lutes *The Country Kitchen* 1938

ONION: humble kindred of the lily clan, rooted from oblivion by Alexander the Great and bestrewn by him, along with learning, to the civilised world, thus lending a touch of wisdom and sophistication to the whole.

Della Lutes *The Country Kitchen* 1938

What I say is that, if a man really likes potatoes, he must be a pretty decent sort of fellow.

A. A. Milne *Not That It Matters*

Vegetarians have wicked, shifty eyes and laugh in a cold calculating manner. They pinch little children, steal stamps, drink water, favour beards.

J. B. Morton (Beachcomber)
in *Daily Express*

First he ate some lettuce and some broad beans, then some radishes, and then, feeling rather sick, he went to look for some parsley.

Beatrix Potter *The Tale of Peter Rabbit* 1902

The effect of eating too much lettuce is 'soporific'.

Beatrix Potter
The Tale of the Flopsy Bunnies 1908

YOU NEED to have the soul of a rabbit to eat lettuce as it is usually served –
green leaves slightly lubricated with oil and flavoured with vinegar. A salad is
only a background; it needs embroidering.

Paul Reboux

Spinach is not worth much essentially. It is susceptible of receiving all imprints: it
is the virgin wax of the kitchen.

Grimod de la Reynière *Almanach des Gourmands* 1804

Fennel is a great encourager of arithmetic . . . fennel is: (1) one of the
ingredients of Chinese five-spice powder; (2) one of the medieval four hot seeds;
(3) one of the (relatively) modern five appetite-encouraging roots: and (4) . . .
one of the nine holy herbs of the Anglo-Saxons.

Waverley Root *Food* 1980

The turnip is a capricious vegetable, which seems reluctant to show itself at its best.

Waverley Root *Food* 1980

Being boiled, baked or roasted (potatoes) are eaten with good butter, salt, juice
of oranges or lemons, and double refined sugar . . . They increase seed and
provoke lust, causing fruitfulness in both sexes.

William Salmon
q. in *The History and Social Influence of the Potato* by R. Salaman 1949

There are four fundamental rules, practically with exceptions, to be remembered
whenever one buys or cooks vegetables: 1. The freshest vegetables are the
best; young and small ones are better than large and old ones; wilted and bruised
ones may cost less but are worthless. 2. Vegetables should be cooked in a
minimum of water and of time; over cooked vegetables lose not only their flavour
but their precious vitamins. 3. Salt should be added to the water in which
vegetables are to be cooked . . . 4. The water in which vegetables have been
cooked must not be thrown away but saved for soups and gravies.

André Simon
The Concise Encyclopedia of Gastronomy 1952

A cooked tomato is like a cooked oyster: ruined.

André Simon *The Concise Encyclopedia of Gastronomy* 1938

Oh herbaceous treat!
'Twould tempt the dying anchorite to eat;
Back to the world he'd turn his fleeting soul,
And plunge his fingers in the salad bowl;
Serenely full, the epicure would say
'Fate cannot harm me – I have dined today.'

Sydney Smith *Recipe for Salad* 1843

Two large potatoes, passed through kitchen sieve
Unwonted softness to the salad give:
Of mordant mustard add a single spoon
Distrust the condiment which bites too soon;
But deem it not, thou man of herbs, a fault
To add a double quantity of salt;
Three times the spoon with oil of Lucca crown,
And once with vinegar, procured from Town;
True flavour needs it, and your poet begs
The pounded yellow of two well-boiled eggs;
Let onion atoms lurk within the bowl,
And, scarce suspected, animate the whole;
And lastly, in the flavoured compound, toss
A magic teaspoon of anchovy sauce.

Sydney Smith recipe for *Potato Mayonnaise* 1843

YOUNG GREEN PEAS! Do not these words sound pleasant to the ear . . . I fancy that, by merely raising my eyes from the paper on which I am now writing, I shall see all our garden in bud and blossom; it not only seems to invigorate the sensitive part of one's appetite, but works upon the mind to that point that you may actually believe you are breathing in a glowing atmosphere, and that the pearly dew is gracefully descending in small globules from heaven, to fix their sparkling eyes on the pinky bloom of myriads of roses.

Alexis Soyer *The Modern Housewife* 1851

SOME PEOPLE shop at a market on the theory that it represents their only hope of coming across fruit and vegetables that have not been bred by the agribusiness Frankensteins to have a shelf life approximately that of a mop handle. They hope, for instance, to find a tomato that does not have a bright-red skin so hard that anyone who wanted to indulge in the good old-fashioned American pleasure of slinging it at a windy political stump speaker would risk being arrested for assault with intent to kill.

Calvin Trillin *Alice, Let's Eat* 1978

Cauliflower is nothing but cabbage with a college education.

Mark Twain

No-one has feared developing leprosy from eating French fries, or any potato, but we all do know that fries make us fat (or fatter), cause blemishes, induce indigestion, nourish ulcers, and make havoc of cholesterol counts. Yet everybody keeps on stuffing them down, at steak and fish houses, at thousands of fast-food operations, on street corners, in the air – and in the finest restaurants too. So much I understand. But the odd thing is that for most people the greasier and more awful the French fry the better.

James Villas
Esquire February 1974

One of the greatest luxuries . . . in dining is to be able to command plenty of good vegetables, well served up. Excellent potatoes, smoking hot, and accompanied by melted butter of the first quality, would alone stamp merit on any dinner: but they are as rare on state occasions, so served, as if they were of the cost of pearls.

Thomas Walker *The Original* 1835

Lettuce, like conversation, requires a good deal of oil, to avoid friction and to keep the company smooth.

Charles Dudley Warner *My Summer in a Garden* 1871

You can put everything, and the more things the better, into a salad, as into a conversation; but everything depends on the skill of mixing.

Charles Dudley Warner
My Summer in a Garden 1871

T O MAKE a good salad is to be a brilliant diplomatist – the problem is entirely the same in both cases. To know how much oil one must mix with one's vinegar.

Oscar Wilde *Vera, or the Nihilists* 1880

CHAPTER SEVENTEEN

FRUIT OF OUR LABOURS

O precious food! Delight of the mouth!
Oh, much better than gold, masterpiece of Apollo!
O flower of all the fruits! O ravishing melon!

Marc Antoine de Saint-Amant q. in *Food* by Waverley Root 1980

He that will not a wife wed
Must eat an apple on going to bed.

Anonymous *English proverb*

An apple a day keeps the doctor away.

Anonymous *English proverb*

A grapefruit is a lemon that had a chance and took advantage of it.

Anonymous

He who fills his stomach with melons is like him who fills it with light – there is a blessing in it.

Anonymous *Arab saying*

A year in which there are plenty of almonds and dates increases prosperity and life.

Anonymous *Arab proverb*

Give me a good working woman and a breadfruit tree and I need never work again.

Anonymous q. in *Food* by Waverley Root 1980

H E WHO PLANTS a coconut tree plants food and drink, vessels and clothing, a habitation for himself and a heritage for his children.

Anonymous q. in *Food* by Waverley Root 1980

Strawberries, and only strawberries, could now be thought or spoken of. 'The best fruit in England – everybody's favourite – always wholesome. These the finest beds and finest sorts. Delightful to gather for oneself – the only way of really enjoying them. Morning decidedly the best time – never tired – every sort good – hautboy infinitely superior – no comparison – the others hardly eatable – hautboys very scarce – Chili preferred – white wood finest flavour of all – price of strawberries in London . . . only objection to gathering strawberries the stooping – glaring sun – tired to death – could bear it no longer – must go and sit in the shade.' Such, for half an hour, was the conversation.

Jane Austen *Emma* 1815

Rightly thought of there is poetry in peaches, even when they are canned.

Harley Granville Barker *The Madras House* 1910

Comfort me with apples: for I am sick of love.

The Bible *The Song of Solomon* c. 200

Rhubarb, n: the vegetable essence of stomach ache.

Ambrose Bierce *The Devil's Dictionary* 1911

O N STRAWBERRIES: Doubtless God could have made a better berry, but doubtless God never did.

William Butler 1600

At Gloucester we furnished ourselves with nuts and apples, which, first a handful of nuts and then an apple, are, I can assure the reader, excellent and most wholesome fare. They say that nuts of all sorts are unwholesome; if they had been, I should never have written Registers and if they were now, I should have ceased to write ere this for upon an average, I have eaten a pint a day since I left home.

William Cobbett *Rural Rides* 1830

CHESTNUTS IN THEIR spiky cases, squashy medlars, and tart-tasting sorb apples – the autumn drives before it a profusion of modest fruits which one does not pick, but which fall into one's hands, which wait patiently at the foot of the tree until man deigns to collect them.

Colette *Earthly Paradise* 1966

A handsomely contrived, and well furnished Fruit Garden is an Epitome of Paradise, which was a most glorious place without a palace.

John Evelyn
Compleat Gard'ner 1693

Fruit, as it was our primitive, and most excellent as well as most innocent food, whilst it grew in Paradise; a climate so benign, and a soil so richly impregnated with all that the influence of Heaven could communicate to it; so it has still preserved, and retained no small tincture of its original and celestial virtue.

John Evelyn
Compleat Gard'ner 1693

A little peach in an orchard grew, – A little peach of emerald hue;
Warmed by the sun and wet by the dew,
It grew.

Eugene Field *The Little Peach* 1889

The grape that can with logic absolute
The two-and-seventy jarring sects confute;
The sovereign alchemist that in a trice
Life's leaden metal into gold transmute.

Edward Fitzgerald
The Rubaiyat of Omar Khayyam c. 1100, trans. 1857

Blueberries as big as the end of your thumb,
Real sky-blue, and heavy, and ready to drum
In the cavernous pail of the first one to come!
All ripe together, none of them green.

Robert Frost *The Poetry of Robert Frost*

My apple trees will never get across
And eat the cones under his pines, I tell him.
He only says 'Good fences make good neighbours.

Robert Frost *North of Boston*

Now sing of the fig, Simiane,
Because its loves are hidden
I sing the fig, said she
Whose beautiful loves are hidden,
Its flowering is folded away
Closed room where marriages are made:
No perfume tells the tale outside.

André Gide

A little sour is the juice of the pomegranate like the juice of unripe raspberries.
Waxlike is the flower
Coloured as the fruit is coloured.
Close-guarded this item of treasure, beehive partitioned,
Richness of savour,
Architecture of pentagons.
The rind splits; out tumble the seeds,
In cups of azure some seeds are blood;
On plates of enamelled bronze, others are drops of gold.

André Gide *Les Nourritures Terrestres*

I came across excellent blackberries, – ate of them heartily. It was mid-day, &
when I left the brambles, I found I had a sufficient meal so there was no need to go
to an inn. Of a sudden it struck me as an extraordinary thing. Here had I satisfied
my hunger without payment, without indebtedness to any man. The vividness
with which I felt that this was extraordinary seems to me a shrewd comment on a
social state which practically denies a man's right to food unless he have money.

George Gissing *Commonplace Book* 1887

THIS SPECIAL feeling towards fruit, its glory and abundance, is I would say universal. We have to bear the burden of it being good for us . . . An apple a day, an orange a day have not spoilt our feelings. We respond to strawberry fields or cherry orchards with a delight that a cabbage patch or even an elegant vegetable garden cannot provoke.

Jane Grigson *Jane Grigson's Fruit Book* 1982

THE APPLE WAS the first fruit of the world, according to Genesis, but it was no Cox's orange pippin. God gave the crab apple and left the rest to man. This is perhaps what has made some suspect that the Tree of the Knowledge of Good and Evil was really a banana. After all, it was the earliest fruit taken into civilisation.

Jane Grigson *Jane Grigson's Fruit Book* 1982

If you can get hold of a branch (of mulberry) from someone else's tree, and put it into the ground, it will grow. Just as the willow tree does – but far more slowly. Give a mulberry tree for a wedding present, if they seem like a staying couple.

Jane Grigson *Jane Grigson's Fruit Book* 1982

TWO OF LIFE's mysteries – how does the ship get into the bottle, and how does the pear get into the bottle of pear eau de vie:

Jane Grigson *Jane Grigson's Fruit Book* 1982

Cool damsons are, and good for health, by reason
They make your entrails soluble and slack,
Let peaches steep in wine of newest season,
Nuts hurt the teeth, that with their teeth they crack,
With every nut 'tis good to eat a raisin.
For though they hurt the spleen, they help the back.

Sir John Harrington
Salerno Regimen – The Englishman's Doctor 1608

Here the currants red and white
In yon green bush at her sight
Peep through their shady leaves, and cry
Come eat me, as she passes by.

Robert Heath *Clarastella* 1650

. . . a chalked notice which I saw outside a greengrocer's shop – 'Rhubarb is good for the Blood' – is about all there is to say for it . . .

Ambrose Heath *Good Food* 1932

Cherry-ripe, ripe, ripe, I cry,
Full and fair ones; come and buy:
If so be, you ask me where
They do grow? I answer, There,
Where Julia's lips do smile;
There's the land, or cherry-isle.
Where plantations fully show
All the year where cherries grow.

Robert Herrick *Hesperides* 1648

Loveliest of trees, the cherry now
Is hung with bloom along the bough,
And stands about the woodland ride
Wearing white for Eastertide.

A. E. Housman *A Shropshire Lad* 1896

THERE IS SOMETHING in the red of a raspberry pie that looks as good to a man as the red in a sheep looks to a wolf.

E. W. Howe *Sinner Sermons* 1926

Talking of Pleasure, this moment I was writing with one hand, and with the other holding to my Mouth a Nectarine – how good how fine. It went down all pulpy, slushy, oozy – all its delicious embonpoint melted down my throat like a large, beatified Strawberry. I shall certainly breed.

John Keats in a letter to Charles Dilke, September 22nd, 1819

While he forth from the closet brought a heap
Of candied apple, quince, and plum and gourd;
With jellies soother than the creamy curd,
And lucent syrops, tinct with cinnamon;
Manna and dates, in argosy transferr'd
From Fez; and spiced dainties, every one
From silken Samarkand to cedar'd Lebanon.

John Keats *St Agnes Eve* 1819

G IVE ME BOOKS, fruit, French wine, fine weather and a little music out of doors, played by somebody I do not know.

John Keats letter to Fanny Keats 29.8.1819

C—— (Samuel Taylor Coleridge) holds that a man cannot have a pure mind who refuses apple-dumplings. I am not certain but he is right. Only I stick to asparagus, which still seems to inspire gentle thoughts.

Charles Lamb *Grace before Meat* 1821

The first rhubarb of the season is to the digestive tract of winter-logged inner man what a good hot bath with plenty of healing soap is to the outer after a bout with plough and harrow. Even the tongue and teeth have a scrubbed feeling after a dish of early rhubarb.

Della Lutes *The Country Kitchen* 1938

There are only two good things in the world, women and roses; and two choice tidbits, women and melons.

Malherbe q. in *Food* by Waverley Root 1980

Friends are like melons. Shall I tell you why?
To find one good you must a hundred try.

Claude Mermet 1600

T HE BANANA is plentiful and cheap; it is enclosed in an almost sterile container; the fat and protein factors are almost negligible, carbohydrates being the chief food constituents. In addition to the easily assimilable carbohydrates, it forms a good source of lime and iron and offers abundant vitamins, except Vitamin D, and as an anti-scorbutic it ranks second only to the orange. Its calorific value is much higher than that of the common fruits, and its energy value is greater than that of the potato.

Von Meysenberg q. in *New Orleans M & S Journal* 1927

There are some fruits which awaken in me feelings deeper than appetite. When I contemplate the musky golden orb of the sugar-melon, or the green and brown seaweed markings of the tiger canteloup, the scales of the pineapple or the texture of figs and nectarines, the disposition of oranges and lemons on the tree or the feign-death coils of the old vine-serpent, I swell in unity with them, I ripen with the sugar-cane, the banana in flower . . .

Palinurus (Cyril Connolly) *The Unquiet Grave* 1945

The quince, coing, membrillo, marmelata, pyrus cydonia or portugalensis; golden emblem of love and happiness to the Ancients, was the golden fruit of the Hesperides and the love-apple which the Greeks used to give to their boys. It was also a Chinese symbol of long life and passion. I behold in it an emblem of the civilization of Europe with its hard flesh, bright colour and unearthly savour.

Palinurus (Cyril Connolly)
The Unquiet Grave 1945

First paint apples and peaches in a fruit bowl.

Auguste Renoir
advice on capturing the skin-tones of the female breast . . .

The flavour of the raspberry stamps it 'Made in Asia'. It breathes of the Orient – rich, exotic, spice-laden and with a hint of musk.

Waverley Root *Food* 1980

F RUIT IS THE WOMB that holds, protects, feeds, matures and eventually delivers the seed responsible for the survival of the species and its propagation. Night and day the roots distil from the moist earth and their leaves distil from the moist air the food and drink which tree, bush, herb or plant needs, not merely to live but also and chiefly to bring forth a living seed.

André Simon *The Concise Encyclopedia of Gastronomy* 1952

Summer's loud laugh
Of scarlet ice
A melon
slice

José Juan Tablada

THE FLESH of the pineapple melts into water and it is so flavourful that one finds in it the aroma of the peach, the apple, the quince and the muscat grape. I can call it with justice the king of fruits because it is the most beautiful and best of all those of the earth.

Père du Tertre   1595

Give me to drink the cocoa's milky bowl,
And from the palm to draw its freshening wine!
More bounteous far than all the frantic juice
Which Bacchus pours . . .

James Thomson   *The Seasons* 1726-30

Mangoes are not cigarettes
mangoes are fleshy skinful passionate fruits
mangoes are hungry to be sucked
mangoes are glad to be stuck in the teeth
mangoes like slush and kissing

Richard Tipping
q. in *The Dictionary of Australian Quotations* ed. S. Murray-Smith 1984

The pear is the grandfather of the apple, its poor relation, a fallen aristocrat, the man-at-arms of our domains, which once, in our humid land, lived lonely and lordly, preserving the memory of its prestige by its haughty comportment.

François Pierre de la Varenne   1650

When the iron blade strikes its guts, the melon throws out gushing streams of juice and many seeds. The cheerful guest divides its bent back into many slices. He tastes this delightful succulence of gardens. Its pure taste charms his throat.

Walafrid Strabo   *Hortulus* (De cultura hortorum)

CHAPTER EIGHTEEN

FISH OUT OF WATER

In Dublin's fair city, where girls are so pretty,
I first set my eyes on sweet Molly Malone,
As she wheeled her wheelbarrow through streets broad and narrow,
Crying, Cockles and mussels! alive, alive oh!

Anonymous

As pheasant is to chicken, so is pike to cod.

Anonymous *Proverb*

Bear in mind that three things, not two, are absolute certainties. Death and Quarter Day are common parables, but it's not generally known that it's a million to one on crab against lobster sauce with a turbot. God bless you. Goodbye.

(also cited by Abraham Hayward in 'The Art of Dining', 1852, as 'an anecdote related of a deceased Irish nobleman who . . . when dying summoned his heir to his bedside and told him he had a secret to communicate that might prove some compensation for the delapidated condition of the family property. It was – that crab sauce is better than lobster sauce.')

Hugo Astley *last words* 1895

FISH IS HELD out to be one of the greatest luxuries of the table and not only necessary, but even indispensable at all dinners where there is any pretence to excellence or fashion.

Mrs Isabella Beeton *The Book of Household Management* 1880

'Will you walk a little faster?' said a whiting to a snail.
'There's a porpoise close behind us, and he's treading on my tail.
See how eagerly the lobsters and the turtles all advance!
They are waiting on the shingle – will you come and join the dance?
Will you, won't you, will you, won't you, will you join the dance?
Will you, won't you, will you, won't you, won't you join the dance?

Lewis Carroll *Alice's Adventures in Wonderland* 1865

'Tis the voice of the lobster; I heard him declare,
'You have baked me too brown, I must sugar my hair.'

Lewis Carroll *Alice's Adventures in Wonderland* 1865

Among all fishes that are pleasant in taste and not wholesome, the Yeele are most in use, which, as they engendered of the very earth, dirt and mire, without generation or Spawne, so they be of a slimie substance, clammie and greatly stopping, whereby they are noysome to the voice.

Thomas Cogan *Haven of Health* 1588

Salmon are like men: too soft a life is not good for them.

James de Coquet in *Le Figaro* 1975

Is the fish or the sauce to play the star part? In traditional English cookery the answer to the question is taken for granted . . . the fish is going to be so delicious that there is little need to bother about the sauce. Therefore the sauces appertaining to English fish cookery are very simple indeed. So far so good. Further on, a great deal less good. Somewhere along the line we began to confuse good plain cooking with plain bad cooking. At this stage our English melted-butter sauce became muddled, not so much with the French sauce blanche, which is what it is, but with béchamel, which is what our white sauce never became. What it did become was billstickers' paste . . .

Elizabeth David *Spices, Salt & Aromatics in the English Kitchen* 1970

If eels only looked a little less like eels more people would want to eat them.

Clement Freud *Freud on Food* 1978

NEVER WITH BUTTER, never with almonds; that is not cooking, that is packaging. (It is, of course, understood that my recipes are not for all comers.) With the exception of truite au bleu nobody knows how to cook a trout. It is the most unfortunate fish on earth. If an atomic bomb destroyed the world tomorrow the human race would vanish without ever having known the taste of a trout. Of course, I am no more talking of tank-bred trout than I would give a recipe for cooking a dog or cat.

Jean Giono in *La France à table* magazine 1955

Whitebait, those pathetic little silver darlings . . .

Ambrose Heath *Good Food* 1932

All the ingenious men and all the scientific men, and all the imaginative men in the world could never invent, if all their wits were broiled into one, anything so curious and so ridiculous as a lobster.

Charles Kingsley *The Water Babies* 1863

The herring is one of those products whose use decides the destiny of empires. The coffee bean, the tea leaf, the spices of the torrid zones, the worm which spins silk, had less influence on the wealth of nations than the northern ocean.

Comte de Lacepede q. in *Food* by Waverley Root 1980

MUSSELS HAVE A BAD reputation: something mysterious has to be done to them before they can be eaten with safety and no-one seems able to tell one exactly what it is.

James Laver q. in *A Wine and Food Bedside Book* ed. C. Morny 1972

Let us hail the shad, which arrives just at the moment when we are beginning to have enough of fish. It is the last word of Lent, but a word which triumphs. What a beautiful fish, shining with silver! The banks of the river are all but lighted up by it when the fishing boats are emptied at twilight. It is the aquatic hazelnut!

Charles Monselet
Lettres gourmandes 1974

Kippers: Semper Augustus of the sea's finny freeholders.

Thomas Nashe

Our plenteous streams a various race supply,
The bright-eyed perch with fins of Tyrian dye,
The silver eel, in shining volumes roll'd,
The yellow carp, in scales bedropp'd with gold,
Swift trouts, diversified with crimson stains
And pikes, the tyrants of the wat'ry plains.

Alexander Pope

Fish must swim thrice – once in the water, a second time in the sauce, and a third time in wine in the stomach.

John Ray *English Proverbs* 1670

HE ORDERS A Bismarck herring with sliced onions to come along, which is a dish that is considered most invigorating.

Damon Runyon *More Than Somewhat* 1937

From the beginning of Time to this day, the sea has been man's magic larder: without plough and without pay there has always been – and there still is – in the sea a ready supply of fish for man to catch and woman to cook. The same applies to all the waters of the earth: the sleepy or rushing waters of the humblest streams and noblest rivers, the icy cold waters of deep lakes in the mountains, and the shallow, brackish waters of lowlands and sea coasts – all are inhabited by fish, and mostly fish that is food for man.

André Simon *The Concise Encyclopedia of Gastronomy* 1952

Born from a test-tube, from parents which had never seen each other, the trout, once a feast for gourmets, is perhaps the most disinherited (of our fish). Brought up in a basin where the . . . water necessary for its survival is measured out for it with parsimony, this free rover of the torrents, whose appetite for savoury and varied foods is well known to fishermen, finds itself being fed at fixed hours with bits of spleen or even of spoiled meat unfit for human consumption . . . Such a trout, served up with almonds in the fallacious hope of distracting the attention of the gourmet, or else served smoked to play the card of Nordic exoticism, can hardly maintain the illusion after the first mouthful.

Albert Simonin q. in *Food* by Waverley Root 1980

FLOUNDER: to appreciate this fish it should never be eaten in London; they ought to be placed almost alive in the frying-pan; at any rate, five minutes ought not to elapse from the time they are swimming in water till they are swimming in fat, and five minutes more before they are consumed.

Alexis Soyer *The Modern Housewife* 1851

Perhaps it has not been sufficiently remarked that the science of ichthyophagy is generally developed in a direct ratio with the civilization of a people.

Alexis Soyer *The Pantropheon* 1853

What transformation, then, what preternatural alchemy transmutes the lobster to such sweet, miraculous meat? The philosopher increases his knowledge as he grows old and rots. Oysters are generated in scummy foam. The worst soil commonly yields the best air. The wolf spider impairs her womb to furnish the material for her beautiful silk. In the slopped and muddied palette of Botticelli patiently sat the 'Birth of Venus'. Isn't there a metaphysics in the making here?

Alexander Theroux *Esquire* July 1975

Anchova's, the famous meat of drunkards, and of them that desire to have their drinke, oblectate the pallat, doe nourish nothing at all, but a naughty cholericke blood . . . and are therefore chiefly profitable for vintners.

Tobias Venner *Via recta ad Vitam Longam* 1620

The Perch is a very good and very bold biting fish . . . He is of great esteem in Italy, saith Aldrovandus: and especially the least are esteemed a dainty dish. Gesner prefers the Perch and Pike above the Trout, or any fresh-water fish . . . and he says the River Perch is so wholesome that physicians allow him to be eaten by wounded men, or by men in fevers, or by women in childbed.

Izaak Walton *The Compleat Angler* 1653

T HE TROUT is a fish highly valued, both in this and foreign nations. It may be justly said, as the old poet said of wine, and we English say of venison, to be a generous fish: a fish that is so like the buck that he also has his seasons; for it is observed that he comes in and goes out of season with the stag and the buck . . . He may justly contend with all fresh-water fish for precedency and daintiness of taste: and that being in the right season, the most dainty palates have allowed precedency to him.

Izaak Walton *The Compleat Angler* 1653

'Turbot, sir' said the waiter, placing before me two fishbones, two eyeballs on a bit of wet mackintosh.

Thomas Earle Welby *The Dinner Knell*

I could not restrain a wistful sigh. 'Jeeves is a wonder.' 'A marvel.' 'What a brain!' 'Size nine-and-a-quarter, I should say.' 'He eats a lot of fish.'

P. G. Wodehouse *Thank You, Jeeves* 1934

CHAPTER NINETEEN

BEAUTIFUL SOUP

Beautiful soup, so rich and green,
Waiting in a hot tureen!
Who for such dainties would not stoop?
Soup of the evening, beautiful soup!
Beautiful soup! Who cares for fish,
Game, or any other dish?
Who would not give all else for two
Pennyworth only of beautiful Soup!
Pennyworth only of Beautiful Soup?

Lewis Carroll *Alice's Adventures in Wonderland* 1865

The great dish of New Orleans, and which it claims the honour of having invented, is the Gumbo. There is no dish which at the same time so tickles the palate, satisfies the appetite, furnishes the body with nutriment sufficient to carry on the physical requirements, and costs so little, as a Creole gumbo. It is a dinner in itself, being soup, pièce de résistance and vegetable in one. Healthy, not heating to the stomach, and easy of digestion, it should grace every table.

William Coleman 1885

*T*INNED SOUPS, *unless you happen to like the taste of tin, are universally displeasing . . .*

Elizabeth David *French Country Cooking* 1951

A whole chapter could be devoted to the bouillabaisse. Every French gastronomic writer and cook . . . has expounded his theories upon the dish so beloved of the Marseillais, and each one gives his own recipe – the only authentic one . . . you will never get the same instructions twice. There is no authentic bouillabaisse without white wine, you are told; it is a heresy of the most deadly kind to add white wine; the best bouillabaisse includes a langouste and mussels; langouste and mussels are only added in Paris because they haven't the other requisite fish; you must rub the croutons with garlic; you must on no account rub the croutons with garlic, and so on and so on.

Elizabeth David *French Provincial Cooking* 1960

B OUILLABAISSE is only good because cooked by the French, who, if they cared to try, could produce an excellent and nutritious substitute out of cigar stumps and empty matchboxes.

Norman Douglas *Siren Lands* 1911

C OLD SOUP is a very tricky thing and it is the rare hostess who can carry it off. More often than not the dinner guest is left with the impression that had he only come a little earlier he could have gotten it while it was still hot.

Fran Lebowitz
Metropolitan Life 1978

T HE MAKING OF A GOOD SOUP is quite an art, and many otherwise clever cooks do not possess the tour de main necessary to its successful preparation. Either they over-complicate the composition of the dish, or they attach only minor importance to it, reserving their talents for the meal itself, and so it frequently happens that the soup does not correspond to the quality of the rest of the dishes; nevertheless, the quality of the soup should foretell that of the entire meal.

Madame Seignobos
Comment on forme une cuisinière

This Bouillabaisse a noble dish is –
A sort of soup, or broth, or brew,
Or hotchpotch of all sorts of fishes,
That Greenwich never could outdo;
Green herbs, red peppers, mussels, saffron,
Soles, onions, garlic, roach and dace . . .

William Thackeray *The Ballad of Bouillabaisse* 1849

CHAPTER TWENTY

BUTTER & EGG MEN

An apple-pie without some cheese
Is like a kiss without a squeeze.

Anonymous *English rhyme*

Eat butter first and eat it last,
And live till a hundred years be past.

Anonymous *Dutch proverb*

The egg is to cuisine what the article is to speech.

Anonymous q. in *Food* by Waverley Root 1980

Be content to remember that those who can make omelettes properly can do nothing else.

Hilaire Belloc *A Conversation with a Cat*

223

Without butter, without eggs, there is no reason to come to France.

Paul Bocuse q. in *Alice, Let's Eat* by Calvin Trillin 1978

God of the country, bless today Thy cheese,
For which we give Thee thanks on bended knees.
Let them be fat or light, with onions blent,
Shallots, brine, pepper, honey; whether scent
Of sheep or fields is in them, in the yard
Let them, good Lord, be beaten hard.
And let their edges take on silvery shades
Under the most red hands of dairymaids;
And round, and greenish, let them go to town
Weighing the shepherd's folding mantle down.

Thomas Braun
Ode to Cheese

A last course at dinner, wanting cheese, is like a pretty woman with only one eye.

Jean-Anthelme Brillat-Savarin
La Physiologie du goût 1825

A hen is only an egg's way of making another egg.
Samuel Butler *Notebooks* 1912

I NEVER SEE an egg brought on my table but I feel penetrated with the wonderful change it would have undergone but for my gluttony; it might have been a gentle, useful hen, leading her chickens with a care and vigilance which speaks shame to many women.

St John de Crèvecoeur *Letters from an American Farmer* 1782

Egg dishes have a kind of elegance, a freshness, an allure, which sets them quite apart from any other kind of food, so that it becomes a great pleasure to be able to cook them properly and to serve them in just the right condition.

Elizabeth David
French Provincial Cooking 1960

As everybody knows, there is only one infallible recipe for the perfect omelette: your own.

Elizabeth David *French Provincial Cooking* 1950

A S TO THE OMELETTE itself, it seems to me to be a confection which demands the most straightforward approach. What one wants is the taste of the fresh eggs and the fresh butter and, visually, a soft, bright golden roll plump and spilling out a little at the edges. It should not be a busy, important urban dish but something gentle and pastoral, with the clean scent of the dairy, the kitchen garden, the basket of early morning mushrooms or the sharp tang of freshly picked herbs, sorrel, chives, tarragon.

Elizabeth David *An Omelette and a Glass of Wine* 1984

Where did all our own home-made cream and milk cheeses go? . . . Some of these cheeses were eaten the day they were made, with cream and sugar, some were for almond cheesecakes, some for the fillings of covered pies called Florentines, some for spiced cheese loaves baked in stoneware porringers. Some were salted and stored in brine in stoneware jars, some were laid between rushes and turned daily until ripe for eating. Some were whipped up with egg whites, lemon peel, and extra cream, some were served with raspberry, strawberry, redcurrant, apple, quince or medlar jelly.

Elizabeth David *Nova* 1965

Ah, Wensleydale! The Mozart of cheeses.

T. S. Eliot q. in *Observer* 1965

I T WAS OBVIOUS that the egg had come first. There was something dignified about a silent passive egg, whereas Aunt Irene found it difficult to envisage an angel bearing a hen – which despite its undoubted merits, was a foolish and largely intractable bird.

Alice Thomas Ellis *The 27th Kingdom* 1982

There is always a best way of doing everything, if it be to boil an egg.

Ralph Waldo Emerson
Conduct of Life 1860

Cheese – milk's leap towards immortality.

Clifton Fadiman
Any Number Can Play 1957

But I, when I undress me
Each night upon my knees
Will ask the Lord to bless me
With apple pie and cheese.

Eugene Field *Apple Pie and Cheese* 1896

Probably one of the most private things in the world is an egg until it is broken.

M. F. K. Fisher *How to Cook a Wolf* 1951

Cheese and salt meat should be sparingly eat.

Benjamin Franklin *Poor Richard's Almanac* 1733

On a chalkwhite plate you lie
With loathing in your yellow eye
Swimming in sickly fat
ugh!

Lucian Freud q. in *Freud on Food* by C. Freud 1978

CHEESE, as a food, is as wholesome as its use is widespread; as an item in a coursed dinner there is nothing known to the world of gastronomy which can so quickly rectify the palate, between the sweets and the dessert, like the tang of a true cheese.

Frederick W. Hackwood *Good Cheer* 1911

An omelette ought never to be stiff enough to retain a very rolled-up appearance. If cooked with proper rapidity it should be too light to present a fixed form, and on reaching the hot dish should spread itself, rather, on account of the delicacy of its substance. Books that counsel you to turn an omelette, to fold it, to let it brown on one side, to let it fry for five minutes, etc., are not to be trusted. If you follow such advice you will produce, at best, a neat-looking egg pudding.

Col. A. Kenney-Herbert (Wyvern) *Fifty Luncheons*

Soufflés: the soufflé is par excellence the kind of sweet that is suited to the cosy home dinner, or a party of three or four friends. It is a thing that few men refuse. Sportsmen who, as a rule, shake their heads at creams, trifles, rich jellies and the like, rarely permit a soufflé – a tempting, well-made soufflé – to pass them by. It is so light, so simple and attractive, that it cannot 'lie like lead upon the bosom'; while it cannot but afford a pleasant stepping-stone between the pheasant's wing and the Gorgonzola – or twixt the teal and Gruyère.

Col. A. Kenney-Herbert
(Wyvern) *Wyvern's Sweet Dishes* 1881

I had an excellent repast – the best repast possible – which consisted simply of boiled eggs and bread and butter. It was the quality of these simple ingredients that made the occasion memorable. The eggs were so good that I am ashamed to say how many of them I consumed . . . it might seem that an egg which has succeeded in being fresh has done all that can reasonably be expected of it.

Henry James *A Little Tour in France*

CHEESE that is compelled by law to append the word 'food' to its title does not go well with red wine or fruit.

Fran Lebowitz *Metropolitan Life* 1978

Fromage, poesie!
Parfum de nos repas,
Que deviendrait la vie
Si l'on ne t'avait pas?
(Cheese, poetry!
Perfume of our meal
What would become of life
if we didn't have you?)

Charles Monselet *La cuisinière poetique* c. 1850

Hickety, pickety, my black hen
She lays eggs for gentlemen;
Gentlemen come every day
To see what my black hen doth lay. (parodied by Dorothy Parker, at dinner
with G. K. Chesterton, as 'Hickety, pickety, my red hen
She lays eggs for gentlemen;
But you cannot persuade her with a gun or lariat
To come across for the proletariat.')

Nursery Rhymes *Nursery Rhymes* ed. J. O. Halliwell 1853

Cheese it is a peevish elf,
It digests all things but itself.

John Ray *English Proverbs* 1670

Toasted cheese hath no master.

John Ray *English Proverbs* 1670

Butter should smell sweet as a nosegay.

Maria Rundell
A New System of Domestic Cookery 1806

When you have decided to serve an omelette, everything but its care must be banished from your mind. Once made, an omelette, like a soufflé, must not and cannot wait, even a minute.

André Simon *The Concise Encyclopedia of Gastronomy* 1952

Many's the long night I've dreamed of cheese – toasted, mostly.

Robert Louis Stevenson
Treasure Island 1883

The friendly cow, all red and white,
I love with all my heart;
She gives me cream with all her might,
To eat with apple-tart.

Robert Louis Stevenson
A Child's Garden of Verses 1885

CREAM . . . is the very head and flower of milk; but it is somewhat of a gross nourishment, and by reason of the unctuosity of it, quickly cloyeth the stomach, relaxeth and weakeneth the retentive faculty thereof, and is easily converted into phlegm and vaporous fumes.

Tobias Venner *Via recta ad Vitam Longam* 1620

HE WAS AN OLD buster who, a few years later, came down to breakfast one morning, lifted the first cover he saw, said 'Eggs! Eggs! Eggs! Damn all eggs' in an overwrought sort of voice and instantly legged it for France, never to return to the bosom of his family.

P. G. Wodehouse *Carry On, Jeeves!* 1925

CHAPTER TWENTY-ONE

TO CHEER BUT NOT INEBRIATE

No honey or spice can make wine so sweet, as real thirst makes cold water.

Saint Ailred of Rievaulx *Christian Friendship*

Coffee . . . having many excellent vertues, closes the Orifice of the Stomack, fortifies the heart within, helpeth Dijestion, quickneth the Spirits, maketh the heart lightsome, is good against Eyesores, coughs, or Colds, Rhumes, Consumptions, Head-ache, Dropsie, Gout, Scurvy, King's Evil and many others.

Anonymous
English Newspaper Advertisement 1657

Coffee should be black as Hell, strong as death and sweet as love.

Anonymous *Turkish proverb*

The chocolate bar is an edible American flag, a security blanket for the distraught, a barometer of the nation's economic health.

Anonymous
in *New York Times* 25th February 1979

The Amorous Gallant, whose hot Reins do fail,
Stung by conjunction with the Dragon's-Tail:
Let him but Tipple here, shall find his Grief
Discharg'd, without the Sweting-Tub's Relief;
Nor have the Ladies reason to Complain,
As fumbling Doe-litles are apt to Faign;
Coffee's no Foe to their obliging Trade,
By it Men rather are more active made;
'Tis stronger Drink, and base adulterate Wine,
Enfeebles Vigour and makes Nature Pine;
Loaden with which, th'Impotent Sott is Led
Like a Sowc'd Hogshead to a Misses Bed;
But this Rare Settle-Brain prevents those Harms
Conquers Old Sherry and Brisk Claret Calms,
Sack, I defy thee with an open Throat,
Whilst truly Coffee is my Antedote.

Anonymous   broadside promoting coffee, 1674

Oh Coffee! Thou dost dispel all cares;
thou art the object of desire to the scholar.
This is the beverage of the friends of God; it gives health in its service who
strive after wisdom.
Prepared from the simple shell of the berry, it has the odour of musk and the
colour of ink.
The intelligent man who empties these cups of foaming coffee, he alone knows
truth.

Anonymous   Arabic poem *In Praise of Coffee* c. 1512

How our ancestors managed to do without tea
I must fairly confess is a mystery to me;
Yet your Lydgates and Chaucers
Had no cups and saucers.

Richard Harris Barham
The Ingoldsby Legends 1840

A cup of coffee – real coffee – home-browned, home-ground, home made, that
comes to you dark as a hazel-eye, but changes to a golden bronze as you temper it
with cream that never cheated, but was real cream from its birth, thick, tenderly
yellow, perfectly sweet, neither lumpy nor frothing on the Java: such a cup of
coffee is a match for twenty blue devils, and will exorcise them all.

Henry Ward Beecher *Eyes and Ears*

CHOCOLATE is not only pleasant to taste, but it is a veritable balm of the mouth, for the maintaining of all glands and humours in a good state of health. Thus it is that all who drink it possess a sweet breath.

Dr S. Blancardi 1705

If any man has drunk a little too deeply from the cup of physical pleasure; if he has spent too much time at his desk that should have been spent asleep; if his fine spirits have become temporarily dulled; if he finds the air too damp, the minutes too slow, and the atmosphere too heavy to withstand; if he is obsessed by a fixed idea which bars him from any freedom of thought: if he is any of these poor creatures, we say, let him be given a good pint of amber-flavoured chocolate . . . and marvels will be performed.

Jean-Anthelme Brillat-Savarin *La Physiologie du goût* 1825

WATER IS THE only beverage that effectually quenches thirst, and it is for this reason that it can only be drunk in very small quantities.

Jean-Anthelme Brillat-Savarin *La Physiologie du goût* 1825

Persons who drink chocolate regularly are conspicuous for unfailing health and immunity from the host of minor ailments which mar the enjoyment of life.

Jean-Anthelme Brillat-Savarin *La Physiologie du goût* 1825

WATER IS INSIPID, inodorous, colourless, and smooth; it is found, when not cold, to be a great resolver of spasms, and lubricator of the fibres; this power it probably owes to its smoothness.

Edmund Burke *The Sublime and Beautiful* 1756

Of all the times for refreshment in the house early morning tea, to the conservatively minded, is the one that must be run to inflexible rule. To those whom tea is served, the slightest deviation from the normal works like sandpaper upon a nervous system already strained by the ascent from the soft valleys of sleep to the dizzy and jagged heights of consciousness.

Patrick Campbell
q. in *Writers' Favourite Recipes* ed. G. Vincent 1978

Heaven sent us soda water
As a torment for our crimes.

G. K. Chesterton
q. in *Simple French Cooking for English Homes* by M. Boulestin 1923

Tea, although an Oriental,
Is a gentleman at least;
Cocoa is a cad and coward,
Cocoa is a vulgar beast.

G. K. Chesterton *The Song of Right and Wrong*

Strong wine it is a mocker, strong wine it is a beast,
It grips you when it starts to rise; it is the Fabled Yeast.
You should not offer ale or beer from hops that are freshly picked,
Nor even Benedictine to tempt a benedict.
For wine has a spell like the lure of hell, and the devil has mixed the brew,
And the friends of Ale are a sort of pale and weary, witless crew –
And the taste of beer is a sort of a queer and undecided brown –
But Comrades, I give you Coffee – drink it up, drink it down.

G. K. Chesterton

Tea! thou soft, thou sober, sage and venerable liquid, thou female
tongue-running, smile-soothing, heart-opening, wink-tippling cordial, to whose
glorious insipidity I owe the happiest moments of my life, let me fall prostrate.

Colley Cibber *The Lady's Last Stake* 1708

On tea: Now stir the fire, and close the shutters fast,
Let fall the curtains, wheel the sofa round,
And while the bubbling and loud-hissing urn
Throws up a steady column, and the cups
That cheer but not inebriate, wait on each,
So let us welcome peaceful evening in.

William Cowper *The Task* 1785

REGARDING CHOCOLATE, I judge it to be of neutral effect; a cloying product fit for serving maids; yet possessed of value as an endearment, an incentive not working upon body but upon mind; it generates, in those who relish it, a complacent and yielding disposition. Deprived of chocolate, your lover of serving maids is deprived of a persuasive helpmate.

Norman Douglas *Paneros* privately published

I hate water – fish fuck in it.

W. C. Fields
q. in *The Book of Hollywood Quotes* 1979

It is disgusting to note the increase in the quantity of coffee used by my subjects and the amount of money that goes out of the country in consequence. Everybody is using coffee . . . My people must drink beer. His Majesty was brought up on beer, and so were his officers. Many battles have been fought and won by soldiers nourished on beer; and the King does not believe that coffee-drinking soldiers can be depended upon to endure hardships or to beat his enemies in the case of the occurrence of another war.

Frederick the Great proclamation against coffee, 1777

TEA . . . is declared to be . . . most wholesome, preserving in perfect health until extreme Old Age. The particular vertues are these: It maketh the Body active and lusty. It helpeth the Headache giddiness and heaviness thereof. It removeth the Obstructions of the Spleen. It is very good against the Stone or Gravel, cleansing the Kidneys and Uriters being drank with Virgins Honey instead of Sugar . . . It removeth Lassitude, and cleanseth and purifieth adult Humors and a hot Liver. It is good against Crudities, strengthening the weakness of the Ventricle or Stomach, causing good Appetite and Digestion, and particularly for Men of a Corpulent Body, and such as are great eaters of Flesh . . .

Thomas Garway broadsheet advertisement, 1660

If you are cold, tea will warm you – if you are too heated, it will cool you – if you are depressed, it will cheer you – if you are excited, it will calm you.

William Gladstone q. in *Talking of Tea* by Gervase Huxley 1956

The best proof that tea or coffee are favourable to intellectual expression is that all nations use one or the other as aids to conversation.

Philip G. Hamerton *The Intellectual Life*

I like a nice cup of tea in the morning
For to start the day you see
And at half-past eleven
Well my idea of Heaven
Is a nice cup of tea.
I like a nice cup of tea with my dinner
And a nice cup of tea with my tea
And when it's time for bed
There's a lot to be said
For a nice cup of tea.

A. P. Herbert *Home and Beauty*

A soft drink turneth away company.

Oliver Herford 1901

The morning cup of coffee has an exhilaration about it which the cheering influence of the afternoon or evening cup of tea cannot be expected to reproduce.

Oliver Wendell Holmes *Over the Teacups* 1891

NOTHING'LL MAKE a father swear before the children quicker than a cup of poor coffee.

Frank McKinney 'Kin' Hubbard *Abe Martin on Things in General*

And if from man's vile arts I flee
And drink pure water from the pump,
I gulp down infusoria
And quarts of raw bacteria,
And hideous rotatorae
And wriggling polygastricae,
And slimy diatomacae,
And various animalculae
Of middle, high and low degree.

William Juniper
The True Drunkard's Delight 1933

You may talk o' gin and beer
When you're quartered safe out 'ere,
When you're sent to penny-fights an' Aldershot it;
But when it comes to slaughter
You will do your work on water
An' you'll lick the bloomin' boots of 'im that's got it.

Rudyard Kipling
Gunga Din 1888

In Europe the most obstreperous nations are those most addicted to coffee . . .
We rightly speak of a storm in a teacup as the tiniest disturbance in the world, but
out of a coffee-cup come great hurricanes.

Robert Lynd *The Blue Lion*

Milk chocolate is a yokel taste.

Nieman Marcus *Quest for the Best*

ONE or two cups of (tea) taken on an empty stomach remove fever, headache,
stomach ache, pain in the side or in the joints, and it should be taken as hot as you
can bear it . . .

Haji Muhammad
q. in *Cathay and the Way Thither* by Sir Henry Yule 1913-16

As long as Mocha's happy tree shall grow,
While berries crackle, or while mills shall go;
While smoking stream from silver spouts shall glide,
Or China's earth receive the sable tide,
While coffee shall to British nymphs be dear,
While fragrant steams the bended head shall cheer,
Our grateful bitters shall delight the taste,
So long her honours name and praise shall last.

Alexander Pope

Coffee is a fleeting moment and a fragrance.

Claudia Roden *Coffee* 1977

AMONG THE NUMEROUS luxuries of the table, unknown to our forefathers, coffee may be considered as one of the most valuable. Its taste is very agreeable, and its flavour uncommonly so; but its principle excellence depends on its salubrity, and on its exhilarating quality. It excites cheerfulness, without intoxication; and the pleasing flow of spirits which it occasions . . . is never followed by sadness, langour or debility. It diffuses over the whole frame a glow of health, and sense of ease and well-being which is extremely delightful: existence is felt to be a positive enjoyment, and the mental powers are awakened, and rendered uncommonly active.

Benjamin Thompson, Count Rumford *Essays*

What should mightily recommend the use of Tea to Gentlemen of a sprightly Genius, who would preserve the Continuance of the their lively and distinct Ideas, is its eminent and unequalled Power to take off, or prevent Drowsiness and Dulness, Damps and Clouds on the Brain, and intellectual Faculties. It begets a watchful Briskness, dispels Heaviness; it keep the Eyes wakeful the Head clear, animates the intellectual Powers, maintains or raises lively Ideas, excites and sharpeneth the Thoughts, gives fresh Vigour and Force to Invention, awakes the Senses and clears the Mind.

Dr Thomas Short *Discourse on Tea* 1750

Thank God for tea! What would the world do without tea?

Sydney Smith q. in *Talking of Tea* by Gervase Huxley 1946

Tea is, without doubt, one of the most useful herbs ever introduced into this country; it was in the year of the fire of London, 1666, and has displaced an unwholesome and heavy drink (ale) which used to be partaken of previously, and has created habits of sobriety . . . It is exceedingly useful in many cases of sickness, and particularly after having partaken of any liquor to excess, or after extraordinary fatigue.

Alexis Soyer *The Modern Housewife* 1851

WATER, WHICH in the general way is thought so lightly of, is one of those elements used in cookery which is of the most important character. The best receipts in cookery may often be spoilt in consequence of the water, as it is by that the flavour of everything is extracted, and upon the quality of the water much depends the nature of the extract.

Alexis Soyer *The Modern Housewife* 1851

It is no longer true that the sun never sets on the British Empire. But it doesn't set on the Coca Cola Company and hasn't for a long time.

Jean Stafford *Esquire* December 1975

A ND AS CHOCOLATA provokes other Evacuations through the several Emunctories of the body, so it doth that of Seed, and becomes provocative to lust upon no other account.

Henry Stubbs *The Indian Nectar* c. 1630

T HE best maxim I know in life, is to drink your coffee when you can, and when you cannot, to be easy without it.

Jonathan Swift letter to Esther Vanhomrigh 1722

A cup of coffee detracts nothing from your intellect; on the contrary your stomach is freed by it and no longer distresses your brain; it will not hamper your mind with troubles but give freedom to its working. Suave molecules of Mocha stir up your blood without causing excessive heat; the organ of thought receives from it a feeling of sympathy; work becomes easier and you will sit down without distress to your principal repast which will restore your body and afford you a calm delicious night.

Charles Maurice de Talleyrand — Perigord
q. in *Coffee* by Claudia Roden 1977

Water is the only drink for a wise man.

H. D. Thoreau *Walden* 1854

Tea possesses an acid astringent quality, peculiar to most leaves and exterior bark of trees, and corrodes and paralyses the nerves.

Jessey Torrey *The Moral Instructor* 1819

I TURNED on the pillow with a little moan, and at this juncture Jeeves entered with the vital oolong. I clutched at it like a drowning man at a straw hat. A deep sip or two, and I felt – I won't say restored, because a birthday party like Pongo Twistleton's isn't a thing you get restored after with a mere mouthful of tea, but sufficiently the old Bertram to be able to bend the mind on this awful thing which had come upon me.

P. G. Wodehouse *Right Ho, Jeeves* 1934

CHAPTER TWENTY-TWO

A CHICKEN IN EVERY POT

We all look on with anxious eyes
When father carves the duck,
And mother almost always sighs
When father carves the duck.
Then all of us prepare to rise
And hold our bibs before our eyes
And be prepared for some surprise
When father carves the duck.

Anonymous
q. in *Pleasures of the Table* by G. Ellwanger 1903

Those who eat goose on Michaelmas Day
Shall have money all year their debts for to pay.

Anonymous
traditional English rhyme 1588

Turkey boiled is turkey spoiled
And turkey roast is turkey lost
But for turkey braised
The Lord be praised.

Anonymous q. in *Food* by Waverley Root 1980

The whole race of fowls was solely created to fill our larders and enrich our banquets. It is undeniable that from quail to turkey-cock, wherever we meet with a member of this large family, we may be sure of finding food that is both light and savoury, and agrees equally with the convalescent and the man in the best of health . . . fowls are to the kitchen what his canvas is to the painter. (cf: Soyer)

Jean-Anthelme Brillat-Savarin
La Physiologie du goût 1825

When the vine-grower or ploughman wants a treat on some long winter evening, what do we see roasting over a bright fire in the kitchen where the table is laid? A turkey. When the hard-working artisan invites a few friends to his house to enjoy a holiday which is all the more precious for being rare, what is sure to be the principal dish of the feast? A turkey, stuffed with sausages or Lyons chestnuts. And in the high places of gastronomy, at those select gatherings where politics are forced to give way to dissertations on taste, what do the guests hope for and long for as the second course? A truffled turkey!

Jean-Anthelme Brillat-Savarin
La Physiologie du goût 1825

The turkey has practically no taste except a dry fibrous flavour reminiscent of warmed-up plaster of Paris and horsehair. The texture is like wet sawdust and the whole vast feathered swindle has the piquancy of a boiled mattress.

William Connor (Cassandra)
in *Daily Mirror* 1953

It was a turkey. He could never have stood upon his legs, that bird. He would have snapped 'em off short in a minute, like sticks of sealing-wax.

Charles Dickens
A Christmas Carol 1843

THERE WAS NEVER such a goose. Bob said he didn't believe there was ever such a goose cooked. Its tenderness and flavour, size and cheapness, were the themes of universal admiration. Eked out by apple sauce and mashed potatoes, it was sufficient dinner for the whole family: indeed as Mrs. Cratchit said with great delight (surveying one small atom of a bone upon the dish) they hadn't ate it all at last!

Charles Dickens *A Christmas Carol* 1843

SERVE A DUCK whole, but eat only the breast and neck; the rest send back to the cook.

Martial *Epigrams XII* c. 100

We all know that in spring a young man's fancy lightly turns to thoughts of love, but it is not such common knowledge that in the early summer the thoughts of a man of mature age turn with equal agility to duckling and green peas.

Lt-Col. Nathaniel Newnham-Davies
The Gourmet's Guide to London 1914

The goose is a snappy brunette, with whom we get along very well, especially in the absence of our dear blonde.

Grimod de la Reynière *Almanach des Gourmands* 1804

A good many things taste like chicken except, nowadays, chicken, which tastes like damp cardboard – a small price to pay for the triumph of having produced the battery-fed square-foot chicken reared on scientifically compounded foods which bring it to a weight of two pounds on four pounds of feed instead of yesterday's six and a half.

Waverley Root *Esquire* June 1974

A Chicken is just a barnyard fowl, and it may be rightly called the best of all birds covered by the name of Poultry. It is a more important article of food, all the world over, than any other domesticated fowl, and its claim to being the best of them all rests upon the fact that, like bread, potatoes and rice, Chicken may be eaten constantly without becoming nauseating.

André Simon *A Concise Encyclopedia of Gastronomy* 1952

Poultry . . . is the best and most delicious of the various matters with which man furnishes himself as food; although containing but little nourishment, it gives a delightful variety to our repast: from the sparrow to the turkey, we find everywhere, in this numerous class, that which gives a meal equally as good for the invalid as the robust. (cf: Brillat-Savarin).

Alexis Soyer *The Modern Housewife* 1851

Boiled Turkey: This is a dish I rarely have, as I never could relish it boiled as it generally is, by putting it into that pure and chaste element, into which has been thrown some salt . . . I often reflect to myself, why should this innocent and well brought-up bird have its remains condemned to this watery, bubbling inquisition, especially when alive it has the greatest horror of this temperate fluid.

Alexis Soyer *The Modern Housewife* 1851

Madame, she said, poor Blanchette (one of our Barbary ducks) is no more. That wretched dog frightened her to death. Her heart was beating so furiously I saw that there was but one thing to do. I gave her three tablespoons full of 'eau-de-vie', that will give her a good flavour. And then I killed her. How does Madame wish her to be cooked? . . . I answered feebly, with orange sauce.

Alice B. Toklas *The Alice B. Toklas Cookbook* 1954

CHAPTER TWENTY-THREE

HERBS FOR ALL SEASONS

Here capers grace a sauce vermilion
Whose fragrant odours to the soul are blown . . .
Here pungent garlic meets the eager sight
And whets with savour sharp the appetite,
While olives turn to shadowed night the day,
And salted fish in slices rims the tray . . .

Ibn al-Mu'tazz
q. in *The Islamic Culture* by A. J. Arberry 1939

Why should a man die who has sage in his garden?

Anonymous

Even the worm inside a stone eats herbs.

Anonymous *Persian saying*

Coriander is essentially a cultivated weed.

Anonymous q. in *Food* by Waverley Root 1980

There is no such thing as a little garlic.

Arthur Baer q. in *The Frank Muir Book*

245

Nose, nose, jolly red nose,
And who gave thee this jolly red nose?
Nutmegs and ginger, cinnamon and cloves,
And they gave me this jolly red nose.

Francis Beaumont & John Fletcher
The Knight of the Burning Pestle 1609

It is not really an exaggeration to say that peace and happiness begin, geographically, where garlic is used in cooking.

X. Marcel Boulestin

Wel loved he garleek, oynons, and eek lekes,
And for to drinken strong wyn, reed as blood.

Geoffrey Chaucer
The Canterbury Tales c. 1387

Neither witch nor devil, thunder nor lightning will hurt a man where a bay tree is.

Nicholas Culpeper
Complete Herbal 1653

TO TAKE PARSLEY away from the cook would make it almost impossible for him to exercise his art.

Louis Bosc d'Antic 1790

A man who is stingy with the saffron is capable of seducing his own grandmother.

Norman Douglas
q. in *An Omelette and a Glass of Wine* Elizabeth David 1984

It has been said of garlic that everyone knows its odour save he who has eaten it, and who wonders why everyone flies at his approach. But the onion tribe is prophylactic and highly invigorating, and even more necessary to cookery than parsley itself. What were a salad without the onion, whey-cheese without chives, a bouillabaisse, or a brandade of cod without garlic, certain soups and ragouts without leeks, and a bordelaise sauce without shallots!

George Ellwanger *Pleasures of the Table* 1903

The savour or smell of the water mint rejoiceth the heart of man.

John Gerard
Gerard's Herbal 1597

T O TURN TO spices, mace – that aesthetically beautiful by-product of the nutmeg-tree, a network husk of deep and brilliant laquer-red while it is with its singularly piquant aroma. Nutmeg itself, grated, is also a help in soups . . . no less than in bread sauce and a rum punch. Saffron is as indispensable to a good Milanese risotto as it is to a bouillabaisse and a paella. A touch of cardamom or coriander seed transforms a humdrum stew with the aroma of a Middle Eastern suq. And what a rich evocative aroma they have, those ancient vaulted bazaars of Aleppo and Damascus and the old City of Jerusalem, of Qazvin and Meshhed and Isfahan . . .

Sir Harry Luke *The Tenth Muse* 1954

He who bears chives on his breath
Is safe from being kissed to death.

Martial *Epigrams* c. 80

Garlick hath properties that make a man winke, drinke and stinke.

Thomas Nashe
The Unfortunate Traveller 1594

All Italy is in the fine, penetrating smell; and all Provence; and all Spain. An onion or garlic – scented atmosphere hovers alike over the narrow calli of Venice, the cool courts of Cordova, and the thronged amphitheatre of Arles. It is the only atmosphere breathed by the Latin peoples of the South, so that ever it must suggest blue skies and endless sunshine, cypress groves and olive orchards. For the traveller it is interwoven with memories of the golden canvases of Titian, the song of Dante, the music of Mascagni.

Elisabeth Pennell *The Feasts of Autolycus* 1896

It is the destiny of mint to be crushed.

Waverley Root *Food* 1980

Nature was indeed at her artistic best when she created the nutmeg, a delight to the eye in all its avatars, from the completely garbed to nudity.

Waverley Root *Food* 1980

CHAPTER TWENTY-FOUR

SPICY STUFF

Always have lobster sauce with salmon,
And put mint sauce your roasted lamb on.
Roast pork sans apple sauce, past doubt,
Is 'Hamlet' with the Prince left out.
Nice oyster sauce gives zest to cod –
A fish, when fresh, to feast a god!
It gives true epicures the vapours
To see boiled mutton minus capers.

Anonymous q. in *Good Cheer* by Frederick W. Hackwood 1911

Cook, see all your sauces be sharp and poynant
in the palate, that they may commend you . . .

Francis Beaumont & John Fletcher

Mayonnaise, n: One of the sauces which serve the French in place of a state religion.

Ambrose Bierce *The Devil's Dictionary* 1911

Salt is the policeman of taste: it keeps the various flavours of a dish in order and
restrains the stronger from tyrannizing over the weaker.

Malcolm de Chazal *Sens Plastique* 1949

No sauce, no health, no cooking.

Marquis de Cussy *L'Art Culinaire*

Although I regard (the liquidiser) with the utmost gratitude, since it is a mechanical kitchen-maid rather than a gadget, I do not care, unless I am in a great hurry, to let it deprive me of the pleasure and satisfaction to be obtained from sitting down quietly with bowl, spoon, eggs and oil to the peaceful kitchen task of concocting the beautiful shining golden ointment which is mayonnaise.

Elizabeth David
French Provincial Cooking 1960

AUNT IRENE really inclined to that simplest of all views: the one expressed so cogently in the book of Genesis, which explained everything with appealing clarity. This was the only view that explained, for instance, mayonnaise. It was patently absurd to suppose that mayonnaise had come about through random chance, that anyone could ever have been silly or brilliant enough to predict what would happen if he slowly trickled oil onto egg yolks and then gone ahead and tried it.

Alice Thomas Ellis *The 27th Kingdom* 1982

Malicious salt makes human beings alter.
Employed with measure, it leaves things well
But taken in excess provokes its private hell:
Makes women hot, but men inclined to falter.

Léon de Fos 1870

Salt is white and pure – there is something holy in salt.

Nathaniel Hawthorne *American Notebooks* 1840

AMONGST SAUCES I consider Harvey's the best for general use; Sutton's 'Empress of India' is a strong sauce with a real flavour of mushrooms; Moir's sauces and 'Reading sauce' are very trustworthy, and there are others which, no doubt, commend themselves to different palates, but I denounce 'Worcester Sauce' and 'Tapp's Sauce' as agents far too powerful to be entrusted to the hands of the native cook.

Col. A. Kenney-Herbert (Wyvern)
Culinary Jottings for Madras 1885

The precious salt, that gold of cookery!
For when its particles the palate thrill'd
The source of seasonings, charm of cookery! came.

Hesiod c. 750 BC

Condiments are like old friends – highly thought of, but often taken for granted.

Marilyn Kaytor in *Look* magazine 1963

The fundamental principle of all,
Is what ingenious cooks, the 'relish' call;
For when the markets send in loads of food,
They are tasteless till that makes them good.

William King
The Art of Cookery 1708

Peter Piper picked a peck of pickled pepper;
A peck of pickled pepper
Peter Piper picked;
If Peter Piper picked a peck of pickled pepper,
Where's the peck of pickled pepper Peter Piper picked?

Nursery Rhymes
Peter Piper's Practical Principles of Perfect Pronunciation 1819

Pepper is small in quantity and great in virtue.

Plato *Laws* 360 BC

Mustard . . . a frightful poison which does not permit itself to be crushed without making the eyes water.

Titus Maccius Plautus 190 BC

An overturned salt-cellar is to be feared only when it is overturned in a good dish.

Grimod de la Reynière *Almanach des Gourmands* 1804

With a well-prepared anchovy sauce, one might eat an elephant.

Grimod de la Reynière *Almanach des Gourmands* 1803

SALT . . . nothing is perfect without it; the health of every individual depends on it, being an ingredient in our blood; it is as much required to be partaken of as food or drink . . . and the great Author of all has bountifully provided the whole human race, in every clime and country, with it.

Alexis Soyer *The Modern Housewife* 1851

Sauces in cookery are like the first rudiments of grammar, which consist of certain rules called Syntax, and the foundation of all languages: these fundamental rules are nine, so has cookery the same number of sauces, which are the foundation of all others; but these, like its prototype the grammar, have two – brown and white, which bear a resemblance to the noun and verb, as they are the first and most easily learnt, and most constantly in use; the others are the adjuncts, pronouns, adverbs and interjections; upon the proper use of the two principal ones depends the quality of all others, and the proper making of which tends to the enjoyment of the dinner.

Alexis Soyer *The Modern Housewife* 1851

SAUCES ARE TO COOKERY what the gamut is to the composition of music, as it is by the arrangement of notes that harmony is produced, so should the ingredients in the sauce be nicely blended, and that delightful concord should exist, which would equally delight the palate, as a masterpiece of a Mozart or a Rossini should delight the ear.

Alexis Soyer *The Modern Housewife* 1851

CHAPTER TWENTY-FIVE

THE PROOF OF THE PUDDING

The Charlotte brown, within whose crusty sides
A belly soft the pulpy apple hides.

Anonymous 1796

'Tis the dessert that graces all the feast,
For an ill end disparages the rest:
Make your transparent sweet-meats timely rise,
With Indian sugar and Arabian spice;
And let your various creams enriched be
With swelling fruit just ravished from the tree . . .

Anonymous *Apician Morsels*

Sugar harms nothing but the purse.

Jean-Anthelme Brillat-Savarin
La Physiologie du goût 1825

Good apple pies are a considerable part of our domestic happiness.

Jane Austen

CUSTARD, n: a detestable substance produced by a malevolent conspiracy of the hen, the cow and the cook.

Ambrose Bierce *The Devil's Dictionary* 1911

Pie, n: an advance agent of the reaper whose name is Indigestion.

Ambrose Bierce *The Devil's Dictionary* 1911

Bring on the dessert. I think I am about to die.

Pierette Brillat-Savarin
last words, 1911

THE FINE ARTS are five in number: Painting, Music, Sculpture, Poetry and Architecture – whereof the principal branch is confectionery.

Antonin Carème

The rule is, jam tomorrow and jam yesterday – but never jam today.

Lewis Carroll
Through the Looking-Glass 1871

Don't eat too many almonds. They add weight to the breasts.

Colette *Gigi* 1945

Hallo! A great deal of steam! The pudding was out of the copper. A smell like washing day! A smell like an eating-house and a pastry-cook's next door to each other, with a laundress's next door to that. That was the pudding . . . like a speckled cannon-ball, so hard and firm, blazing in a half of a half-a-quarten of ignited brandy, and bedight with Christmas holly stuck into the top.

Charles Dickens *A Christmas Carol* 1843

The dessert is said to be to the dinner what the madrigal is to literature – it is the light poetry of the kitchen.

George Ellwanger *Pleasures of the Table* 1903

A LOT OF PEOPLE have never really had the chance to eat a decent apple pie, but after a minute's sensual reflection will know positively what they would expect if they did. They can taste it on their mind's tongue: thin flaky pastry and hunks of sweet apple bathed in a syrup; rich but sturdy dough filled with finely sliced tart apples seasoned with cinnamon; an upper and lower crust in a traditional pie pan; an upper crust only, in a deep dish; a bottom crust with crosses of dough over the filling . . .

M. F. K. Fisher *Esquire* December 1975

In moments of considerable strain I tend to take to bread-and-butter pudding. There is something about the blandness of soggy bread, the crispness of the golden outer crust and the unadulterated pleasure of a lightly set custard that makes the world seem a better place to live.

Clement Freud *Freud on Food* 1978

The proof of the pudding is in the eating.

Henry Glapthorne *The Hollander* 1635

Trifle: that time-honoured, excellent dish, so dear to the hearts of our elderly cousins and our maiden aunts.

Col. A. Kenney-Herbert (Wyvern) *Wyvern's Sweet Dishes* 1881

Like Albion's rich plum-pudding, famous grown,
The mince-pie reigns in realms beyond his own,
Through foreign latitudes his power extends,
And only terminates where eating ends.

William Hone *Ode to the Mince-pie*

Of all the delicates which Britons try
To please the palate or delight the eye,
Of all the sev'ral kinds of sumptuous fare.
There is none that can with apple pie compare.
Ranged in thick order let your Quinces lie
They give a charming relish to the Pie.
If you are wise you'll not brown sugar slight,
The browner (if I form my judgement right)
A deep vermillion tincture will dispense,
And make your Pippin redder than the Quince.
When this is done there will be wanting still
The just reserve of cloves and candied peel;
Nor can I blame you, if a drop you take
Of orangewater for perfuming's sake.
But here the nicety of art is such,
There must not be too little nor too much.

William King
The Art of Cookery 1708

I was presented . . . with a card on which some thirty different types of ices were listed. The temptation was atrocious. My soul responds to a mere vanilla ice cream smeared out into the thick glass of an Italian ice-cream vendor; but here was an opportunity to sample ices which were to the ordinary vanilla as Hyperion to a satyr. Although I knew nothing could be worse for my complaint . . . I really did feel that life was less important than sampling these ices . . . Some of the fervour which has given martyrs to science was mine . . . Even without dysentry and cystitis it would have been impossible for any man to sample every ice . . . I do not remember that ever in my life was I so anxious to make a right choice.

Compton Mackenzie
First Athenian Memories

Blessed be he that invented pudding, for it is a Manna that hits the Palates of all Sortes of People; a Manna, better than that of the Wilderness, because the People are never weary of it. Ah, what an excellent Thing is an English Pudding! 'To come in Pudding time' is as much as to say, to come in the most lucky Moment in the World.

H. Misson *Memoirs* 1719

Little Jack Horner sat in the corner,
Eating a Christmas pie:
He put in his thumb, and pulled out a plum,
And said, 'What a good boy am I!'

Nursery Rhymes in *Namby Pamby* by Henry Carey c. 1720

The Queen of Hearts
She made some tarts,
All on a summer's day;
The Knave of Hearts
He stole the tarts,
And took them clean away.

Nursery Rhymes *The European Magazine* 1782

Simple Simon met a pieman
Going to the fair;
Said Simple Simon to the pieman
'Let me taste your ware.'

Nursery Rhymes *Simple Simon* 1764

Sing a song of sixpence,
A pocket full of rye,
Four and twenty blackbirds,
Baked in a pie;
When the pie was opened,
The birds began to sing;
Was that not a dainty dish
To set before the king?

Nursery Rhymes
in *Tom Thumb's Pretty Song Book* c 1744

THEN, as though touching her waist had reminded her of something, she felt in the pocket of her overalls and produced a small slab of chocolate. She broke it in half and gave one of the pieces to Winston. Even before he had taken it he knew by the smell that it was very unusual chocolate. It was dark and shiny and wrapped in silver paper. Chocolate normally was dull-brown crumbly stuff that tasted, as nearly as one could describe it, like the smoke of a rubbish fire. But at some time or another he had tasted chocolate like the piece she had given him. The first whiff of its scent had stirred up some memory which he could not pin down, but which was powerful and troubling.

George Orwell *1984* 1949

Though we eat little flesh and drink no wine,
Yet let's be merry; we'll have tea and toast;
Custards for supper, and an endless host
Of syllabubs and jellies and mince-pies,
And other lady-like luxuries.

Percy Bysshe Shelley
Letter to Maria Gisborne 1821

Graceful monuments, delicious fortresses, seductive ramparts, which as soon as they are on all sides attacked, totter, crumble, and no longer present anything but glorious and ephemeral ruins, like every work of man – all pass away be they temples, columns, pyramids or pies.

Alexis Soyer *The Pantropheon* 1853

WHAT IS SWEETER than honey? What is more pure or more nourishing? It is the milk of the aged, it prolongs their existence, and when they descend into the tomb, it still serves to embalm them.

Alexis Soyer *The Pantropheon* 1853

Promises and pie-crust are made to be broken.

Jonathan Swift *Polite Conversation* 1738

PIE, often foolishly abused, is a good creature at the right time and in angles of thirty and forty degrees, although in semicircles and quadrants it may sometimes prove too much for delicate stomachs.

Artemus Ward

CHAPTER TWENTY-SIX

ONE MAN'S MEAT

Next to Habeas Corpus and the freedom of the Press there are few things that the English people have a greater respect for and a livelier faith in than beef.

Anonymous
in *Household Words* magazine

L UCKILY FOR HIM the average Englishman has no culinary sense at all. His palate is burned by tobacco, cocktails and whisky, and cannot appreciate fine savoury sauces.

Anonymous in *L'Epoque* 1947

The Irishman loves usquebah,
The Scot loves ale called blue cap,
The Welshman he loves toasted cheese,
And makes his mouth like a mouse trap.

Anonymous
q. in F. Accum Cookbook, 1821

B EEF IS A GOOD MEATE for an Englysshman so be the beest be younge . . . Old beefe and cow flesshe doth ingender melancolye humoures. (Yet) . . . if it be moderately powdeyd and the grose blode by salte be exhawtyed it doth make an Englysshman strong.

Anonymous manuscript c. 1350

A Frenchman drinks his native wine,
A German drinks his beer;
An Englishman his 'alf-and-'alf,
Because it brings good cheer.
The Scotsman drinks his whisky straight
Because it brings on dizziness;
An American has no choice at all –
He drinks the whole damn business.

Anonymous

Everything in France is a pretext for a good dinner.

Jean Anouilh *Cecile* 1949

T HERE ARE CERTAIN tastes which those who have never experienced them as children can neither understand nor cure: who but an Englishman, for example, can know the delights of stone-cold leathery toast for breakfast, or the wonders of 'Dead Man's Leg'?

W. H. Auden
introduction to *The Art of Eating* by M. F. K. Fisher 1963

Roast beef has long been a national dish in England. In most of our patriotic songs it is contrasted with the fricasseed frogs, popularly supposed to be the exclusive diet of Frenchmen. 'O the roast beef of old England, And O the old English roast beef.' This national chorus is appealed to whenever a song-writer wishes to account for the valour displayed by an Englishman at sea or on land.

Mrs Isabella Beeton
The Book of Household Management 1861

France . . . is a land of milk and honey, the best milk and the most perfumed honey, where all the good things of the earth overflow and are cooked to perfection.

William Bolitho *Camera Obscura*

G ENIAL AND GLADDENING is the power of good ale, the true and proper drink of Englishmen. He is not deserving of the name of Englishman who speaketh against ale.

George Borrow *Lavengro* 1851

The northern nations are more addicted to the use of strong liquors than the southern, in order to supply by art the want of that genial warmth of blood which the sun produces.

James Boswell *Journal* 1780

One cannot help wondering if an English salad is the result of ignorance or the aim of a curiously perverted taste. A salad must be fresh and crisp, its flavour sharp and appetising. The ingredients with which it is made all have these qualities; so has the seasoning. Indeed, to make it sickly amounts to a tour de force which must be very difficult to accomplish. Still, most English cooks seem to be very successful in their attempt with the help of cream sauces, sham mayonnaises and the additon of the fatal radish, the strong taste of which absolutely kills that of the other vegetables.

X. Marcel Boulestin
Simple French Cooking for English Homes 1923

The destiny of nations depends upon what and how they eat.

Jean-Anthelme Brillat-Savarin *La Physiologie du goût* 1825

Fish when it has passed the Hands of a French Cook is no more Fish: it has neither the Taste, Smell nor Appearance of Fish. It, and everything else, is dressed in masquerade, seasoned with slow poisons, and every Dish pregnant with nothing but the Seeds of Diseases both Chronick and acute . . .

Robert Campbell *The London Tradesman* 1747

THE ESSENTIALS of English cooking are roasts of beef, mutton and lamb, the various meats cooked in salt water, in the manner of fish and vegetables . . . fruit, preserves, puddings of all kinds, chicken and turkey with cauliflower, salt beef, country ham and several similar ragouts – that is the sum of English cooking.

Antonin Carème

But since he stood for England
And knew what England means,
Unless you give him bacon
You must not give him beans.

G. K. Chesterton *The Englishman*

NOBODY HAS EVER been able to find out why the English regard a glass of wine added to a soup or stew as a reckless foreign extravagance and at the same time spend pounds on bottled sauces, gravy powders, soup cubes, ketchups and artifical flavourings. If every kitchen contained a bottle each of red wine, white wine and inexpensive port for cooking, hundreds of store cupboards could be swept clean for ever of the cluttering debris of commercial sauce bottles and all synthetic aids to flavouring.

Elizabeth David *French Country Cooking* 1951

In a French town of any size at all we find perhaps three or four rival charcutiers displaying trays of shining olives, black and green, large and small, pickled gherkins, capers, home-made mayonnaise, grated carrot salad, shredded celeriac in remoulade sauce, several sorts of tomato salad, sweet-sour onions, champignons à la Grecque, ox or pig's muzzle finely sliced and dressed with a vinaigrette sauce and fresh parsley, a salad of mussels, another of cervelas sausage, several kinds of pork pâté; sausages for grilling, sausages for boiling, sausages for hors-d'oeuvre, flat sausages called crepinettes for baking or frying, salt pork to enrich stews and soups and vegetable dishes, pig's trotters ready cooked and bread-crumbed, so that all you need to do is take them home and grill them; cooked ham, raw ham, a galantine of tongue, cold pork and veal roasts, boned stuffed ducks and chickens . . .

Elizabeth David *Vogue* 1960

When one tries to analyse the real reasons for the respect which French cookery has so long exacted from the rest of the world, the French genius for presentation must be counted as a very relevant point, and its humble beginnings can be seen on the market stalls, in the small town charcutiers' and patissiers' shops, in modest little restaurants where even if the cooking is not particularly distinguished, the most ordinary of little dishes will be brought to your table with respect, properly arranged on a serving dish, vegetables separately served, the object of arousing your appetite will be achieved, and the proprietors of the establishment will have made the most of their limited resources.

Elizabeth David

The great British tradition that the food is going to be so bad that you must completely hide all its flavours by dousing them with a supremely hot and aggressive commercial addictive.

Roy Andries de Groot *Esquire* June 1974

An Englishman will fairly drink as much
As will maintain two families of Dutch.

Daniel Defoe
The True-Born Englishman 1701

When mighty roast beef was the Englishman's food
It ennobled our hearts and enriched our blood –
Our soldiers were brave and our courtiers were good.
Oh, the roast beef of England.

Henry Fielding
The Grub Street Opera 1731

Jews are the best indication of good food in a place.

M. F. K. Fisher
Serve It Forth 1937

Our English nature cannot live by roots, by water, by herbs or such beggary baggage. That may well serve for vile, outlandish quarters; give the Englishmen meat after their old usage, beef, mutton, veal to cheer their courage.

William Forrest q. in *Great Cooks and their Recipes* by A. Willan 1977

PORRIDGE OR PRUNES, sir; these are grim words. It is an epitome – not, indeed, of English food, but of the forces which drag it into the dirt. It carries the true spirit of gastronomic joylessness. Porridge fills the Englishman up, prunes clean him out, so their functions are opposed. But their spirit is the same: they eschew pleasure and consider delicacy immoral.

E. M. Forster *Wine and Food* 1939

The depressing thing about an Englishman's traditional love of animals is the dishonesty thereof . . . Get a barbed hook into the upper lip of a salmon, drag him endlessly around the water until he loses his strength, pull him to the bank, hit him on the head with a stone, and you may well become fisherman of the year. Shoot the salmon and you'll never be asked again.

Clement Freud *Freud on Food* 1978

The French cook: we open tins.

John Galsworthy

No draught of wine amid the old tombs under the violet sky but made me for the time a better man, larger of brain, more courageous, more gentle. 'Twas a revelry whereon came no repentance. Could I but live for ever in thoughts and feelings such as those born to me in the shadow of the Italian vine!

George Gissing
The Private Papers of Henry Ryecroft 1903

IN THE EIGHTEENTH CENTURY, before the difficult era of the soup kitchen, the English were famous for the abundance and quality of their meat and game, and for dishes made from them, such as pies and soups. Foreign travellers exclaimed . . . that the British working classes ate meat, and not just occasionally but often. The unspoken conclusion was that it would all come to no good. But in fact we escaped the excesses of revolution. Can we ascribe this to meat-eating by the lower orders in the eighteenth century?

Jane Grigson *The Mushroom Feast* 1975

On the assumption that the metaphysical depends on the physical, it has been argued that national food forms the national character; in proof of which have often been put forward the contrast between the smooth, slippery, volatile character of the soup-, snail-, and frog-eating Frenchman and of the heavy, stolid and imperturbable character of our own beef- and pudding-eating countrymen.

Frederick W. Hackwood
Good Cheer 1911

The English system of cookery it would be impertinent for me to describe, but still, when I think of that huge round of parboiled ox-flesh, with sodden dumplings floating in a saline, greasy mixture surrounded by carrots looking red with disgust and turnips pale with dismay, I cannot help a sort of inward shudder, and making comparisons unfavourable to English gastronomy.

Himself
Memoirs of a Stomach by 'A Minister of the Interior' 1835

Nearly every woman in England is competent to write an authoritative article on how not to cook a cabbage.

Vyvyan Holland *Wine and Food* 1935

Many things have struck me as prodigious in this country, none so much as the restraint that the ordinary Englishman practises towards the woman, wife or servant, who prepares his meals. Why he does not murder her is a great and insoluble mystery.

Odette Keun
q. in *A Wine and Food Bedside Book* ed. C. Morny 1972

JAPANESE FOOD is very pretty and undoubtedly a suitable cuisine in Japan, which is largely populated by people of below average size. Hostesses hell-bent on serving such food to occidentals would be well advised to supplement it with something more substantial and to keep in mind that almost everybody likes french fries.

Fran Lebowitz *Metropolitan Life* 1978

IT MAY BE A CHARACTERISTIC of a nation's imperialistic moment that its citizens insist on eating their national dishes, whether tea or toast or hamburgers, wherever its citizens travel. There is also the tendency to assume that the natives really prefer manufactured breakfast foods, roast beef and Yorkshire, or whatever the dishes prized back home, in preference to their (often more sophisticated) local cuisine.

David Leitch *Deadline* 1984

What is patriotism but the love of the good things of our childhood?

Lin Yutang q. in *The Art of Eating* by M. F. K. Fisher 1963

To eat well in England you should have breakfast three times a day.
Somerset Maugham
q. in *The Breakfast Book* by D. St. John Thomas 1981

If every Frenchwoman is born with a wooden spoon in her hand, every Scotswoman is born with a rolling-pin under her arm.

F. Marian McNeill
q. in *A Taste of Scotland* by Theodora Fitzgibbon 1970

Americans can eat garbage, provided you sprinkle it liberally with ketchup, mustard, chilli sauce, tabasco sauce, cayenne pepper, or any other condiment which destroys the original flavour of the dish.

Henry Miller *Remember to Remember* 1947

We begin with brochet. Why is brochet so good and pike so nasty, since the dictionary affirms that they are one and the same? Then partridges, followed by thick, juicy French cutlets quite unlike the penny on the end of a brittle bone which is the English butcher's presentation of that piece of meat. They were burnt on the outside, inside, almost raw. Boiled eggs suddenly appeared, with fingers of buttered toast, in case anybody should still be famished. Then a whole brie on bed of straw; the chocolate profiteroles.

Nancy Mitford *Don't Tell Alfred* 1960

Mutton old and claret good were Caledonia's forte,
Before the Southron taxed her drink and poisoned her with port.
Also cited: Firm and erect the Highland chieftain stood
Old was his mutton and his claret good.
'Thou shalt drink port', the English statesman cried.
He drank the poison – and his spirit died.

Charles, Lord Neaves
Beef and Potatoes

In the matter of cookery, the Anglo-Saxon is about as advanced as a rabbit.

Max O'Rell (Leon Blouet) *John Bull & Co* 1894

The English have only three vegetables – and two of them are cabbage.

Walter Page

Every country possesses, it seems, the sort of cuisine it deserves, which is to say the sort of cuisine it is appreciative enough to want. I used to think that the notoriously bad cooking of the English was an example to the contrary, and that the English cook the way they do because, through sheer technical deficiency, they had not been able to master the art of cooking. I have discovered to my stupefaction that the English cook that way because that is the way they like it.

Waverley Root *The Food of France*

LET THE GOYIM sink their teeth into whatever lowly creature crawls and grunts across the face of the dirty earth, we will not contaminate our humanity thus. Let them . . . gorge themselves upon anything and everything that moves, no matter how odious and abject the animal, no matter how grotesque or shmutzig or dumb . . . Let them eat eels and frogs and pigs and crabs and lobsters; let them eat vulture, let them eat ape-meat and skunk if they like – a diet of abominable creatures well befits a breed of mankind so hopelessly shallow and empty-headed as to drink, to divorce, and to fight with their fists . . . Thus saith the kosher laws, and who am I to argue that they're wrong. For look at Alex himself . . . sucks one night at a lobster's claw and within the hour his cock is out and aimed at a shikse on a Public Service bus. And his superior Jewish brain might as well be made of matzoh brei!

Philip Roth *Portnoy's Complaint* 1969

It is a fact that great eaters of meat are in general more cruel and ferocious than other men; this observation holds good in all places and at all times; the barbarism of the English is well known.

Jean-Jacques Rousseau *Emile* 1762

THE AVERAGE ENGLISH middle-class household salad is an abomination, consisting of wet lettuce cut up small with a steel knife, uncored halves of tomatoes, stalky watercress and sliced hard-boiled eggs, with a covering of linseed oil salad 'Cream' from a grocer's bottle.

André Simon *The Concise Encyclopedia of Gastronomy* 1952

Gentlemen do not like food that has been 'messed about with'. Continental cookery gives them diarrhoea.

Douglas Sutherland *The English Gentleman* 1978

If it be true that, while the French eat, the English only feed, we may fairly add that the Australians 'grub'.

Richard Twopeny *Town Life in Australia* 1883

I will venture to say that if a prize were proposed for the scheme of a regimen most calculated to injure the stomach, the teeth and the health in general, no better could be invented than that of the Americans.

Comte de Volney
q. in *Food* by Waverley Root 1980

The English have forty-two religions, but only two sauces.

Voltaire *Philosophical Dictionary* 1764

This is the way of these cursed English: they mind more a play of Shakespeare's, a plum-pudding or a bottle of rum than they do the Pentateuch.

Voltaire *L'Ingenu* 1767

THE BRITISH COOK is a foolish woman – who should be turned for her iniquities into a pillar of salt which she never knows how to use.

Oscar Wilde

Few things bought with money are more delightful than a French breakfast.

N. P. Willis *Pencillings by the Way* 1835

CHAPTER TWENTY-SEVEN

MINE HOST

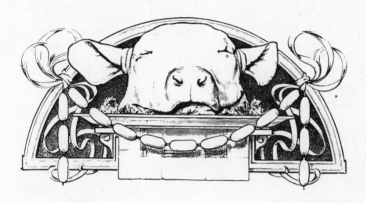

Table d'hôte, n: a caterer's thrifty concession to the universal passion for irresponsibility.

Ambrose Bierce
The Devil's Dictionary 1911

All barmaids who are not fools are philosophers.

Arthur Binstead (The Pitcher) *Pitcher's Proverbs* 1909

VENITE omnes qui stomacho laboratis, et ego restaurato vos (Come all ye who labour with the stomach, and I will restore you.)

M. Boulanger motto of the first ever restaurant, in Paris 1765

Few among those who go to restaurants realize that the man who first opened one must have been a man of genius and a profound observer.

Jean-Anthelme Brillat-Savarin
La Physiologie du goût 1825

Eating alone fosters egotism, encourages one to care only for oneself, isolates one from one's surroundings, dissuades one from paying little polite attentions . . . It is easy, in society, to observe those guests who ordinarily eat in restaurants.

Jean-Anthelme Brillat-Savarin *La Physiologie du goût* 1825

A TAVERN is a little Sodom, where as many vices are daily practised as ever were known in the great one.

Thomas Browne *Talks Round London* c. 1700

I can't count the number of delectable hours I've spent in bars, the perfect places for the meditation and contemplation indispensable to life . . . The bar . . . is an exercise in solitude. Above all else, it must be quiet, dark, very comfortable – and, contrary to modern mores, no music of any kind, no matter how faint. In sum, there should be no more than a dozen tables, and a clientele that doesn't like to talk.

Luis Buñuel *My Last Breath* 1983

Establishing centres for wartime mass catering: I hope the term 'communal feeding centres' is not going to be adapted. It is an odious expression, suggestive of Communism and the workhouse. I suggest you call them 'British Restaurants.' Everybody associates the word 'restaurant' with a good meal, and they may as well have the word if they cannot get anything else.

Winston Churchill speech, 1941

Along the varying road of life,
In calm content, in toil or strife,
At morn or noon, by night or day,
As time conducts him on his way,
How oft doth man, by care oppressed,
Find in an Inn a place of rest.

William Combe
Dr Syntax in Search of the Picturesque 1809-1811

I dream of a starless restaurant with a plush banquette where the owner wears the chef's white cap, where the young and decorative and the old and talented would eat for nothing and the rich pass a stiff examination and pay an entrance fee.

Cyril Connolly *Sunday Times* 1953

. . . the bar;
Where a grand priestess of the temple sway'd,
The most obedient, and the most obey'd,
Rosy and round, adorned in crimson vest,
And flaming ribands at her ample breast . . .
Her port in bottles stood, a well-stain'd row
Drawn for the evening from the pipe below;
Three powerful spirits fill'd a parted case,
Some cordial bottles stood in secret place;
Fair acid-fruits in nets above were seen,
Her plate was splendid and her glasses clean;
Basins and bowls were ready on the stand,
And measures clatter'd in her powerful hand.

George Crabbe 1810

He goes not out of his way that goes to a good inn.

George Herbert *Outlandish Proverbs* 1640

Few of us are adventurous in the matter of food; in fact, most of us think there is
something disgusting in a bill of fare to which we are unused.

William James q. in *Food* by Waverley Root 1980

THERE IS NOTHING which has been contrived by man by which so much
happiness is produced as by a good tavern or inn.

Dr Samuel Johnson
q. in *The Life of Samuel Johnson* by James Boswell 1791

As soon as I enter the door of a tavern, I experience an oblivion of care, and a
freedom from solicitude: Wine there exhilarates my spirits, and prompts me to
free conversation and an interchange of discourse with those whom I most love: I
dogmatize and am contradicted, and in this conflict of opinions and sentiments I
find delights . . . There is no private house in which people can enjoy themselves
so well as at a capital tavern.

Dr Samuel Johnson
q. in *The Life of Samuel Johnson* by James Boswell 1791

The finest landscape in the world is improved by a good inn in the foreground.

Samuel Johnson q. in *Pleasures of the Table* by G. Ellwanger 1903

The three never-failing accompaniments of advancing civilisation are a racecourse, a public house and a gaol.

John Lang 1834

Technological innovation has done great damage not only to reading habits but also to eating habits. Food is now available in such unpleasant forms that one frequently finds smoking between courses to be an aid to the digestion.

Fran Lebowitz
Metropolitan Life 1978

PUBS MAKE YOU as drunk as they can, as soon as they can, and turn nasty when they succeed.

Colin MacInnes *England Half-English* 1961

Restaurants have this in common with ladies: the best are often not the most enjoyable, nor the grandest the most friendly, and the pleasures of the evening are frequently spoiled by the final writing of an exorbitant cheque.

John Mortimer in *The Observer* 1978

AVOID ANY RESTAURANT where a waiter arrives with a handful of knives and forks just as you reach the punchline of your best story and says 'Which of you is having the fish?'

John Mortimer in *The Observer* 1978

> Tavern, how dear you are to me;
> Nothing on earth or under sky
> Was ever quite so good to see,
> For every need you do supply.
> Even your dishcloths are so fair
> They can with Holland cloth compare . . .
> Wine beckons me, invites my kiss,
> It drives my sadness far away,
> And fills me with unending bliss;
> We love each other more each day.
> I burn for it, it does me burn;
> I drink it up, am drunk in turn.

Motin drinking song.

The golden rule when reading the menu in a restaurant is, if you can't pronounce it you can't afford it.

Frank Muir *English Digest*

In the highly mechanised countries, thanks to tinned food, cold storage, synthetic flavouring matters, etc., the palate is almost a dead organ . . . Look at the factory-made, foil-wrapped cheeses and 'blended' butter in any grocer's; look at the hideous rows of tins which usurp more and more of the space in any food-shop, even a dairy; look at the sixpenny Swiss roll or a twopenny ice-cream; look at the filthy chemical by-product that people will pour down their throats under the name of beer. Wherever you go you will see some slick machine-made article triumphing over the old-fashioned article that still tastes of something other than sawdust.

George Orwell *The Road To Wigan Pier* 1937

We joined a swelling stream . . . all following a series of notices marked 'British Restaurant', to a huge elephant house, where thousands of human beings were eating as we did an enormous all-beige meal, starting with beige soup thickened to the consistency of paste, followed by beige mince full of lumps and garnished with beige beans and a few beige potatoes, thin beige apple stew and a sort of skilly. Very satisfying and crushing, and calling up a vision of our future planned World – all beige also.

Francis Partridge *A Pacifist's War* 1978

A TAVERN IS a common consumption of the afternoon and the murderer . . . of a rainy day. It is the busy man's recreation, the idle man's business, the melancholy man's sanctuary, the stranger's welcome, the inns of court man's entertainment, the scholar's kindness, and the citizen's country. It is the study of sparkling wits, and the cup of canary their book.

Reuben & Sholto Percy *The Percy Anecdotes*

'Tis the greatest good of our tradesmen, their felicity, life and soul, their chiefest comfort, to be merry together in a tavern.

Pliny c. 60

Everyone has a penny to spend at a new ale-house.

John Ray *A Collection of English Proverbs* 1670

It takes much art
To choose à la carte
For less than they quote
For the table d'hôte

Justin Richardson *La Carte*

The earlier stages of the dinner had worn off. The wine lists had been consulted, by some with the blank embarrassment of a schoolboy suddenly called on to locate a Minor Prophet in the tangled hinterland of the Old Testament, by others with the severe scrutiny which suggests that they have visited most of the higher-priced wines in their own homes and probed their family weaknesses.

Saki (H. H. Munro) *The Chronicles of Clovis* 1911

By insisting on having your bottle pointing to the north when the cork is being drawn, and calling the waiter Max, you may induce an impression on the guests which hours of laboured boasting might be powerless to achieve. For this purpose, however, the guests must be as carefully chosen as the wine.

Saki (H. H. Munro) *The Chronicles of Clovis* 1911

It is a matter for future anthropologists to ponder that the two favourite companions of business are Bottle and Board . . . Deep drinking and intrigue are part of all the noble professions. These, combined with the studious avoidance of exercise, have conspired to produce a whole race of voluptuaries who, by twos and threes from noon till three, sit in dim restaurants, picking at their sideburns and destroying the furniture with their gigantic buttocks.

Richard Selzer *The Drinking Man's Liver* 1974

Taverns are places where madness is sold by the bottle.

Jonathan Swift 1738

'What'll youse 'ave,' said the waiter,
Reflectively pickin' 'is nose.
'I'll 'ave two boiled eggs, you bastard,
You can't get yer fingers in those.'

George Wallace Snr.
q. in *The Dictionary of Australian Quotations* ed. S. Murray-Smith 1984

We can go to any restaurant at all and be made uncomfortable by the waiters, waiters seem to be a breed gifted in making guests ill at ease. They are always older, wearier, and wiser than we are; and they have us at a disadvantage because we are sitting down and they are standing up. We should very much like to discover a restaurant where we would be allowed to stand up to our food, and the waiters be compelled to sit down, so we could lord it over them!

E. B. White *Every Day Is Saturday*

THE REASON for eating in a restaurant is to have food which would be cooked less well, or not at all, at home.

Woodrow Wyatt *To the Point* 1981

The restaurant is the tank in the warfare of cookery, because it has always been a major instrument for the smashing of old eating habits . . . Take-away food is the guerilla of cooking, and a more ancient institution . . . The counterpart to the jeans revolution in clothes is the replacing of good table manners based on the habits of the rich, by those of the student.

Theodore Zeldin quoted in *The Listener* 1982

CHAPTER TWENTY-EIGHT

A LITTLE OF WHAT YOU FANCY

If you want to feel important – go on a diet.

Joey Adams *Cindy and I* 1959

Should we not think a man mad who at one meal will devour fowl, flesh and fish; swallow oil, and vinegar, salt, wines and spices; throw down salads of twenty different herbs, sauces of an hundred ingredients, confections and fruits of numberless sweets and flavours? For my part, when I behold a table set out in all its magnificence, I fancy that I see gouts and dropsies, fevers and lethargies, and other innumerable distempers, lying in ambuscade among the dishes.

Joseph Addison in *Spectator*

To miss a meal sometimes is good,
It ventilates and cools the blood,
Gives Nature time to clean her streets
From filth and crudities of meats;
Far too much meat the bowels fur,
And fasting's Nature's scavenger.

Anonymous
q. in *Good Cheer* by Frederick W. Hackwood 1911

PULSE ARE WINDY, cheese offends the stomach, milk hurts the head, water the lungs, whence it happens that in all the rivers, fields, gardens and markets, there is scarce to be anything fitting for man to eat.

St Bernard of Clairvaux

When there appears in society a vivacious, pink-cheeked young person, with a pert nose, rounded contours, and short, plump hands and feet, everybody is entranced and finds her charming; everyone that is, but I. For, taught by experience, I look at her with the eyes of twelve years hence, see the ravages which obesity will have wrought on those fresh young charms and groan inwardly over ills so far non-existent.

Jean-Anthelme Brillat-Savarin
La Physiologie du goût 1825

OF ALL MEDICAL prescriptions (against obesity) dieting is best, because it acts incessantly, day and night, in sleep and in waking; its effort is reinforced with every meal, and it ends up by subjugating every part of the individual's constitution.

Jean-Anthelme Brillat-Savarin *La Physiologie du goût* 1825

Dieting makes you fat.

Geoffrey Cannon book title 1983

Obesity is a mental state, a disease brought on by boredom and disappointment.

Cyril Connolly *The Unquiet Grave* 1945

EXERCISE IS the most awful illusion.
The secret is a lot of aspirin and marrons glacés.

Noel Coward q. in *Observer* 1959

It does seem to me that with so much talk about art versus fine ingredients somebody might mention that there is also the art, or the discipline, call it what you like, of leaving well alone. This is a prerequisite of any first class meal . . .

Elizabeth David *Spectator* July, 1961

THE FURTHER I TRAVEL in search of the ideal slimming method the more I am convinced that food is one of the oldest and greatest comforters. If this comforter – this secret return to the womb – is suddenly taken away from me, I begin to feel anxiety, depression, tension. I may suddenly find myself suffering from diarrhoea, dry mouth, faintness, fatigue, giddiness, headaches, uncontrollable hunger, irritability, lethargy, nausea, palpitations, weakness, to name only a few of the possibilities.

Roy Andries de Groot *Esquire* December 1972

Plain food and plainly cooked and not too much of it.

Auguste Escoffier q. in *Wine and Food* 1935

The popular concept of a strengthening diet is a chicken wrung out in hot water.

Martin Fischer

One of the stupidest things in an earnest but stupid school of culinary thought is that each of the three daily meals should be 'balanced'. This still goes on in big-magazine advertising, but there seems less and less insistence on it in real life: baby-doctors and even gynaecologists admit that most human bodies choose their own satisfactions, dietetically and otherwise . . . Not all people need or want three meals every day. Many of the them feel better with two, or one and one-half, or five.

M. F. K. Fisher *How to Cook a Wolf* 1951

TIME: Easter holidays. 'Good for you, dear. Good for you.' And there it lay, pink and slightly green. Livid. Bird's custard yellowing on one side of the plate, and pastry – admittedly the pastry was nice – a little pink and flavoured, but not too much, with rhubarb juice. Nanny-food. Governess-food. School-meal-food (cold porridge with rhubarb for breakfast).

Jane Grigson *Jane Grigson's Fruit Book* 1982

Great harms have grown, and maladies exceeding,
By keeping in a little blast of wind:
So cramps and dropsies, colics have their breeding,
And mazed brains for want of vent behind.

Sir John Harrington
The Salerno Regimen – The Englishman's Doctor 1608

Eat, drink and be merry, for tomorrow ye diet.

Lewis C. Henry (ed.) *Toasts for All Occasions*

We . . . have become a bastion of sugar addicts . . . We give our babies a formula that provides something like two teaspoons of sugar per feeding, wean them on heavily sweetened baby foods, and raise them on double-sweetened frankfurter and hamburger buns, sweet ketchup, candy and drinks. We consume more of this poor nutrient than any other society ever has . . . and we look for it in everything we eat – bread, meat, even soups, vegetables and salads.

John & Karen Hess *The Taste of America* 1977

Most people eat as if they were fattening themselves for the market.
E. W. Howe

Whenever I feel like exercise I lie down until the feeling passes.
Robert M. Hutchins
q. in *Young Man Looking Backwards* by J. P. McEvoy 1938

W E ARE . . . eating too much of some things, notably sugar. Nutritionally speaking sugar is little more than potted energy. Of course we need energy, but less of it than we did, now that fewer of us are employed in hewing coal, wielding picks, humping sacks or scrubbing floors, and more in sitting still, and therefore should be eating foods with fewer calories – units of energy – and more vitamins and proteins. But actually we are sopping up many more calories because of our sweet tooth. Today we eat in a fortnight as much sugar as our ancestors, a couple of centuries back, ate in a year.

Elspeth Huxley *Brave New Victuals* 1965

Who ever hears of fat men heading a riot, or herding together in turbulent mobs.

Washington Irving
Knickerbocker's History of New York 1809

We never repent of having eaten too little.
Thomas Jefferson *Writings* c. 1820

If you have formed the habit of checking on every new diet that comes along, you will find that, mercifully, they all blur together, leaving you with only one definite piece of information: french-fried potatoes are out.

Jean Kerr *Please Don't Eat the Daisies* 1957

WHEN A GOOD fellow has been sacrificing rather too liberally at the throne of the Jolly God, the best remedy to help the Stomach to get rid of its burden is to take for Supper some Gruel with half an ounce of Butter and a teaspoon of Epsom salts in it.

William Kitchiner *The Cook's Oracle* 1822

Forbidden to you are carrion, blood, the flesh of swine, what has been hallowed to other than God, the beast strangled.

The Koran c. 650

Thoroughly distasteful as synthetic foods might be, one cannot help but accord them a certain value when confronted with the health food buff . . . Brown rice is ponderous, overly chewy, and possessed of unpleasant religious overtones.

Fran Lebowitz *Metropolitan Life* 1978

If you wish to grow thinner, diminish your dinner,
And take to light claret instead of pale ale;
Look down with an utter contempt upon butter
And never touch bread till it's toasted – or stale.

Harry Leigh
Carols of Cockayne 1869

On those who prescribe diets: If they do no other good, they do this at least, that they prepare their patients betimes for death, by gradually undermining and cutting off their enjoyment of life.

Michel de Montaigne *Essais* 1595

Has it ever struck you that there is a thin man inside every fat man, just as they say there is a statue inside every block of stone.

George Orwell
Coming Up for Air 1939

Imprisoned in every fat man a thin one is wildly signalling to be let out.

Palinurus (Cyril Connolly)
The Unquiet Grave 1945

YOU CAN NOW take any protein you want, cottonseed, or peanut, or groundnut or fishmeal, purify it, dissolve it in alkali, extrude it through tiny holes, wind it up like a great hank of wool, cut it across the fibres, and lo and behold you have beef, mutton, turkey or smoked salmon according to the flavour you care to give it that day.

Dr Magnus Pyke in *The Guardian* 1970

We are wealthy and wasteful but this can't go on. If we don't eat dog biscuits, we could end up eating our dog instead.

Magnus Pyke in *The Observer* 1975

'I want the truth from you. I wouldn't tell your father . . . but I must have the truth from you . . . Is it just French fries, darling, or is it more? . . . Tell me, please, what other kind of garbage you're putting into your mouth so that we can get to the bottom of this diarrhea! I want a straight answer from you, Alex. Are you eating hamburgers out? Answer me, please, is that why you flushed the toilet – was there hamburger in it?'

Philip Roth *Portnoy's Complaint* 1969

'He eats French fries,' she says and sinks into kitchen chair to Weep Her Heart Out once and for all. 'He goes after school with Melvyn Weiner and stuffs himself with French-fried potatoes. Jack, you tell him. I'm only his mother. Tell him what the end is going to be. Alex . . . tateleh, it begins with diarrhea, but do you know how it ends? With a sensitive stomach like yours, do you know how it finally ends? *Wearing a plastic bag to do your business in!'*

Philip Roth *Portnoy's Complaint* 1969

Let no man snub his stomach. Come, be very kind to the stomach. You had better . . . Living with your stomach is not unlike living with a petulant spouse upon whose bounty you must depend.

Richard Selzer *Moral Lessons* 1981

Jack Sprat could eat no fat
His wife could eat no lean
A real sweet pair of neurotics.

Jack Sharkey *Playboy* May 1965

EVERYTHING I eat has been proved by some doctor or other to be a deadly poison, and everything I don't eat has been proved to be indispensable for life . . . But I go marching on.

George Bernard Shaw
q. in *Days with Bernard Shaw* by S. Winsten

There is no disease, bodily or mental, which adoption of vegetable diet, and pure water has not infallibly mitigated, wherever the experiment has been fairly tried.

Percy Bysshe Shelley *Queen Mab* 1813

If you wish for anything like happiness in the fifth act of life, eat and drink about half of what you could eat and drink . . . My calculation about eating and drinking: between ten and seventy years of age I had eaten and drunk forty four-horse wagon-loads of meat and drink more than would have preserved me in life and health! The value of this mass of nourishment I considered to be worth seven thousand pounds sterling. It occurred to me that I must, by my voracity, have starved to death fully a hundred persons.

Sydney Smith q. in *The Smith of Smiths* by Hesketh Pearson 1934

Do you want to know who the most exploited person in the world is? The fat man, the fat person. Fat people are almost like an ethnic group, but one that nobody has any qualms about doing a job on. You never hear on radio and TV any more any jokes about spades or Jews or PRs, but the fat man gets it from everybody. Ha-ha the jolly fat man. Give us a yuk, fat man. Make us howl, fat lady. Do you have any idea what it's like to be made aware every day of your life that you're a freak?

Burr Snider *Esquire* March 1973

A sportsman's diet: No side dishes – no liqueurs. Only two or three wines. Whatever your stomach fancies – give it . . . Breakfast – fried ham and eggs, brown bread and a walk. Luncheon – a roast pigeon and fried potatoes and then a ride. Dinner at six, not later, mind; gravy soup, glass of sherry, nice fresh turbot and lobster sauce – wouldn't recommend salmon – another glass of sherry – then a good cut out of the middle of a well-browned saddle of mutton, wash it over with a few glasses of iced champagne, and if you like, a little light pastry to end up with. A pint of old port and a devilled biscuit can hurt no man. Mind, no salads or cucumbers or celery at dinner, or fruit after. Turtle soup is very wholsome, so is venison. Don't let the punch be too acid, though.

Robert Surtees *Handley Cross* 1843

A cure for asthma. Live for a fortnight on boiled carrots only.

John Wesley *Primitive Physic* 1789

I NEVER WORRY about diets. The only carrots that interest me are the number you get in a diamond.

Mae West q. in *The Wit & Wisdom of Mae West* 1967

Lurking somewhere behind every expressed motive for eating yogurt is the myth, rumour or suspicion, nurtured throughout the ages, that yogurt is invested with the ability to cure a variety of ills: cancer, arthritis, colitis, gallstones, hepatitis, migraines and virtually everything else. In addition to guaranteeing good health, it is supposed to assure sexual vigour well into a lifetime at least a century long.

Leslie Aldridge Westoff *Esquire* June 1973

You can never be too rich or too thin.

Duchess of Windsor
q. in *A Dictionary of Contemporary Quotations* by Jonathon Green 1982

Nancy was taken very ill this Afternoon with a pain within her, blown up so as if poisoned, attended with a vomiting. I supposed it proceeded in great measure from what she ate at Dinner . . . some boiled Beef rather fat and salt, a good deal of a nice roast duck, and plenty of boiled Damson Pudding. After Dinner, by way of Dessert, she eat some green-gage Plumbs, some Figgs, and Rasberries and Cream. I desired her to drink a good half-pint Glass of warm Rum and Water which she did and was soon a little better.

James Woodforde *Diary of a Country Parson* September 24, 1790

MY BOY JACK had another touch of the Ague about noon. I gave him a dram of gin at the beginning of the fit and pushed him headlong into one of my Ponds and ordered him to bed immediately and he was better after it and had nothing of the cold fit after, but was very hot . . .

James Woodforde *Diary of a Country Parson* May 22, 1779

Let no man snub his stomach. Come, be very kind to the stomach. You had better . . . Living with your stomach is not unlike living with a petulant spouse upon whose bounty you must depend.

Richard Selzer *Moral Lesson* 1981

INDEX OF AUTHORS

INDEX OF AUTHORS

Cicero, Marcus Tullius, 106-43 BC
Roman jurist and philosopher, 138
Clarisse, 172
Clarke, M'Donald, 94
Clarke, Marcus, 1846-1881,
Australian journalist, 119
Claudel, Paul, 1868-1955, French
diplomat and poet, 58, 71, 158
Cobb, Irvin S., 72
Cobbett, William, 1763-1835, British
radical journalist and politician, 138,
205
Cogan, Thomas, 1545?-1607, British
physician, 119, 172, 214
Coleman, William, 219
Colette (Sidonie-Gabrielle Colette),
1873-1954, French novelist, 58,
205, 251
Colton, John, & Rudolph, Clemence,
138
Combe, William, 1741-1823, British
poet, 270
Condon, Eddie, 1904-1973, American
jazz musician, 95
Condon, Richard, 1915-, American
novelist, 6
Congreve, William, 1670-1729,
British dramatist, 95
Connolly, Cyril, 1903-1974, British
man of letters, 30, 210, 270, 278,
282
Connor, William, (Cassandra), 1909-
1967, British journalist, 242
Conran, Shirley, 1932-, British
writer, 192
Croft-Cooke, Rupert, 1903-, 36
Copley, Esther, British cookery
writer, 182
Coquet, James de, French food
writer, 192, 214
Cosmopolite, A, 6
Cotton, Charles, 1630-1687, British
writer, 95
Coward, Noel, 1899-1973, British

playwright and actor, 59, 278
Cowley, Abraham, 1618-1667,
British diplomat, scholar and poet,
95, 119
Cowper, William, 1731-1800, British
writer, 234
Crabbe, George, 1754-1832, British
writer, 72, 95, 271
Creighton, Bishop, c. 1871, British
clergyman, 6
Crèvecoeur, St John de, 1735-1813,
224
Culpeper, Nicholas, British herbalist,
192, 246

d'Antic, Louis Bosc, French gourmet,
246
Dargent, Joseph, French vintner, 59
d'Aussy, Legrand, 18th century,
French historian, 193
David, Elizabeth, 1913-, English
cookery writer, 6, 44-5, 138, 158,
182, 193, 214, 220, 224-5, 246,
250, 262, 278
Davies, Robertson, 1913-1949, 36,
139
De Groot, Roy Andries, American
food writer, 72, 262, 279
De la Mare, Walter, 1873-1956,
British poet, 139
De Quincey, Thomas, 1785-1859,
British writer, 7, 147
De Voto, Bernard, 1897-1955, 72
De Vries, Peter, 1910-, American
writer, 153
Defoe, Daniel, 1660?-1731, British
author and pamphleteer, 263
Deighton, Len, 1929-, British writer,
7
Deloney, Thomas, 1543?-1607?,
British ballad-writer and
pamphleteer, 36
Dibdin, Charles, 1745-1814, British
song-writer, 95

Jonathon Green has compiled and collected many
anthologies of quotations, the most notable of which are
*A Dictionary of Contemporary Quotations; The Book of
Political Quotes* and *Famous Last Words*. He lives in
London.